Linking Up!

●●

D1629333

This project was made possible by the generous support of The William and Flora Hewlett Founda- tion, the Lippincott Foundation of the Peace Development Fund, and individual contributors.

Linking Up!
by Sarah Pirtle

Copyright © 1998 Educators for Social Responsibility, Inc. and Sarah Pirtle
All rights reserved.
Published 1998.

Editor: Laura Parker Roerden
Production Editor: Jeffrey Perkins

Pirtle, Sarah

ISBN 0-942349-10-5

Inquiries regarding permission to reprint all or part of Linking Up! should be addressed to:
Permissions Editor, Educators for Social Responsibility, 23 Garden Street, Cambridge, MA
02138

Cover Photo: Children at Brightwood Magnet School in Springfield, Massachusetts play
"Let's Get Together": Jonathan Díaz, Latoya Hall, Carlos Reyes, and Vicenta Cruz.
Cover Photo by Will Elwell, Shooting Star Photography, Greenfield, Massachusetts
Cover Design by Dave Miranda
Page Layout by Christine McGee
Music Consulting by Douglas Parker Roerden, Bedrock Barn Productions
Music Transcription and Preparation by Chris Hull, Forté Music Services
Bilingual Advisors: Roberto Díaz and Dale Kasal
Production Assistants: Priya Natarajan and Molly Marsh
Linking Up! was recorded at Avocet Studios by Joe Podlesny.

Linking Up!

BY SARAH PIRTLE

esr

EDUCATORS
for
SOCIAL
RESPONSIBILITY

23 Garden Street
Cambridge, MA 02138
(617) 492-1764

Table of Contents

Linking Up!

Building The Peaceable Classroom With Music And Movement

For preschool through grade 3

● ●

by Sarah Pirtle

Dedication

Some people preserve endangered species of animals, rainforest plants, or seeds. Early childhood teachers preserve endangered human values and abilities: cooperation, mutual regard, and respect for diversity.

It is to this important work and to all the teachers and parents connected in this common effort that this book and these songs are dedicated.

> *Who can see the grass grow?*
> *Day by day it grows so slow.*
> *You are important in this world.*
> *Who can see the roots grow?*
> *Underground the roots don't show.*
> *You are important in this world.*
> *Linking up like the grasses, linking up like the trees,*
> *Linking up like the river as it goes into the sea.*
> *Who can see the love shining very near?*
> *I see it. I feel it. It's here.*
> — from "Linking Up!" (Song 46)

SONGS LINK PEOPLE

What memories of group play do you have from childhood? Building tree houses, flipping baseball cards, playing kick the can, or carving acorn cups?

I grew up in a neighborhood where a large pack of children played together. All were included, which was unusual because we spanned ages five to twelve. Boys and girls joined in kick ball, bicycle tag, or went off to mess around in the woods. We shaped the games together. One child would announce under a neighbor's tree, "This is our house." "Okay, and here's the door," another would chime in. "And I'm cooking dinner over here," added a third. We built upon what others offered.

We squabbled plenty. We dealt with bullying, bossiness, and name-calling, but there was an unwritten rule that no individual would tear apart the essential fabric of our neighborhood. The values I hold now as a teacher—inclusion, conflict resolution, fairness—I experienced in our play.

Collaborative play has been the seed-bed for constructing knowledge of cooperative social skills in societies throughout history. Children today spontaneously take up this kind of collaborative activity during free play or choice time and at home with their friends.

Yet, it appears that children today have less chance to fashion these understandings by playing and negotiating together. Toys are scripted. Fewer wooded areas remain. Television beckons. Children can't always roam a neighborhood with the same safety. As a result, children arrive in our schools and our child care centers less savvy about how to negotiate and get along with other people.

Linking Up will help you provide avenues for constructing social learning in your early childhood program.

The Peaceable Classroom

What positive social skills are we trying to foster in our Peaceable Classroom? We can help children learn how to:

- cooperate together on shared activities;
- connect to and express their feelings;
- communicate their needs and concerns;
- respond appropriately to the messages others communicate;
- transform conflicts by problem solving;
- share power with others rather than using power over others;
- notice and affirm diversity;
- actively promote fairness;
- seek nourishment from friendship, community, and self-worth.

Linking Up! includes songs that address each of these skills. Moreover, the songs set up opportunities to explore the skills in direct ways. Young children are concrete thinkers. They construct their knowledge by social interaction. By living and learning in a Peaceable Classroom—a safe place where cooperation, the healthy expression of feelings, communication, conflict resolution, appreciation for diversity, and responsible decision making is valued—children can both experience and begin to develop the skills of participating in a caring community.

Music and Social Skills

The words "linking up" are for me the essence of what music does in the Peaceable Classroom. I learned this phrase from Riane Eisler, author of *The Chalice and the Blade* (New York: Harper and Row, 1987). She contrasts "linking," a system of collaboration and partnership, with "ranking," a system of stratification and domination. She maintains that violence is a direct outcome of ranking. I believe that in every group experience we have a choice between ranking or linking with each other.

When music enters our classroom, the mood can shift in a moment. Joy erupts. New thoughts and feelings are shared. What was stuck can become unstuck. Moreover, we reach the place where children construct their basic social understandings.

Songs tell the news of the village, help children learn how to interact, and teach the basic joy of community. Songs are a glue that link us to rhythm and breath, to nature, and to the mystery of ourselves as individuals and within a community.

I first saw the powerful effect of music and movement in my first-grade classroom in Cleveland, Ohio over twenty years ago. At that time I did not think of myself as a musician or even a singer. If another adult entered the room while I was singing the latest song I'd learned from an Ella Jenkins record, I clammed up. But the children's joy in singing and dancing broke through my inhibitions. By my fourth year of teaching, I set aside time each day that I called "Discovery Time" to open the door to all the discoveries we'd be making as we sang and moved together.

The parents, who were primarily African American, supported my decision to set aside a half-hour each day before lunch to explore cooperation skills through music and movement. Children moved independently, then rejoined their small group—which we called a "family"—to create a group shape together. The children reinforced their individuality and also their membership in a group, and they discovered how this works as a rhythm. They told me it was their favorite time of day. I watched them learn essential lessons harder to measure than math skills.

In September one boy in that class named Marcus ran away to the far side of the room, hoping someone would coax him back. Gradually, though, Marcus came to prefer a physical link with his "family" members instead of isolation. I also watched Joshua's motions change from guarded and withdrawn to expansive and courageous. I learned from Georgianna the importance of trusting the unique ways children explore the world. One day she kept falling down on the floor, and calling, "Stop that!" When I asked her, "Who are you talking to?" she replied, "Gravity."

As you hear the song on the tape, "Let's Get Together" (Song 40), you can picture these first explorations we did as "family"—small groups creating shapes together. I've also included a favorite traditional song, "This Little Light of Mine" (Song 3), to stitch African-American music into this body of songs.

Eventually, I needed to find more songs to use in that classroom. I wanted to write a song that spoke to the children's needs at the end of the school day when they were just itching to move. They wanted to jump. But there was the potential for chaos. I wanted to construct an activity where there would be periods of jumping with times for resting. It would be fun *and* safe. From this intention, I formulated a simple song where we sat during the verses and jumped during the chorus.

We then began a custom where the children themselves created the verses. Each person took a turn naming something they liked that day—kickball, new shoes, a loose tooth—and we sang their words with them.

> *Oh, I like my new braids. I like my new braids.*
> *You ask me what I like? Oh! I like my new braids.*

Then, during the chorus, they popped out of their chairs and jumped to their heart's content until the last line where they sat back into their seats.

> *Now, jump, jump, jump, jump jump.*
> *Jump, jump, jump, jump jump.*
> *Jump, jump, jump, jump jump.*
> *And get back to your place.*

This last line of the chorus was an important element. We didn't jump indefinitely. We were due back in our chairs by the word "place." The children would leap exuberantly as if they would never stop and then arrive back deftly in their chairs, precisely at the last second, looking over at me with a gleam in their eye that seemed to say, "You didn't think I would make it back, but I did." This element of self-control was part of the learning. The children took as much pride in this exercise as they did in timing their exit from a jump rope game on the playground.

The verses had their own magic. They didn't just provide a moment of calm before everyone returned to jumping wildly. They built closeness. By that simple act of singing whatever a classmate wanted to contribute to the song, in effect, they were saying: "Your ideas matter to me." In a concrete way we were noticing and affirming each person.

Each day the verses were re-created. The children often collaborated together as they jumped. Sometimes they grabbed hands and devised tricky ways to hop with a partner. They counted on the familiar framework of the song, and they also made it new every day. That year they asked for "Jump, Jump, Jump"* over and over again for months.

With these first graders, I learned I didn't have to tell them about mutual respect or cooperation. We could experience it directly in the way we shared music together. It's not that I didn't say the words. I would remind them about agreements for cooperation. But I didn't rely on words alone to communicate. I helped them to construct their social understanding so that phrases like, "Each person matters here," and "We won't leave anyone out," had meaning for them that was experienced personally.

HOW TO USE THIS GUIDE

Using music and movement in your classroom can help young children experience cooperation, communication, and community and thereby increase their understanding of social relationships.

There are different ways that interactive music can be integrated into the day to help develop these skills. You can gather the group together to participate in several songs, insert a single song to amplify a study unit, or teach a movement game for an energizing group experience. This is the basis for the three sections of the book.

---

* I've included "Jump, Jump, Jump" on the recording. It comes at the end of "Sitting in the Soup," (Song 7), which is a cousin of this first creation. You'll hear a member of our Children's Chorus, Emily Caffrey, in the spirit of these students from Cleveland, invent her own verse, "Oh, I like strawberries a lot." Information about the lesson plan I used to lead these Discovery Time sessions can be found in the extension activities for "Let's Get Together" (Song 40).

Part I: Songs for Circle Time

Part II: Songs for the Social Skills Curriculum

Part III: Songs for Movement Games

Each section of the book includes the words and music for the appropriate songs, activities (called song games) to try in your classroom, extensions for the song games, song sequences (programmatic suggestions for building your curriculum), and tips and ideas for implementing the curriculum. But how should a teacher respond if

- a conflict breaks out during a cooperation song game?
- children unexpectedly start doing an entirely different movement than the one you are leading?
- children don't want to sit in song circle?
- children exclude each other during a group game?
- a child mentions information about the foods they like or who is in their family and another child expresses disapproval?

The answers to these questions are provided throughout *Linking Up* with summaries of teacher strategies and anecdotes from real-life situations provided.

Part I: Songs for Circle Time

You can use the song games provided in Part I for Circle Time—a regular time when your class meets as a group and participates in several song games. Songs used this way during Circle Time are referred to throughout the curriculum as Song Sequences. Bracketed by a clear beginning and ending song, Song Sequences can help develop communication skills, cooperation, and build community. The songs are sequenced to 1) unify, 2) anchor, 3) build, 4) expand, and 5) end.

Here is a sample Song Sequence:

1. To unify the group: "¡Hola!/Hello" (Song 11)
   Each child is greeted by name.
2. To anchor the children and help them focus: "This Little Light of Mine" (Song 3)
   Moving hands in unison, the group affirms that they each bring their own light to the classroom community.
3. To build community: "Creeping Mouse" (Song 9)
   The children creep towards each other in a circle and use gentle touch to greet one another.
4. To expand cooperation skills: "Step by Step/Paso a Paso" (Song 13)
   All stand to sing in Spanish and English and move different body parts.
5. To end clearly: "Llegó la Hora/Now's the Time" (Song 15)

The closing song informs that it's time to end Circle Time and prepares the children for the next activity.

Part II: Songs for the Social Skills Curriculum

Use the song games in Part II to develop and infuse music, appreciating diversity, and conflict resolution into your curriculum. For example:

- If the class is studying their neighborhood, interview people who help their community and write verses about them using the song pattern, "I Want to Know Your Name" (Song 18).
- If the class is celebrating its families, draw pictures about who is in your students' families and reflect upon the drawings using the song, "Sing About Us" (Song 21).
- If the class is increasing its skills in conflict resolution, focus on positive choices when confronted with a conflict by using the bilingual song, "¡Dilo!/Talk to Me" (Song 31).

Part III: Songs for Movement Games

Use the movement song games provided in Part III to help children learn how to collaborate and bond as a classroom community through movement. Many of these songs are used during the day when children are in need of an energizing experience. For example:

- "Build A Boat" (Song 35) asks children to connect to each other as they walk together across the floor.
- "Let's Get Together" (Song 40) is the basis for the game in small groups that you see illustrated on the *Linking Up!* cover.

Other Features of the Guide

I'm an inveterate note-taker and have notebooks full of old lesson plans, activity designs, and descriptions of how children responded. Throughout this guide you'll find that the activity directions for the songs are peppered with anecdotes of actual places I've used them over the past twenty years. This feature is called "Snapshot."

Sequenced lesson plans combining several songs to meet a particular curricular goal are also included in each chapter and are called "Song Sequences." Song lyrics are italicized. Other suggested words to use in dialoguing with children are marked with quotations. Tips are provided throughout to help you implement the curriculum.

The procedures provided in these pages are not meant to be a set of rules. Rather this is a collection of suggestions. The activities share with you the discoveries I've made. Step by step, day by day, like a plant turning toward the light, children incrementally develop life-affirming social skills.

HOW TO USE THE RECORDING

This book is accompanied by a recording of forty-six songs available on cassette or CD. The songs appear in the same order in the book and on the recording.

The recording is intended primarily for teaching the songs to you and to your students. Many songs are very short. Instead of repeating a song several times, just enough of the song is provided for you and your class to learn it. Our intention is to provide the maximum number of songs so that you have a wide variety available to use in your classroom.

Most of the songs presented here will be unfamiliar. Here are ways to become acquainted with them and to find songs that will help your teaching:

- Listen for songs that jump out at you as you play the recording, that feel catchy and easy to learn.
- Skim the book in search of themes that echo what you are promoting in your classroom, such as "We Won't Leave Anyone Out" (Song 20).
- Choose songs to complement sharing time or class meetings, such as "Come Join in the Circle" (Song 4).
- Select songs for teachable moments or to intervene in a conflict, such as "When I Say Stop, I Mean Stop" (Song 29) or "There's Always Something You Can Do" (Song 30).
- Check the social skills listed in the objectives for each song. Locate skills you want to develop. For example, "How Can We Be Friends Again/Amigos de Nuevo" (Song 25) helps children recognize what escalates a problem.
- Look for songs that enhance curricular units on the family or community, such as "Sing About Us" (Song 21) and "I Want to Know Your Name" (Song 18).
- Look for complementary songs for science—snails, clouds, the water cycle, spiders, nocturnal animals.
- Find music to accompany studies of Puerto Rico, Mexico, and two Native American nations. Hear a Guatemalan contemporary poem put to music.
- Turn to "Carry the Candle" (Song 44) for ceremonies or friendship circles.
- Play songs for your class and watch their response.

When we watch children learn songs, we see various learning approaches. Some watch our lips intently. Some are silent and follow along with the motions before they begin singing. Some pick up the words so fast it feels like they already knew the song.

- *Linking Up!* was designed to take into account the different learning styles of both children and adults. You can listen to the songs on the recording, read the lyrics in the book, or use the notation to learn the melody on an instrument.
- You don't have to read music to use this book. The notation is provided as an optional aid.

You can lead Linking Up! activities without leading songs. Play the recording to:

- Lead a game.
- Practice a conflict resolution extension activity from Chapter Five introduced by a song.
- Provide a short energizing movement activity.
- Learn bilingual lyrics for reading practice.
- Hear lively music for free-style dancing.
- Start a discussion about the meaning of the words.
- Spark ideas for poetry and creative writing.

While the book includes step-by-step instructions for each song game, when useful, instructions are provided also on the recording itself. For example, children are led through the back patting game, "Sleeping Birds/Los Pajaritos Duermen" (Song 23). When additional information would interfere with listening, instructions are included only in the book—such as the hand motions to Grandmother Spider (Song 19). All of the songs in this collection have been classroom tested and revised like stones worn smooth by use.

Ten songs were recorded with young people and include dialogue that illustrates how to use a song directly with children.

- "Come Join in the Circle" (Song 4) shows how to use the news that children offer to create a new verse.
- "My Roots Go Down" (Song 33) models how to create new verses for a movement game and shows how to respond to pushing or grabbing by establishing group agreements.

Twenty songs are bilingual and can be sung in English, Spanish, or both.

To learn which language is used at the start of a bilingual song, look at the title. Whichever language is first in the title of the song is the first language sung.

Some songs, like "Step by Step/Paso a Paso" (Song 13), alternate languages with simple vocabulary and lend themselves to bilingual language development.

Most songs involve hand motions or active games. You'll find details on these options in the book. Many songs have lively percussion or piano accompaniment for dancing. These include:

- "My Space/Mi Espacio" (Song 6)
- "Mi Cuerpo Hace Música/There's Music Inside Me" (Song 37)
- "Peace is Me Being Me" (Song 43).

Song Sequences

When several related songs are used together, their impact is increased. Recognizing that it will be easier to use a sequence of songs if they appear in the same order on the recording, the selections have been arranged so that there are fourteen complete sequences featured on the recording.

Song Sequences are models. They are one way to construct a lesson plan. They provide a starting place for you to group songs together in thematic sequences.

In the appendix you will find the Song Sequences grouping songs together. These lead you to the detailed lesson plan for each song activity. For example, Song Sequence 14 describes a spiral handshake which the whole class can do as they sing Song 46, "Linking Up." This handshake is not described in the Song Sequence, but rather is found in the lesson plan of the song activity itself.

OVERVIEW OF THE RECORDING

Part I: Songs for Circle Time

Chapter Two: Starting Songs

1. The Colors of Earth
2. Good Morning to the Sky/ Buenos Días al Cielo*
3. This Little Light of Mine
4. Come Join in the Circle

Chapter Three: Friendship Songs

5. Chocolate*
6. My Space/ Mi Espacio*
7. Sitting in the Soup and Jump, Jump, Jump
8. Our Own Song and the Spoony Song
9. Creeping Mouse Game
10. Across the Wide Ocean/A Través Del Inmenso Mar*
11. ¡Hola!/Hello*
12. Pajarito/Little Bird - traditional*
13. Step by Step/Paso a Paso*
14. En La Feria /At the Fair*
15. Llegó la Hora /Now's the Time*

Part II: Songs for the Social Curriculum

Chapter Four: Diversity Songs

16. In the Very Middle
17. Speak Up
18. I Want to Know Your Name
19. Grandmother Spider
20. We Won't Leave Anyone Out
21. Sing About Us/ Cantemos De Nosotros **
22. Canción de la Nube/ Song of the Cloud*
23. Sleeping Birds / Los Pajaritos Duermen (Back Patting Game)*
24. Full Circle (The Village)

SIDE TWO (of audio recording)
Chapter Five: Conflict Resolution Songs

25. How Can We Be Friends Again?/Amigos de Nuevo*
26. Two in the Fight/Dos en una Pelea **
27. Heart to Heart/Corazón a Corazón*
28. The Anger Chant
29. When I Say Stop/Cuando Digo Ya*
30. There is Always Something You Can Do
31. ¡Dilo!/Talk to Me*

* Song in English and Spanish on the recording.
**Spanish lyrics provided in the book but not on the recording.

You can sing any song in Linking Up wherever you want—in a classroom, a camp, a concert, or an assembly. Photocopy the lyrics and pass them out. The formality of copyright ownership applies when someone is making a recording of a song to sell. Like the sun and the trees and the grass, songs are meant to belong to everyone.

Included with the purchase of the CD is one license to copy the recording in its entirety onto tape for your own classroom use only. We do, however, ask that you do not copy the recording—either CD or tape—for distribution to others.

> *Take these songs in your hands.*
> *They are yours now, too.*
> *I hope you'll enjoy making your own discoveries*
> *as you adapt them to your group*
> *and learn how they work best for you.*

MUSIC BELONGS TO EVERYONE

My son Ryan burst into song as we drove to his nursery school when he was three. The open car windows let in the sweet smells of the April day. He sang:

> *I am the glory of the spring, spring, spring!*
> *And I go to school, and I go to school!*

I remember being his age and inventing songs. One of my earliest memories is swinging in my backyard, making up hums with words to the oak tree, the grass, and the wind.

---

* *Song in English and Spanish on the recording.*

** *Spanish lyrics provided in the book but not on the recording.*

These forty-six songs and their activities arrive to you in this same spirit—on a breeze not just of one spring day but propelled by a long gust of wind, carrying the flavor of song sessions with children over the past twenty-five years, deep late night thoughts, and dreams as old as the earth. I want these songs to say to you: music is yours.

As I talk to other teachers my impression is that in many schools people are singing less. This collection is here to contradict the message that some of us are musicians and some of us aren't. Part of our innate human ability is our musical intelligence. At ages two or three we all explored the world by playing with words and tunes. If we encourage children's first songs as we encourage their first words, they can have more access to this musical intelligence within.

- Encourage children to make music their own by using a whole language approach that features children's contributions to songs. Many songs in this collection have simple patterns that invite children to add their own words.
- Just as we work to honor the diversity of our identities, honor the diverse ways we express our musical intelligence. Some children write songs and learn melodies quicker than others. But try not to turn these differences into a musical hierarchy in your classroom. Instead, encourage musical gifts as gifts for the community. Say, for example:

    "If you find yourself writing a song at home, bring it in. We'd love to hear it. We can all write songs."

    "The two of you learned that melody really fast. Would you be our tune keepers for this song? I'm going to turn the tape off now. Can you help us remember the tune while we sing the words?"

- Avoid any messages that separate people on the basis of how they express their musical intelligence. This means we never need to apologize for our singing voices. Model for children that everyone's voice is welcome. We can create safety to sing without jokes or put-downs.
- Let the reasons for singing shine forth—we sing together to have fun and feel closer as a group.

As surely as we need food, water, and shelter, we need human connection. Every day children need to feel in a concrete way that they are linked to others. We do that in many ways—with hugs, jokes, acknowledging nods, smiles, and words of warmth and encouragement. This social bonding provides its own kind of essential daily food.

Singing together is one of our sources of nourishment. Simply put, music is a direct way to show love. In our schools, family day care settings, early childhood centers, families, and summer camps, let's encourage each other to gather together for shared music.

BILINGUAL SINGING IS FOR EVERYONE

The National Association for Bilingual Education (NABE) states, "According to the 1990 Census, nearly 9.9 million children ages five to seventeen—one out of every five children of school age—spoke a language other than English at home. These children, language-minority children, are the fastest-growing segment of our school-age population. One of every three teachers in American schools has language-minority students in his/her classroom."

Of these languages spoken, Spanish is the most frequently used. The 1990 census revealed that over seventeen million of the 230 million people in the United States speak Spanish in their homes.

What is it like to learn a second language? It's like the emerging of new growth on a tree. It takes time and support. When Roberto Díaz and I presented the bilingual songs in this collection at the 1997 International Bilingual/Multicultural Education Conference of NABE, teachers told us why they felt this music was an important learning tool:

- Songs increase the comfort level in a classroom and reinforce the natural approach to learning a language by immersion.
- Bilingual action songs like "Step by Step/Paso a Paso" allow students to say it, hear it, see it done, and act it out.
- Songs help build the confidence of many groups of learners—mono-lingual Spanish speakers who are learning English, bilingual students who are preserving their Spanish heritage, and Spanish as a second language students. Melodic repetition combined with physical movements makes the meaning clear and allows easy absorption.

Twenty songs in this collection are presented in Spanish and in English on the recording. In addition, a translation into Spanish for seven other songs is provided within the text. This book and the recording are designed so that you can adapt the language to the needs of your group. Use the song games just in Spanish, just in English, or bilingually.

Songs in Spanish can be found in every chapter—starting songs, connecting songs, friendship songs, conflict resolution songs, movement songs, and peace songs.

For those, like myself, who are learning Spanish, here's my advice. Don't let fear of mispronunciation keep you away. I'm not a fluent speaker, but I wanted to sing in the language of friends, and the teachers and students I work with. I suggest consulting with students and colleagues who speak Spanish to check the accurate pronunciation. Practice with the recording. Feel free to ask for help. Music can be a doorway for learning more Spanish.

If You Want to Sing in Spanish Only

If you teach children in Spanish, you'll find new songs like "¡Dilo!/Talk to Me" (Song 31) that help as well as traditional songs like "El Caracol/The Snail's Dance" (Song 32). You'll also find lively songs like, "My Space/Mi Espacio," (Song 6) and a Guatemalan poem by Adrián Ramírez Flores set to music, "Canción de la Nube/Song of the Cloud" (Song 22). Also, "Llegó la Hora/Now's the Time" (Song 15) begins in Spanish. You can play just the first section and teach the song only in Spanish.

In addition, a complete sequence of songs in Spanish is found in Chapter 2, Connecting Songs. These selections follow in order on the recording to make a complete lesson:

1. Starting Song: ¡Hola!/Hello (Song 11)
2. Seated song with hand motions: Pajarito/Little Bird (Song 12)
3. Dancing song: Step by Step/Paso a Paso (Song 13)
4. Active song with hand motions: En la Feria/At the Fair (Song 14)
5. Ending or transition song: Llegó la Hora/Now's the Time (Song 15)

If You Want to Sing Bilingually

Begin with any song in the most familiar language. Once the meaning is clear, expand to the other language.

- "Step by Step/Paso a Paso" (Song 13) alternates short phrases in both languages. Additional verses in the book ask children to move their fingers—los dedos—and do other simple motions.
- Dancing to "Mi Cuerpo Hace Música/There's Music Inside Me" (Song 37) helps children learn the names of four parts of their body in both languages.
- You can study the process of translation with students in grade two or older. "Canto Por La Paz" (Song 42) was written by Roberto Díaz in Spanish. The second verse provides an English text, and the third verse alternates languages. Students can locate the same word or phrase in both languages, such as "verdadera paz" and "true peace."

If Speaking Spanish is New for You

Here are easy-to-learn bilingual tunes. They are listed in order of increasing complexity:

¡Hola!/Hello (Song 11)

Good Morning to the Sky/Buenos Días al Cielo (Song 2)

Step by Step/Paso a Paso (Song 13)

Mi Cuerpo Hace Música/There's Music Inside (Song 37)

My Space/Mi Espacio (Song 6)

Adiós/Goodbye (Song 45)

Llegó la Hora/Now's the Time (Song 15)

These bilingual songs have greater complexity. Learn them first in the language which is home-base for your students.

Across the Wide Ocean/A Través Del Inmenso Mar (Song 10)

Cuando Digo ¡Ya!/When I say Stop (Song 29)

¡Dilo!/ Talk to Me (Song 31)

How Can We Be Friends Again?/Amigos de Nuevo (Song 25)

Two Hands Hold the Earth/Mis Dos Manos (Song 41)

Sleeping Bird/Los Pajaritos Duermen (Song 23)

El Caracol/The Snail's Dance (Song 32)

Canción de la Nube/Song of the Cloud (Song 22)

Simple songs helps students of every age develop their ability to speak Spanish. In addition to the songs listed above, these also provide an easy starting place:

- "Chocolate" (Song 5) is one of the quickest songs to learn in the collection. Singers count to three and sing the syllables of "Cho-co-la-te."
- "En La Feria/At the Fair" (Song 14) names instruments like the guitar and drum. It begins in English to provide the meaning, and then continues only in Spanish.

- Although the verses of "Heart to Heart/Corazón a Corazón" (Song 27) are entirely in English, the chorus alternates Spanish and English using simple phrases like "hand in hand" and "mano a mano."

If You Want to Sing in English Only

If you enjoy a song presented in both languages but aren't ready to use the Spanish portion, sing it just in English.

- A song in both languages—such as "Across the Wide Ocean/A Través Del Inmenso Mar" (Song 10)—can be learned entirely in English. Play the beginning of the song, then stop the recording and help children to continue singing and repeating the two basic phrases in English.
- "Sleeping Bird/Los Pajaritos Duermen" (Song 23) is a back-patting game where words in Spanish are more complex. The song is sung four times—twice in English followed by twice in Spanish. Whether or not children are familiar with Spanish, they can play the game four times through and the meaning of the game will be clear.

More Songs in Spanish

Use the Spanish translations provided in this book for seven additional songs and games, that are presented only in English on the recording.

Our Own Song/Nuestra Canción (Song 8)

Creeping Mouse Game/Los Ratoncitos (Song 9)

Sing About Us/Cantemos de Nosotros (Song 21)

Two in a Fight/Dos en una Pelea (Song 26)

Shake, Shake, Freeze/Muévete, Muévete, Para (Song 36)

Cloud Hands/Manos Como Las Nubes (Song 38)

Let's Get Together/Juntémonos (Song 40)

ACKNOWLEDGMENTS

Thank you to friends and neighbors in western Massachusetts who gave me encouragement during these four years of work. Thanks to Leslie Fraser who suggested the name "Linking Up" and all the members of our Monday meditation circle, and thanks to Deborah Kruger and Paula Green, to name but a few of the many important supportive people in this region.

Thanks to the teachers and principals at the schools I've worked with over the past twenty-five years. I want to single out Mary Ann Larkin, of the Independent School in East Cleveland now a teacher at Howard University, for her support of my teaching since 1973, and Lois Bascom, most recent collaborator, for welcoming me to work with her students at Mohawk Nursery School.

In the mid-1980's a team of us teachers, songwriters, parents, and performers founded the Children's Music Network. Helping to build this community has transformed my life and made a big difference for my family. A tremendous thank you goes to Ruth Pelham, Marcia Berman, Joanne Hammil, Phil Hoose, Sandy Byer, and Bob Blue for their friendship, inspiration, and perseverance. Across the miles, in Syracuse, New York the Sapon-Shevin family—Mara, Mayer, Dalia, and Leora— and Karen Mihalyi, Robin Smith, and Eugene Marcus have also been a foundation for me. Thanks to all these people for what they do to make the world a place that sustains everyone.

In this collection you'll meet music from three Children's Music Network members—Carol Johnson, Ernest Siva, and Jose-Luis Orozco. Thanks also to Pete Seeger who has been a beacon for us in this network. Pete and my first music teacher Capitola Dickerson inspired me to follow the path of music since I was a girl. My friends in the People's Music Network, and especially Ray Korona, have shown me that music can be a lifetime journey.

I particularly want to thank Jill and Donald Person of A Gentle Wind in Albany, New York. They not only produced my first three recordings, but over the past dozen years, have given me encouragement as a songwriter to create words that have meaning for children. For nearly two decades, Jill and Donald have pioneered music with important values, setting a standard in the children's music field. "The Colors of Earth" and five other songs have been previously released by A Gentle Wind on the recordings, "Magical Earth," "The Wind is Telling Secrets," or "Two Hands Hold the Earth." The other 40 songs—mostly original, some written by or with Roberto Díaz, and some traditional—I've recorded for the first time.

Thanks to all those who helped make the Linking Up! recording. Thank you to the children from Full Circle School in Bernardston, Massachusetts and the other children who sang on the recording, and Eveline MacDougall who helped coach them.

Engineer: Joe Podlesny, Avocet Studio, Bernardston, MA
Producer: Sarah Pirtle
Musicians:
Piano - Roberto Díaz
Percussion - Morning Star
Guitar on "The Colors of Earth"—Joe Podlesny
Guitar on other songs - Sarah Pirtle
Vocalists: Sarah Pirtle and Roberto Díaz
The Children's Chorus, directed by Sarah Pirtle and Eveline MacDougall
Members:
Krista Bascom, Emily Caffery
Peter Jaros, Isabelle McKusick
Emma Nolan-Thomas, Ryan Pirtle-McVeigh
Ishana Strazzero-Wild, Felicity Watts

At Full Circle School self-directed learning and group projects intertwine; it's a place where children can still go out and "mess around" in the woods every day. The song "Full Circle/ The Village" (Song 24) is dedicated to this place that has nourished my son Ryan.

Thank you to Traprock Peace Center in Deerfield, Massachusetts where I first became involved in developing the field of peace education in 1981. Joining the efforts of Educators for Social Responsibility and others in the early 1980s, I helped forge activities that taught conflict resolution and cooperation skills. I wrote activities for the first edition of *Perspectives* by ESR that have been widely used by William Kreidler and other trainers. At Traprock I met elders in the field who had a lifetime of experience living what we were teaching. For instance, at a workshop I asked Charles Walker of Peace Brigades International if there was one thing he wanted to pass on to children about peacemaking. His answer, "There's always something you can do," became the seed of Song 30.

People all over the country have been developing their own way to teach conflict resolution. I think it's because you can't just work from someone else's recipe. You have to take the skills into your life and invent your own way of expressing the very same concepts. I have been lucky to meet Sue Liedl in Bemidji, Minnesota, who has helped change the lives of children in her community because she approaches conflict resolution teaching from her wealth of common sense. Thanks also to my mentors Marianne Hurley, Edith Sullwold, and Lynn Hoffman for their knowledge. This book is here because of all the people working in partnership to preserve essential human values.

Three years ago, I became a music consultant at Brightwood Magnet School in Springfield, Massachusetts, which specializes in integrating the arts. It's a bilingual school; 70 percent of the children are Latino. As soon as I learned that a second grade teacher, Roberto Díaz, led music every day in his classroom, I couldn't wait to meet him. Our meeting at Brightwood launched an ongoing collaboration. You'll find his songs here, like "Canto Por La Paz" (Song 42) and the melody of Linking Up!, and hear his voice and piano playing on the recording. When Roberto and I play music together, I feel like leaping dolphins. There are always new tunes to find, new words to make up. Singing with him in the studio helped old songs come alive and new songs like "Cuando Digo ¡Ya!/When I Say Stop" (Song 29) to be created.

Thank you to the dedicated group of people at Educators for Social Responsibility. First, thanks to my editor Laura Parker Roerden for her skill at getting to the heart of the matter and her unflagging enthusiasm. Thanks to Jeff Perkins, Jeremy Rehwaldt-Alexander, and Priya Natarajan for all their hard work and for seeing to all the details with thoroughness and care; thanks to Bill Kreidler, Carol Miller Lieber, Nan Doty, and ESR's early childhood training group for their advice (Lisa M. Cureton, Chris Gerzon, Rebecca Johns, Kim D. Jones, William J. Kreidler, Carol Miller Lieber, Sandy Tsubokawa Whittall). And thanks to Doug Parker Roerden and Chris Hull for all their help with the music production. Thanks to Betsy Evans and Dan Gartrell for reviewing sections of this manuscript. Thanks to Roberto Díaz and Dale Kasal for bilingual expertise and to Will Elwell at Shooting Star Photography for documenting work at Brightwood Magnet School and donating the cover photograph.

Finally, I heartily thank my son Ryan for his honest insights, his ability to make ingenious song parodies, his wisdom, and his humor.

A NOTE BEFORE YOU GO

Linking Up! has the foundational belief, exemplified in the third song "This Little Light of Mine," that we can all shine our light at the same time.

There is not only room for every light—what sustains us as a culture is each of us being at full blaze, each of us empowered to discover and give our unique gifts. Every new generation gives to the next. Each new individual refreshes their culture with who they are, like new leaves bursting forth on the branches of the same enduring tree. As said in the final song, "Linking Up,"

> *You are important in this world.*

I hope you enjoy exploring with these songs, developing your own variations, and making your own discoveries!

GLOSSARY

Circle Time: A group meeting time for developing social skills such as cooperation, communication, and respect for diversity. Children ages three to seven years old sing, play movement games, share news, talk about events in the class, or do communication activities. The purpose of the time is to provide an experience of being part of a caring community.

Discovery Time: A Song Circle for grades one and older. An exploratory approach is used to allow children to construct their social understanding. Instead of didactic instruction, interactive methods are employed such as role plays, music, creative movement and dramatics, cooperative games, listening activities, and discussion. These sessions relate directly to language arts and/or social studies goals. The emphasis is on discovery.

Song Circle: A Circle Time or Discovery Time that primarily uses music and movement.

song game: A lesson plan for one song.

group agreements: Norms for group behavior which have been developed with input from children and agreed to by all members of the group. These rules have increased import because of the shared ownership. They could also be called "our promises," or "our contract."

holding a group: Taking responsibility for all members of the group. A teacher "holds" a group when she or he makes sure all children feel physically and emotionally safe and guides the group to interact with mutual respect. This phrase comes from the work of Robert Kegan, author of the *Evolving Self* (Cambridge: Harvard University Press, 1982) where he describes a classroom as one of the "holding environments" for children.

teachable moment: An opportunity to help children learn from what is happening in the moment. In this book we'll look at how we can use interactions with children to provide guidance on social skills. By focusing on the events as a chance for learning, a teacher makes a decision to move out of the sphere of discipline and into the realm of guidance.

movement song game: A song that engages children in interaction and involves movement.

Song Sequence: A programmatic plan of two or more songs. We can assemble songs and movement song games in a sequence to be used at Circle Time or to link to your day's curriculum. We can construct a song sequence that meets our specific goals, such as developing conflict resolution skills, or helping us study community members in social studies, or providing lively, active movement.

the wave: A description of the way group experiences build and develop and then crest like a wave. As we notice the clear periods of beginning, middle, and end of a song activity we can create song sequences that are structured for increasing interaction and then end with a deliberate closing.

zipper songs: Songs with a clear pattern where the lyrics can be readily modified. Folk singer Lee Hayes invented this term to describe the way you could "zip" out the old words and "zip" new ones in their place. Using a whole language orientation, we can seek out zipper songs and invite children to add their own words into the pattern of a song.

CHAPTER 1 Implementing Linking Up!

There is always something
you can do, do, do
when you're getting
in a stew, stew, stew.

— from "There's Always Something You Can Do" (Song 30)

Whenever I enter a classroom to lead interactive music, I bring along four tools. Only one of these is something visible in my hand—a piece of paper with a lesson plan organized around a clear goal—and even this I'm prepared to change if necessary. The rest I carry in my heart and mind—these are orientations of how I'm going to interact.

TOOL 1: SOCIAL AGREEMENTS

- I know I will begin by making clear social agreements so that all children will feel physically and emotionally safe.
- I create these agreements through a conversation with the children rather than through imposing my rules.
- I am responsible for maintaining safety the whole time we are together.

TOOL 2: A GUIDANCE APPROACH

- I know that if there are conflicts or disagreements, if children are upset or if someone is excluded or mistreated, I will step in.
- I provide guidance rather than punishment so that the event can be a learning experience.
- No matter what kind of hurt or mistaken behavior they show me, I will stand by them with respect and assistance.
- I try to balance the needs of individuals with the needs of the whole group.

Five Key Elements in Teaching Social Skills

1. *Holding*

   "Hold" the group together.

   Think about all the members of the group.

   Look around and notice everyone.

   Maintain the group agreements and intervene when needed.

   Make sure both girls and boys receive equal attention.

   Create an anti-bias framework.

2. *Responding*

   Invite feedback and contributions.

   Provide opportunities to collaborate.

   Include suggestions.

   Identify what's not working and step in.

---

3. Energizing

Help each child feel engaged and involved. Provide games with lively full-body movement. Include strong powerful motions in dancing. Affirm children's need to move.

4. Guiding

Model how to talk to one another and listen. Use social situations as teachable moments. Reflect back feelings and thoughts. Ask children how a problem can be solved. Help children think of options.

5. Connecting

Use songs that ask children to look at each other. Use collaboration games to help children connect. Respond to movements. Increase children's interactions with you and with others. Through eye contact and responsive body language acknowledge every child.

TOOL 3: STRUCTURE

- I think about the specific situation—the needs of the children that time of day, and the space available in the room—and make deliberate decisions about how to structure the experience.
- I think about all kinds of diversity present and include all children.
- I bring a clear lesson plan with a clear beginning, middle, and end that is organized around a theme like diversity of families or a goal like learning about personal space.
- I prepare one or two additional song activities as options if the plan goes differently than I expect.

TOOL 4: RESPONSIVENESS

- I notice the signals the children are giving me—what things they are interested in right now, whether they need to move, and what conflicts are brewing—and respond to these signals.
- I use movements and thoughts they contribute for new verses of the songs.
- I ask questions to learn more about their suggestions and ideas.
- If necessary, I change songs and revise my plan to meet them where they are.
- I am both very firm and very flexible—I clearly "hold the group" at every moment and I am willing to incorporate their contributions.

1. MAKING SOCIAL AGREEMENTS

As a first-grade teacher at the Independent School, East Cleveland, Ohio, I led an activity period called Discovery Time that used music and movement collaboration games for a half hour before lunch. On the first day of Discovery, we sat in a circle and made a "Contract." I asked the first graders to think of one or two agreements we could make to help the group feel safe. They created these:

- No pushing or bumping.
- Stop if someone gets hurt and find out if they need help.

"Contract" became an empowering vocabulary word. If anyone felt unsafe or felt that our agreements weren't honored, they could call out—Contract! This was like calling "Freeze!" It meant all activities came to a halt while we stopped to handle the situation.

The children liked it so much that they began to use the contract when we weren't in Discovery Time. On the playground if someone fell down, others yelled "Contract!" and they all came running to see what help was needed.

It's the *process* employed with these agreements more than the particular agreements they chose that I want to recommend. Let's look at what made the contract work:

- I repeated the contract at the beginning of each session for the first two weeks. After that we reviewed weekly.
- I ended the sessions by asking, "How did we do today on the contract?" or "How could you tell the contract was working today?" This also assisted them in noticing what people did that was helpful, such as how one student helped another feel included.
- I expected the contract to be tested in the beginning, and every time an agreement wasn't kept, I intervened.
- The process belonged to them. Every month I checked back with them and asked if they wanted to change the contract. Moreover, each day they had as much power as I did to intervene if the contract wasn't kept.

Expect Your Agreements To Be Tested

When children test our agreements, that doesn't mean the method has failed. Testing is part of the learning process. It's one way children see that the agreements are real. The group needs to watch the agreements in action; when they are broken, children can observe that the teacher gives a reminder and holds them to their promises. This is how children experience that the agreements work.

Some Basics of Creating Agreements for a Song Circle

1. Three things children need to feel safe in a Song Circle that you can express in contracts:
   - Children don't want to be bumped, hit, or squeezed. They want to feel that their body is safe.
   - Children want to make sure that they won't be made fun of. They want their self-image to be safe.
   - Children want to feel they won't be made to do something they don't want to do. They want their autonomy safe.

2. Such agreements can be expressed to children using simple phrases, such as:
   - Keep it fun for everyone.
   - No bumping.
   - Friendly talking.
   - Let's treat everyone—including ourselves—in a friendly way.
   - It's okay to pass.

3. Select a term to represent your agreement that you like, such as: promises, class contract, agreements, ground rules.

4. Find phrases to insure physical safety: no bumping, look all around you, keep things safe.

5. Find phrases for social safety: friendly talking, everyone belongs here, we won't leave anyone out, there's room for everyone.

6. Respect autonomy: allow children to pass or just to observe.

7. Keep it simple:
   - Use phrases that are easy to remember.
   - Select only one or two at a time for focus.
   - Use other reminders as needed.

8. Promote leadership on group safety. I share my thought process and my reasoning with children of all ages. I talk about what a leader does to look out for everyone and make sure things are safe and fair. Sometimes children take turns at being leaders. Example: Who will watch and make sure there's room for everyone during "Creeping Mouse"?

Tip!

A three- or four-year-old may become motionless when he or she wants to pass. You can say, "It looks to me like you don't want a turn," and add if appropriate, "I'll ask you later if you'd like a turn at the end of the game."

2. A GUIDANCE APPROACH

When children have trouble pronouncing a word or forming a letter we give them help patiently. We don't expect them to get it right the first time. We inform then what they need to do differently and how they can make a change. When children have difficulty in social situations, it is very important that we give them the same quality of patient understanding guidance.

Daniel Gartrell, whose work we will learn more about in chapter 5, Conflict Resolution, suggests that we reorient from thinking in terms of misbehavior to thinking in terms of *mistaken behavior*. Misbehavior assumes that children are willful and want to do something wrong. If instead we see children as active learners, we assist them in developing social skills, just as they learn speaking or writing skills, without being punished as wrongdoers when they have difficulty.

As we work with young children, the unexpected always arises. What to us may feel like an interruption, from a child's perspective is exploration, self-expression, a request for help, or the way they are trying to connect with others. It's more important that we take time for the teachable moments that arise, than that we follow the lesson plan of songs we intended. As young people sing and move together, they actively construct their understandings of individual autonomy and of how to be a member of a community.

Strategies For Intervening

How To Help Children Participate in the Community

1. Enter the situation and provide assistance or structure.
2. Using open and responsive body language, acknowledge the child's feelings and the situation. Move closer and talk calmly.
3. Remind the children about group agreements or other social realities of the classroom community. Give reasons.
4. As needed, present two choices, or give your recommendation.
5. Provide the information and guidance to help the child(ren) try new behaviors.

Example: Leaving the Agreed Area of the Game

Situation: We've agreed to stay on the rug when we dance. As we explore movements in "My Roots Go Down," (Song 33) a four-year-old child takes several steps off the rug and looks at the teacher.

What the Child is Learning: How to keep social agreements

Teacher Response:

1. *Acknowledge*

    Hi, Alisha. I see you're moving off the rug where we're playing our game. Did you notice that, too?

2. *Remind*

    The rug is our marker, isn't it?

3. *Give Reasons*

    We agreed to stay on the rug because on the other side of the room there are blocks and other games we don't want to bump into.

4. *Make a Recommendation*

    Come on back and join us dancing on the rug.

5. *Limit Choices*

    If the recommendation didn't bring Alisha back and instead she ran further away:

    You can come back and join us in Song Circle, or you can do what we've agreed children do when they choose not to join Song Circle; your other choice is to read a book.

Example: Pounding Hands Hard

Situation: We're singing "Chocolate" (Song 5) which includes pounding hands. A five-year-old child is smashing his hands so that they hurt.

What the Child is Learning: How to treat himself respectfully

Teacher Response:

1. *Acknowledge*

    It looks like you're finding out what it feels like to pound your hands hard.

2. *Remind*

    What we're doing in our class is learning how to treat each other in a friendly way and that includes treating ourselves in a friendly way, too.

3. *Give Reasons*

    When you pound really hard, your hand might sting.

4. *Make a Recommendation*

    I bet you can find a way to do it so it's fun, but it doesn't hurt.

Note: *I've run into this situation with a range of ages—from three years old to twelve years old. Usually the person smashing their hands is looking at friends and about to engage other people. Using the guidance approach, each time the child did stop pounding, got engaged, and the tenor of the group was restored.*

Example: Exclusion

Situation: A trio of second graders are working to form a pretzel shape but one child is being excluded. Two of the trio keep their backs turned to her or him.

What the Children are Learning: How to include community members

Teacher Response:

1. *Remind*
   You're trying to figure out a way that all three of you can form a pretzel shape.

2. *Acknowledge*
   So far I see just two of you connected.

3. *Give Reasons*
   We're learning what it's like to include three people at once.

4. *Limit Choices*
   How can you stand together so you can all see each other? Do you want to think of it like a triangle or a circle? Would you like some methods from me for how you could take turns and hear each other's ideas, or would you like to work by yourselves right now?

Note: *Sometimes it is helpful to be explicit that it hurts feelings to be excluded. Other times it's more respectful for the child who is left out to present the situation as shown above.*

Example: Learning How to Collaborate in Small Groups

Situation: A second grader named Matt became angry and impatient during the game of creating a boat for the song, "Build a Boat," when other children in his group didn't take up his ideas. He started to yell at a child in the group named Robin.

Teacher Response:

Matt is yelling at Robin.

Teacher: Matt, it looks like you really want Robin to hear what you're thinking.

Teacher acknowledges feelings.

Matt: Yes, I've got a great idea, but she's not even paying attention to me.

Teacher: You look angry.

Matt: I am.

Teacher: You want to be heard. It looks like all four of you in your group want to have a chance to share your ideas.

Teacher provides the context of the whole situation.

[I'm looking for the next skill that Matt is ready for. I want to provide the information that is missing and set up the amount of social structure needed to carry it out. My understanding of Matt is that his next step is learning the reciprocal nature of collaboration; he's having as much trouble taking in the ideas of others as he is feeling heard.]

Teacher: How could each of you have a chance to tell or show an idea you have for building the boat?

(No one responds.)

Teacher: Who wants to begin?

Matt: I will.

Teacher: Who will go after Matt?

Robin: Me.

Teacher: Looks like you can keep going around the circle. (Points to other two children who will have a turn.)

Teacher: Are you going to try each other's ideas, or listen to all of the ideas first?

Robin: Hear all of them.

Teacher: Will you choose one idea or find a way to put all four ideas together?

Teacher guides the new skill.

Teacher adds more structure to facilitate the skill of taking turns talking.

Teacher moves away to allow them to work independently.

The group came up with this plan: two other children created the sides of the boat, and both Robin and Matt acted out the parts they wanted; Robin stood as the sail and Matt held a spy glass.

What I'm saying to Matt when he's angry and looks ready to explode is:
You want to be heard and you deserve to be heard.
The way you're trying to be heard isn't working.
There are other ways you can try.
I'll stand with you and keep affirming you as you learn.

Summary: The Guidance Approach
To summarize the guidance approach:
guidance=providing information with affirmation

Here's what a guidance approach offers children.
- Adults connect with children and join them where they are. They use responsive body language and non-judgmental words to mirror children's feelings. In this way they help the children feel understood.
- Adults help children become aware that their feelings have legitimacy even if what they are doing isn't recommended or isn't working. Children realize that their feelings are healthy and are sending them important messages.
- Adults help children become aware of other choices they have. They give information about other behaviors to try. Children feel invited into new possibilities instead of feeling blamed.

- Children watch others getting assistance and learn that they are in a community where all people receive help.
- Children take an active role. They are the doers; they feel in charge of themselves.

You can find more information about problem solving with children during a conflict in Chapter 4, Diversity Songs and Chapter 5, Conflict Resolution Songs.

3. PROVIDING STRUCTURE

The structure we provide for children contributes to safety and to helping children connect and build friendships. Here are other issues to consider during your planning.

1. Take space considerations into account:
   - Where in your room are you able to form a circle?
   - Where can children have enough room to move?
   - Can you have one area for a close circle and another section for large movement?
   - What objects in the room do they need to be careful of?
   - If you need to move the furniture, who will do it?
   - In what concrete way can you indicate the boundaries? (e.g., put up a yarn barrier or stay on a particular rug.)

2. Consider any group customs you will need to establish:
   - How will you call children to the Song Circle? (e.g., singing, "Come Join in the Circle" (Song 4) or "This Little Light of Mine" (Song 3), setting up chairs in a circle, then ringing a chime.)
   - How will you signal when everyone needs to be quiet and listen? (e.g., using a sound for a "zero noise signal" like a bell, a chime, a drum, or a rattle; using a visual cue such as a hand signal or raising your arm.)
   - How can children signal when they want to pass? (e.g., shaking their head, a hand signal invented by the group.)

3. Help children learn the group skill of forming a circle:
   - Develop the skill of noticing if someone is physically cut off from the circle because there isn't room. Help children learn how to move over and respond to others.
   - You can ask children to trace their hands around the circle, look, and check if everyone has enough room. "Creeping Mouse" (Song 9) provides a chance to practice looking out for one another.

4. Include democratic methods for empowering children by giving them choices in the Song Circle:
   - Plan a regular part of the Song Circle—such as the second song—where children select what song you will sing.
   - Keep a chart that shows whose turn it is next to pick a song.
   - Use activities that ask the children to add their own ideas to the songs and games.

- Let children have ownership of the group agreement. Check in periodically to see if they want to make any changes. Show them that the agreement is *theirs*.

- If they like the idea of a hand signal that means "I want to pass," engage the group in creating this signal.

- Look for movement games where children are invited to create their own unique motions instead of imitating the motions of the teacher (e.g., "Across the Wide Ocean" (Song 10). I often tell the group, "I'm not going to move, but I'm going to watch all the different ways you are making waves.")

- Allow children to take the lead in inventing new games while you help shape them. Ask a question of the group: "How do you want to use this scarf today? What will it be?" If they respond, go with their ideas. "I see. It's a blanket for our picnic." If they don't have an idea, supply one to keep the activity going at a pace that is engaging. Pose your idea as in invitation or possibility: "How about if it's a sail for our boat?"

- Invite children to take a turn as a leader who notices if the game is safe and fair.

When A Child Doesn't Want To Be Part Of The Song Circle

- Provide an optional activity for three- to five-year-olds who don't want to sit in the circle. We want to promote the child's sense of both individuality and community. This means that the child has the right not to participate, as well as to be invited to participate. Agree together as a staff what other options you can give. Select an alternative to the activity such as looking at books in the book corner.

- Talk with the children about the alternatives you are offering, both those that would work—quiet activities—and which wouldn't—like a noisy marble game. Help them understand the reasons.

- If the children who are sitting out are persuading others to join them so that the unity of the group in Song Circle is eroding, select a compelling movement song like "Jump, Jump, Jump," (Song 7) "Sitting in the Soup," (Song 7) or "Mi Cuerpo Hace Música/ There's Music Inside Me" (Song 37).

How Do We Make Sure All Children Are Included?

As we empathize with our students, we realize how to help them feel more included. Here are some considerations to keep in mind around inclusion:

1. Can the motions be done by all participants? If not, how can they be modified? Can other options be provided?

   - We can change the directions of a song game to fit all the people in the group. If "stand facing your partner and move your arms" is not a direction all children in your class can follow, modify the words: "Face your partner and either stand or sit together. Use your eyes, your head, your fingers, or your arms." This revision makes sure children who, for example, are in wheelchairs, have cerebral palsy, or are on crutches, are acknowledged.

2. Do children understand the different physical and social needs and abilities present in the group?

- "Jarad can't tell you in words that he wants to be with you, so when Jarad pulls you by your shirt, he's asking you to come and play with him."

- "You asked why Lucy is sitting out, yet I urged you to stay in the game. I'll treat each of you with care, but that doesn't mean I'll always treat you the same."

- "Misha and Pedro are meeting with Ms. Lopez now to work on some games that will help develop the muscles in their fingers. This will help make it easier to hold a pencil or a marker. That's why they aren't singing with us. Ms. Lopez said that tomorrow she will do those same games with any child in our group who would like to try them."

3. Do you know the skills of the children in your class with disabilities so that their full abilities are incorporated?

- We acknowledge each child's full capacity. For example, if we're handing out rhythm instruments, instead of assuming that some children don't have the physical dexterity to play, we can offer every child a choice.

4. Has someone had an event in their life that needs to be noticed and honored? How can you acknowledge it?

- If a child has been absent for a length of time with an illness, we can use song games as a chance to welcome them back concretely. For example, create a verse about the child's return and what it was like to be sick. Ask what words they want to put in, and use the tune of "Come Join in the Circle" (Song 4):

  Emmanuel was sick for seven days.
  His throat hurt so much it felt on fire.
  He almost went to the hospital.
  We're glad Emmanuel is back!

5. Do the words to the songs refer to all the individuals?

- Just as children want to know that their feelings and life experiences will be acknowledged and respected, children want to be sure their identities will be acknowledged, too.

- When I'm singing about families, I'll make sure that every family structure in the class is included. Not all students have sisters and brothers and sometimes an onus is put on an "only child." Not all children live with a biological parent. After a divorce, some children travel between two homes, or have step-parents or new siblings from a blended family. For example, if I'm using the song, "Sing About Us," (Song 21) I work with the children to create several family verses to cover all of their family constellations. Here is one of the verses a kindergarten class created:

  Some of us have two homes.
  Some of us have two Moms.
  Some of us live with sisters or brothers.
  Some of us live with our Grandma.

6. Are songs that represent a culture authentic?
    - If you question the authenticity of a song, find a way to research it. For example, I read in two books that "A Ram Sam Sam" was a Moroccan song, yet the words didn't feel authentic. I wanted to know what the words meant. I called up the local university and asked if they had a department of Arabic Studies. A professor was pleased to give help. He burst into laughter when I told him the words, "guli, guli, guli, guli ram sam sam." He said they weren't at all familiar and certainly weren't from Morocco, but maybe that they were nonsense syllables.

    - When I first heard the songs, "The Earth is My Mother," and "Wearing My Long Wing Feathers," they were presented as Native American songs. Later I learned that they had changed so much in the folk process that whatever their origins were, they weren't direct or accurate representatives of Native American music. "The Night Critters Song" (Song 34) is offered from Ernest Siva's teachings of music from his childhood.

7. Do you know the cultural background of members of your class? If not, talk to family members and ask questions.
    - "Tell me more about how you celebrate the Jewish Fall Festival of Sukkoth."
    - "Colleen's mother said she has a favorite lullaby in Gaelic she'd like to teach the class. I'll be asking all of your parents if there are other family songs that we could learn."

8. Do you provide ample opportunities for full body movements?
    - Instead of treating children's exuberance as a nuisance— "Oh, no. They can't sit still!"—we can include many active games. Children need that "whole body stir." We can supply songs and games for stretching and jumping, thereby planning for and affirming the vitality of children.

4. BEING RESPONSIVE

As teachers we are adept at being responsive. If one song isn't working, we can move to another. Or, if we start out planning to sing only a few verses of a song, we can sing it three times longer than anticipated if children become engrossed. Here are five ways we can be responsive to children's needs and interests.

Use Zipper Songs to Make New Verses

Children enjoy being asked to contribute new ideas for songs. Use the structure of a "zipper song" to invite children to add their own words.

How to Encourage Songwriting
1. Study the pattern of a favorite song.
2. Look for places where word substitutions can be made.
3. Encourage children to give ideas for ways to zip new words into songs.

For instance, using "This Little Light of Mine" (Song 3) we see the verse has this pattern:

All around the world, I'm gonna let it shine.

A child's new contribution could be:

All around our playground, I'm gonna let it shine.

Example: Bilingual Language Class

Situation: Second-grade students are discussing what kinds of foods go into a salad.

What the Child is Learning: Language arts skills

Teacher Response:

1. The teacher selects a tune she is familiar with ("Llegó La Hora," Song 15) and makes a song pattern with three open lines.

    We put _____ in the salad. (3x)
    Now's the time for salad.

2. The teacher asks three children at a time to name a food that is used to make salad. Then she asks the whole group to repeat what they said to develop their listening skills. Finally, the three items are inserted into the blanks and the class sings the new verse.

Create a New Song

Circle Time gives us the flexibility to follow the immediate interests of the group. Let's say the weather has made a dramatic change, or a pet has died, or the group has just completed an exciting activity. You could focus on this.

How to Write A New Song

1. Think of a song with which you are familiar.
2. List information related to the topic of interest.
3. Work with the pattern of the song and zip the words from the list into it.

Example: Banana Muffins

Situation: The children have just finished mixing muffins before Circle Time. Now they are in the oven. The smell lingers in the air as the muffins cook.

What the Child are Learning: Language arts skills

Teacher Response:

1. The teacher picks a tune he is familiar with ("She'll Be Coming 'Round the Mountain.")
2. He asks the children to review all the stages of the recipe.
3. He puts their words into the verses, repeating the words children have said in sequence without worrying about finding rhymes. He engages them in pantomiming the actions as they sing.

    First we measure flour in a cup. (2x)
    And then we added baking powder.
    And we added salt.
    And we stirred it around in a bowl.

Expand The Activity When the Unexpected Arises

Another way we are called to respond is when one member of the group does an exploratory motion or behavior like stomping that is outside the perimeters of the song game. It is important to treat this behavior as part of the child's exploration of the world and not misbehavior. Whenever possible, I like to use an interaction strategy to bring what children do into the song, while providing safety.

How to Work With the Unexpected

1. Make the unexpected behavior the next group activity in the song or game if appropriate.
2. To maintain safety, create a clear transition back to the next activity.

Example: Peeking Under Chairs

Situation: Three- and four-year-old children are seated in chairs as they begin to learn a new song game, "Jump, Jump, Jump" (Song 7). Suddenly one child peeks under her chair. Others get interested in what she is doing and start to do the same. They do not respond when the teacher requests that they return their focus to the game.

What the Children are Learning: That responsiveness is an important social skill.

Teacher Response:

1. Use the unexpected behavior.
   The teacher uses the same tune as "Jump, Jump, Jump" and starts the verse with peeking:

   > *We look under our chairs. (2x)*

2. Bring the group back.
   She then ends the verse to re-focus the group:

   > *And then* (she pauses to engage them through the suspense)
   > *We creep, creep, creep back up again.*
   > *And do a silly wave under our chins.*

A different engaging movement is substituted—that of holding your hand under your chin and waving. This refocuses the children to look at each other and at the teacher while they prepare to hear the next direction.

Part 3, "Songs for Movement Games," includes more strategies to use to respond to unexpected behavior and maintain safety using ideas from the group.

Teachable Moments

When a child is upset, more important than the words we use is the attitude we take. When conflicts arise as they always do—if someone's hand is squeezed too hard or a child is elbowed in the ribs—use this as a teachable moment. Song circles provide a time to zero in on the specific assistance in social skills that children need. Look at what problems children are presenting. When we are willing to lay aside a lesson plan to interact with children we model that responding to people is an essential social skill.

Example: Intervening in Hitting

Situation: One day I'd brought a bag of spoons to Circle Time with three-, four-, and five-year-olds. I was intending to share "The Spoony Song," (Song 8). Instead I needed to intervene as a boy named Eddie was hit repeatedly by his younger friend.

What the Child is Learning: I focused primarily not on the boy who was hitting but gave Eddie tools to protect himself and ways to insist that his boundaries be respected. The song activities for "When I Say Stop" (Song 29), describe how I used that song to help. When we sang "The Spoony Song" next, I asked Eddie to suggest a food for the song. He said, "cereal," and there was a gleam in his eye as we sang his words and pantomimed that we were eating cereal. This was the first time he had ever spoken in Circle Time.

Respond to a Specific Problem with a Song Activity

When I enter a classroom, I focus not only on what isn't working, but envision what the classroom would look like if social interactions were healthier. What skills are the children ready to develop next?

How to Increase the Social Health of the Group

1. Identify one way the group is having trouble and describe it in terms of a positive goal. Select the next step.
2. Use a song to offer a positive direction and re-pattern the group.

Example: Personal Space

Situation: First graders were becoming involved in play-fighting and scuffling at recess and were pushing whenever they got in line.

What the Child is Learning: What it means to keep a personal boundary.

Teacher Response:

1. The teacher decided that the children needed work identifying their own space and what it meant to have a personal boundary.

2. He used the song "My Space/Mi Espacio" (Song 6) at Circle Time to help children practice finding their own "space bubble." Each day before recess he asked students to remember their own space and to speak up if someone was entering their space in a way they didn't like. Then after recess he held a class meeting to check how things had gone and discuss any problems. By working on just one concept, he was able to see progress. The song made the idea of personal space concrete.

   In the appendix, you will find "How Songs Develop the Social Health of a Class," which suggests specific songs in "Linking Up" to use to teach particular social skills.

SEQUENCING SONGS: HOW DO YOU DEVELOP A LESSON PLAN?

You can combine several song games into a Song Circle—a circle time devoted to music. I find that Song Circles feel more unified and satisfying when we provide a clear beginning, middle, and ending. Within this framework, I have observed that when children are engaged together, the main activity tends to build like a wave. They are singing, moving, adding more ideas, and actively participating. Then suddenly the children feel finished. It's as if the wave has crested. They are ready to stop and need help making the transition. We can provide a clear closure to the experience, use a calming song, and give guidance about what will happen next.

Simple Steps for Building Your Song Sequence

1. Identify a goal that relates to social interaction and self-awareness. Examples: I want children to be able to get up and move without colliding. I want them to feel calmer and more focused. I want one child to work with another child.

2. Find a main activity that corresponds to this goal. Refer to the objectives listed at the beginning of each song. For example:
   Goal: I want them to be able to get up and move without colliding.
   Objective for Song 36: To help children develop self-control.
   Use: "Shake, Shake, Freeze" (Song 36)

3. Sequence the activities to build like a wave. Picture this main activity as the peak of the wave and work toward it.
   - Begin with a clear starting song.
   - Next, select one or two songs that anchor the group in the present because they are familiar or they use active motions while seated.

4. As needed, add songs that remind children about social agreements. For example, you may want to add "Two in the Fight" (Song 26) or "We Won't Leave Anyone Out" (Song 20).

5. Verbalize the social skill the group is working on at that moment. Examples:
   - Stay in your own space bubble.
   - Be sure to stop and freeze.
   - Move your own way.
   - Look at your partner and work together.

   Focus together on the activity and let it come to full-ness.

6. Sense when the activity is over and the children are ready to stop. Have ready a song that provides clear closure.

Tip!

When you are leading the group, keep your Song Sequence plan in mind and use it to keep you on track, but also be guided by the immediate needs of the group. In other words, structure and responsiveness work as partners in song circles.

I recommend the following pattern for your general plan for the songs to be used in your song:

1. UNIFY 2. ANCHOR 3. BUILD 4. EXPAND 5. END

1. *Unify* the group. Select a starting song to gather and welcome everyone. Children need a chance to connect with the teacher and be noticed in a concrete way.

2. *Anchor* the group in the present. Choose activities that help children become centered physically, that respond to their interests, or that remind them about group

agreements. Familiar songs help provide an anchor. This is also a time when you can ask children to select the song.

3. *Build* a skill. Introduce the main skill you want to develop. Use simple activities to prepare for more difficult ones.

4. *Expand* the children's involvement. Focus upon a main song game which engages children.

5. *End* together. Stop the activity when you sense the children need to stop. Use a song to let them know that it's over. Make a clear closing.

When it Doesn't Go as You Had Planned

Rarely does the plan go exactly as I expect because I am incorporating ideas from where the children are at the moment. The songs I picked in advance aren't always the ones I use. I may have too many songs and need to omit one. Or sometimes something else emerges as a better plan. However, this feeling of a wave that builds and then ends is still an accurate description of what occurs in most successful Song Sequences.

At the heart of this work, however, is responding to the unexpected and following the immediate interest of the children. Make music out of what the children are doing and respond to where they are. For example, while singing "My Space/Mi Espacio" (Song 6) one child starts to jump as high as she can in the air. It's infectious. Jumping looks like fun, and more and more children are trying it. Instead of fighting this direction, we can leverage what appears to be the children's greatest interest while providing a clear form of appropriate boundaries:

"Who are you jumping so high?" responds the teacher.

"A prairie dog," says the child who's just seen prairie dogs in a book.

The teacher uses the tune of "My Space" and sings the children's words:
> *Here I am. I'm a prairie dog.*

"Can you hide in your prairie dog holes and pop up again?" the teacher adds to provide a boundary in the game.

And so it builds. Suddenly this song has become the main activity. We follow it and follow it until it runs its course.

End When the Spirit Says End

> *"Leave them wanting more instead of wanting out."*
> —Barbara Beach, Arts educator, Wolf Trap Center

When we are leading a group, children send signals that tell us when they are ready to stop. The group may seem restless. Some children may be turning around or perhaps starting to talk about what's next. The activity has come to fruition. They are satisfied with the group experience and ready to move on. When it's time to end, end.

Songs to Use in Your Song Sequence

Choose one song from each group.

1. **Starting Songs**
   Unify
   Good Morning to the Sky/Buenos Días al Cielo (Song 2)
   Come Join in the Circle (Song 4)
   ¡Hola!/Hello (Song 11)
   This Little Light of Mine (Song 3)
   Grandmother Spider (Song 19)

2. **Anchoring Songs**
   Anchor using their experience
   Come Join in the Circle (Song 4)
   Our Own Song (Song 8)
   Spoony Song (Song 8)

   or Anchor using seated movement
   Chocolate (Song 5)
   Creeping Mouse (Song 9)
   Pajarito/Little Bird (Song 12)
   En la Feria/At the Fair (Song 14)
   We Won't Leave Anyone Out (Song 20)
   Build a Boat (Song 35), holding hands and rocking

3. **Main Activity to Build Skills and Expand**
   Cooperation Movement Games
   My Space/Mi Espacio (Song 6)
   Sitting in the Soup (Song 7)
   Jump, Jump, Jump (Song 7)
   Across the Wide Ocean/A Través Del Inmenso Mar (Song 10)
   Step by Step/Paso a Paso (Song 13)
   Or, select any movement game songs from chapters 6 or 7.

   Thoughtful Songs
   The Colors of Earth (Song 1)
   Friendship songs from chapter 3
   Diversity or conflict resolution songs from chapter 4 or 5
   Peace songs from chapter 8

4. **Ending Songs**
   Slow, Soothing Closing Songs
   Across the Wide Ocean/A Través Del Inmenso Mar (Song 10)
   Grandmother Spider (Song 19)
   Sleeping Birds/Los Pajaritos Duermen (Song 23)
   Carry the Candle (Song 44)
   Linking Up (Song 46)

Quick, Snappy Transition Songs
Come Join in the Circle (Song 4), revised as "Time to end the circle"
Llegó la Hora/Now's the Time (Song 15)
Two in the Fight (Song 26), as a talk it out reminder before recess
Two Hands Hold the Earth/Mis Dos Manos (Song 41), stand and stretch
Adiós/Goodbye (Song 45)

SNAPSHOT

Song Sequence: Riding the Wave

• •

A circle of four- to six-year-olds are gathered for their usual welcoming song, "Come Join in the Circle" (Song 4).

> *Come join in the circle,*
> *Moon, moon, the moon and sun.*
> *Come join in the circle*
> *there's room for everyone.*

"Let's wave around the circle," I say. "Take a look at each person here."

> *Wave around the circle.*
> *Wave the way you like.*

"Tony, you're waving with your elbow. We'll try it like you."

The song resumes, with everyone waving with our elbows.

"Now let's add our news. Who has news to put in our song today?" I ask.

"Put my cat in," says Juanita.

"What should we say?"

"Last night she hurt her ear."

"Anything else you want to say?"

"I'm sad."

We sing her words to the same tune:

> *Juanita's cat hurt her ear,*
> *her ear, her ear.*
> *Juanita's cat hurt her ear.*
> *She's sad her cat is hurt.*

"We got to sing it like this," says Jamal. He pantomimes that he's petting and soothing a cat. "Yeah," agrees Juanita. We sing it again, adding his motion.

I've posted a chart with the names of each child. Every time they have a chance to pick the second song of the day, I check off their name. I look at the chart. "Gina, it's your turn to pick the next song."

"That one," says four-year-old Gina, rubbing her palms together and pointing to the chart of songs depicted by symbols.

"That's the chocolate song," calls Marguerita.

> *Uno, dos, tres—CHO*
> *Uno, dos, tres—CO*

As we count in Spanish and pound our hands, I notice that a few of the children who'd begun to lose interest in the first song are again engaged. Each time we sing, "Chocolate," children look more involved, more physically anchored.

"Do it the fast way," says Gina. We sing twice more, faster and faster, and then to help the transition, before the last line I call, "Slow down the ending." We stretch out the final words:

> Ba-te..., ba-te..., cho-co-la-te.

I see wiggles in the group. I've planned to bring us gradually into full-bodied movement starting with "Shake, Shake, Freeze" (Song 36). But I remember that last time we sang this song, some children got accidentally bumped, and escalated the problem by pushing. I sense that the group would have more success moving together for the song if we prepared words for when a conflict arises.

I choose the song "Two in a Fight" (Song 26) to help the children practice communication and conflict resolution skills before trying "Shake, Shake, Freeze." We begin the song. Together we raise our index fingers as if they are people talking to each other and sing:

> There were two in the fight and the little one said,
> "I'm angry. I'm angry."

We sing the whole story of the song. It ends,

> Talk it out. We can figure this out.

I tell them, "We might need to talk things out when we start dancing. What can you say if you get bumped while you're dancing?"

"You can say—Don't," says Jamal.

"Or, please stop bumping me," answers Marguerita. She remembers our last conversation.

I add, "Let's look out for each other as we dance today. Everyone agree?"

They nod, and I show them the "Stop and go" song ("Shake, Shake, Freeze" Song 36). Each time the song says, "freeze," children have a chance to practice self-control.

> Shake, shake, shake, shake, shake and freeze.

Tony keeps on shaking while the rest freeze as the music stops. "Stop and freeze," I remind. He notices me looking at him and he freezes. I keep a close eye on the group as we go through a series of different motions. Tony and the rest of the children are exhibiting self-control by the next verse. I'm looking to see what motions they'd want to do next. I read the way they explore each movement to learn how they are yearning to expand. It looks like they are eager for stomping. The song, "My Roots Go Down" (Song 33), with which they are familiar, can provide a safe avenue for strong movements such as stomping.

I reinforce our work on maintaining personal space which we call "your own bubble of space."

"Find a spot where you can stand and have enough room to swing your arms," I say. Lucas glues himself to Brian. I guide him to give himself more room. "Pretend you are a tree, Lucas. Your roots are planted and your branches swing in the breeze."

> My roots go down, down to the earth.

Now there's room for moving safely. "Let's add stomping as we sing those same words," I suggest. The children stomp to the rhythm of the song. After we repeat that chorus, they have more attention for the usual game. I ask, "What shall we put in our song today?"

"Jumping beans," says Kisha.

"Try jumping while you're holding hands with other people." We sing:

> I am a jumping bean, jumping to the sun.
> My roots go down.

"I want to be a bird," says Jamal. "Let's make a nest like yesterday," he suggests. We all bring our hands together as if forming a roof. As we sing, children pretend to fly around the room and then return to the circle as the song calls them back:

> Come on back where you started from
> We're glad you're back.

We repeat the flying birds until Tony collides with Juanita. "Watch out," she says.

"You did it, Juanita," I encourage. "You said what you want with your words," Tony runs behind a shelf. "Come on back. We can figure this out," I tell him, using the same phrase we just sang in the "Two in the Fight" song. "It's more fun to play flying birds when no one is bumped," I guide him. "Try again using your own bubble of space." We do the game again and I watch as he carefully avoids other dancers. "That's it, Tony," I tell him with encouragement.

We continue following their suggestions to include other animals for the "My Roots Go Down" game until they are ready to rest.

"Let's do the Sleeping Bird game (Song 23)," I say. "Who wants to lie down and be a sleeping bird?" Most everyone raises their hands. "And who wants to help pat backs?" Jamal and Gina volunteer.

> We see the birds sleeping, we see the birds sleeping.
> We'll pat you, we'll help you, feel safe in your nest.

Jamal, Gina, and I walk around and make sure each back is patted. After playing the game one time through, I allow time for any children to switch roles as sleeping birds and back-patters. We repeat the song and then they are ready for snack.

"The birds are flying off to eat," says Jamal.

Song Sequence:
1. Come Join in the Circle (Song 4)
2. Chocolate (Song 5)
3. Two in the Fight (Song 26)
4. Shake, Shake, Freeze (Song 36)
5. My Roots Go Down (Song 33)
6. Sleeping Birds/ Los Pajaritos Duermen (Song 23)

Here's How The Wave Worked

The main objectives in the Song Sequence in the Snapshot were 1) to help children to become more aware of each other and 2) to provide opportunity for active movement with self-control.

Here's how the "1. Unify 2. Anchor 3. Build 4. Expand 5. End" sequence worked in this example.

1. *Unify*

   "Come Join in the Circle": Children shared news with a greeting song familiar to them.

2. *Anchor In The Present*

   "Chocolate": Hand motions helped them anchor physically.

   "Two in the Fight": The song reminded them to find the words they need.

3. *Build A Skill*

"Shake, Shake, Freeze": The word "freeze" introduced self-control. This alternated with free movements like shaking.

4. *Expand Their Involvement*

"My Roots Go Down": Children explored their movements within the order of the game. Social agreements were reinforced.

5. *End Together*

"Sleeping Birds/Los Pajaritos Duermen": Children expressed care in a back patting game.

Song Sequences As Discovery Time

When Song Sequences combining music and movement are used during Circle Time, I like to call this Discovery Time.

In the previous snapshot example, what did we discover together? When we use interactive music and movement:

- We discover that our lives are important to each other. Jamal's movement suggestion about patting a cat helps Juanita feels valued.
- We discover our "I am" identity. Making strong movements, we feel physically present.
- We discover our ideas are important to other people. Kisha makes a suggestion for a song, and the teacher responds and sings her idea.
- We discover we can solve social problems by communicating and by intending to cooperate together. Juanita speaks up when Tony collides into her. Tony is guided to try again instead of being punished. This gives an opportunity to progress in the development of social skills.

Summary Of Key Song Circle Facilitation Ideas

When leading a song circle:

1. Help children connect with each other. Encourage them to:
   - look at everyone
   - notice the needs and feelings of others
   - join and move together

2. Look for opportunities to ask children for their suggestions:
   - What do you want to sing next?
   - How do you want to move on this song?
   - What other words could we sing?

3. Give guidance. Children need to practice social skills the same as they practice speaking, reading, or counting. Cooperative songs and movement games provide this opportunity for practice. Use conflicts as an opportunity. Respond to mistaken behavior by guiding children instead of punishing. Go beyond a general statement like "Use your words," and help identify specific words that will help.

PART I

Songs for Circle Time

Here we are sitting in the soup,
sitting in the soup on Monday.
— from "Sitting in the Soup" (Song 7)

We build a caring community when we come together for participatory music. Music provides a means for all children to feel valued at the same time. In Part I: Songs for Circle Time, you'll find songs that are effective for building community during group gatherings.

Chapter 2 features four Starting Songs that help begin a Song Circle because they are compelling and welcoming.

1. The Colors of Earth
2. Good Morning to the Sky/Buenos Días Al Cielo
3. This Little Light of Mine
4. Come Join in the Circle

Chapter 3 presents Friendship Songs that help children become more connected to one another, arranged in three sequenced lesson plans. The last six songs in this chapter are both in English and Spanish.

5. Chocolate
6. My Space/Mi Espacio
7. Sitting in the Soup and Jump, Jump, Jump
8. Our Own Song and the Spoony Song
9. Creeping Mouse Game

10. Across the Wide Ocean/ A Través Del Inmenso Mar
11. ¡Hola!/Hello
12. Pajarito/Little Bird
13. Step by Step/Paso a Paso
14. En La Feria/ At the Fair
15. Llegó la Hora/Now's the Time

Beginning Circle Time

Lois Bascom announces Circle Time to her three- to five-year old students by singing, "Come Join in the Circle" (Song 4) while she walks around the room at Mohawk Nursery School in Shelburne Falls, Massachusetts. The song signals that it's time to come to the circle of chairs around the story rug and greet each other at morning meeting.

Here are five teaching strategies to use at Circle Time:

1. **Eye Contact**
   Look at each child and smile warmly as you are singing.

2. **Sweep the Circle**
   Give each child a turn in a sequence. Help them predict when their turn will come. Teach them that when you say you will "sweep the circle" it means no one will be left out. You will proceed in order until everyone has had a turn.

3. **Lines of Connection**
   When you ask children to look at each other, touch hands, sing each other's words, or mirror each other's motions, it is as if you have drawn a line that links them. With each song activity, look for ways that you can increase children's interactions so that they are not only relating to you the teacher but also to each other.

4. **Make Pairs Deliberately**
   Saying "Everyone get into partners" might mean some children will be excluded. Instead create a deliberate method for forming pairs or small groups which models fairness. (Young children will also need an explanation that "pair" means two people.) Start by setting an agreement: "We're about to form partners. I'm going to ask people not to call out who they'd like to be with. We're learning how to work well with everyone in our class. You'll have a chance to work with many differnt people this year. I'll use a fair method each time we divide into groups."

   Here are suggested strategies:
   * Keep names on index cards and draw names randomly.
   * Place the children in pairs yourself based on where people are sitting.
   * Place the children in pairs yourself, mixing up the group.
   * Count off using numbers or alternate names like apple, orange.
   * Use a method of rotation.

5. **Ask for Their Ideas**
   Look for places in each song where children can provide additional words or give ideas for movement. Example: How shall we wave to the sky this morning? Children may suggest pointing with their fingers, or stretching their whole palm, or making a gesture from their heart.

CHAPTER 2

Starting Songs: Gathering the Group

Come join in the circle,
Moon, moon, the moon, and sun.
Come join in the circle.
There's room for everyone.
I'm so glad you're here. I'm so glad you're here.
Come join in the circle.
There's room for everyone.
— from "Come Join in the Circle" (Song 4)

If you lead a regular circle time with your class, you probably have a favorite song or ritual that greets the children and helps them focus. What makes a starting song work?

- It's upbeat. The joyful tune reinforces the words of the song and helps children feel welcomed.
- The words ask children to notice each other. In a concrete way they know that they are seen. This helps children feel included.

The songs in this chapter:

- **provide important messages**

    I notice you. You're important to me.

    We care about each other.

    Everyone is included. We're all welcome here.

    You can be yourself in this circle and express your uniqueness.

- **ask children to contribute**

    What is your news?

    How do you want to wave your hands?

    What color are your eyes?

- **help children welcome each other**

    Take a look at the other people with you.

    Wave to them and greet them.

Other songs in the book that make effective starting songs include:

Across the Wide Ocean/A Través Del Inmenso Mar (Song 10)

¡Hola!/Hello (Song 11)

Grandmother Spider (Song 19)

We Won't Leave Anyone Out (Song 20)

Build A Boat (Song 26)

Carry the Candle (Song 44)

Ages	3 and older
When to Use	To complement language arts and social studies curricula
Language	English
Location	Side 1, Song 1
Source	Sarah Pirtle

1 The Colors of Earth

Children recognize their diversity
and common connection to the earth.

● ●

OBJECTIVES

- to recognize our basic unity and diversity
- to initiate anti-bias discussions

PROCEDURE

1 Teach the chorus of the song to the children. Variation: Use American Sign Language.

2 Focus on the first verse of the song and facilitate a class discussion on the colors of our eyes. Ask: "How do you describe the color of your eyes? How is the color of your eyes mentioned in the song?" Clarify that "topaz" is a brown gemstone. "Is there a different way you'd describe the color of your eyes?" (For example, first graders have said "seaweed color" and "blueberry.") "Take a look at the eyes of the people next to you. How would you describe them?"

3 Focus on the second verse of the song and facilitate a class exploration of hands. Invite children to work in pairs to look for as many similarities and differences in their hands as they can find. Ask: "How are your hands the same? How are they different?" Discuss the discoveries children have made.

Tip!

Bring colors of the earth into the classroom for this song. Place a multi-colored cloth in the middle of the circle as you introduce the song. Add a bowl of sea shells, chestnuts, acorns, gem stones, and rocks. Each child then selects an item to hold as everyone sings together.

4 If you are playing an instrument to accompany the song, you may prefer to use easier chords than the ones listed in the transcription. The song is recorded and transcribed in the key of A flat. You can also sing it a half step lower in the key of G. Play these chords:

G   C   G
We are made of the colors of earth.

C   G   Amin   D
Each color is different. Each color is true.

```
        G                   C   G
We are made of the colors of earth.
C        G           D   G
I love the colors that made you.
```

Songwriter's Note: *The seed for this song was planted when I heard an ecologist and poet from India named Vandana Shiva comment that if we look around at people we see that we all have the same colors as the earth.*

The Earth's Colors: Our Universal Paintbrush

· ·

Second-grade classroom teacher and educational consultant Barbara Rothenberg, from Fort River School in Amherst, Massachusetts, uses "The Colors of Earth" with her second-grade students every year. She teaches them how to interpret the lyrics in American Sign Language. Here is how she ties the song into her curriculum:

> "In discussing earth's colors the students become aware that these colors are seen by everyone, regardless of where one lives on our planet. There is a sense of a universal paintbrush. This song is a great tool to teach the concept of metaphor. My students explore which colors in nature describe their physical characteristics. We focus on the common frame of reference we all share. By celebrating the beauty of the earth, we celebrate the beauty of every human being. My students not only explore skin and eye color, but extend their comparisons to hair color, teeth, and lips. Their comparisons range from oyster shells and strawberries, to seal skin, sand dunes, and lily pads."

Barbara likes to use these additional verses that are recorded on my cassette, *The Wind is Telling Secrets*. To highlight the complexity of color, I call attention to the variety of purples, including the deep purple in the skin of a peach.

1. *Tell me the names of the colors of earth.*
    The purple of eggplant, the purple of peach.
    The green and the black of the rocks on the beach.
    And the sun on the mountains in the morning.

2. *Earth that I love, do you know how I feel?*
    How much I love seashells? How much I love stones?
    When I walk barefoot through the fields all alone.
    I sing out a song to the morning.

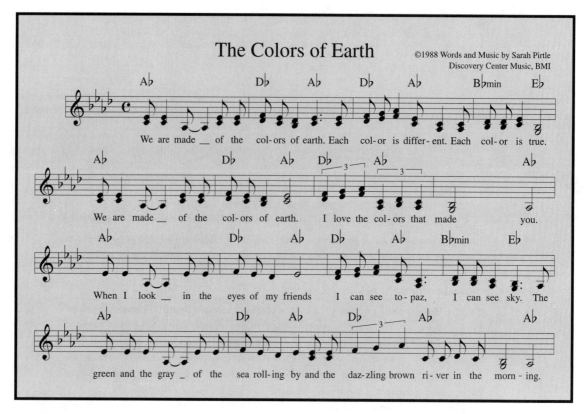

The Colors of Earth

©1988 Words and Music by Sarah Pirtle
Discovery Center Music, BMI

We are made __ of the col-ors of earth. Each col-or is differ-ent. Each col-or is true.

We are made __ of the col-ors of earth. I love the col-ors that made you.

When I look __ in the eyes of my friends I can see to-paz, I can see sky. The

green and the gray __ of the sea roll-ing by and the daz-zling brown ri-ver in the morn-ing.

Chorus

We are made of the colors of earth.
Each color is different.
Each color is true.
We are made of the colors of earth.
I love the colors that made you.

Verse 1

When I look in the eyes of my friends,
I can see topaz, I can see sky.
The green and the gray of the sea

rolling by and the dazzling
brown river in the morning.

Verse 2

When I look at the hands of my friends,
I can see chestnut, I can see corn.
The color of wheat fields and a dappled
brown fawn,
And the rain-kissed black trees in the
morning.

E X T E N S I O N S

Whole Language Songwriting

Option A

Write your own verse about eye color. List all the colors as the children describe their eyes. Make sure that everyone is included in the way they want to be included. Arrange the colors within the verse pattern. The lines do not have to rhyme.

Sample Pattern

When I look in the eyes of my friends.
I can see ____, I see ____,
And ____ like ____, and ____ like ____.
I see ____ when I look at you.

Example

When I look in the eyes of my friends.
I can see seaweed, I see gray ocean,

And brown like the tree trunks and blue like the waves, I see sparkles like cat's eyes when I look at you.

Option B

Write your own verse about hands. Make a list of all the observations partners made (see #3 in the song activity) and craft the words into new verses.

Sample Pattern

When I look at the hands of my friends.
I see ____ and ____.
Some have ____ and____.
And we have ____.

Example

When I look at the hands of my friends,
I see long fingers and short fingers, too.
Some have scars and we all have veins.
And we have lines on our palms like tree branches.

Art Activity

Materials: Multicultural crayons

Have pairs of children compare their hands. Ask the children to focus on all the details that emerge, such as lines, scars, freckles, and the shapes of their fingers. Then help children to pair up with a new partner and use these details to examine more differences and similarities between their hands.

Each child then traces his or her partner's hand on a sheet of drawing paper. Children decorate their own hands by drawing in as many details as they can. They can depict the back of their hand or their palm. Post the hands on a bulletin board with lyrics to the song or with their songwriting.

ADDITIONAL RESOURCES

All The Colors We Are/Todos Los Colores De Nuestra Piel by Katie Kissinger, with photographs by Wernher Krutein (St. Paul, MN: Redleaf Press, 1994). This easy-to-read book provides scientific information about how we get our skin color.

Literature Activity

Materials: All the Colors of the Earth by Sheila Hamanaka (New York: William Morrow, 1994)

Read *All the Colors of the Earth* to the children. Children ages three to nine enjoy the beautiful illustrations and words. Coincidentally, the song and the book relate to each other, although they were written independently. One of the many wonderful aspects of this book is that children who are biracial and children who are albino can find themselves in the illustrations.

Anti-bias Activity

"The Colors of Earth" can help initiate discussions about bias and about ways to change bias to fairness. Share these messages with children: "It's not skin or hair color or any way that we look that creates the problem of discrimination. Discrimination happens when one group of people tries to say they are better and tries, unfairly, to claim more privileges. Who we are right now is beautiful. All eye colors are good eye colors. All skin colors are good skin colors. All kinds of hair are good."

Chapter 3, "Diversity Songs," provides additional activities and songs on related themes.

Ages 3 to 12
When to Use Circle Time or
to start the day
Language Bilingual
Location Side 1, Song 2
Source Sarah Pirtle

2 Good Morning to the Sky/ Buenos Días Al Cielo

Children greet the sky, the ground, and each other.

● ●

OBJECTIVES

- to notice and greet the members of your group
- to honor your relationship to nature

PROCEDURE

1 Gather the children together in a circle. Review the song. Teach the motions as you teach the words. The movements help children feel more physically present and aware of others.

2 Invite children to greet each other by looking, waving, or nodding while singing the song. Encourage children to notice other people looking at them.

Variation If you aren't singing the song in the morning, you can vary the words:

> **English**
> *Good day to the sky*
> *Hello to the sky*
> *Good afternoon to the sky.*
>
> **Spanish**
> *Buenos días al cielo*
> *Hola al cielo*
> *Buenas tardes al cielo*

Tip!

Ask yourself: How can I make it very concrete to each child that she or he is being welcomed by me and by the group?

3 Invite children to develop their own motions: "How shall we greet each other today?" Example: They may choose to wave with all ten fingers. Or ask a child, "How can we wave to you today?" Then insert the child's name into the tune: Hola a _____ or Good morning to _____ (2x).

4 Use the song to emphasize names, and change the pattern to sing the name of every child. Example: *Buenos días a Jorges y Dianne.* You can fit eight names in each verse (two per line).

SNAPSHOT

The Power of Singing Their Words

I like to use the pattern of the song to help children express themselves. In a first-grade classroom at Brightwood Magnet School in Springfield, Massachusetts, Roberto Díaz and I had just finished this song and were starting a new one when a boy shyly raised his hand and said, "I want to say—good morning to the sun." As teachers, we had a choice: we could tell him that we were sorry but we had already started a new song, or we could follow his lead. When we sang his words, the whole tenor of the class shifted as the children saw the potential for adding their own words. Our responsiveness helped them go deeper to what they needed to talk about. Next a girl said, "I want to sing to the dead people in the sky." We knew the reason for her thoughts about death—her mother had just had a stroke—and we found a way to craft the words to speak of continuity. Roberto sang in Spanish, "Buenos días a los que se me adelantaron," and I translated, "Good morning to the ones who've gone before." As we sang in both languages, she smiled and found it comforting to feel her classmates join in her words. Later that day the boy stopped me in the hall and asked with a grin, "How do you like my song—Good morning to the sun?" I was delighted that he thought of it as his song.

Buenos Días Al Cielo

©1997 Words and Music by Sarah Pirtle
Discovery Center Music, BMI

Good morning to the sky, sky, sky.
(Stretch your hands up or point to the sky.)

Good morning to the ground, ground, ground.
(Tap floor or legs or point to the ground.)

Good morning to all the people in the circle.
Let's take a look around.
(Wave to everyone.)

Buenos días al cielo, sí.
(Stretch your hands up.)

Buenos días a la tierra, sí.
(Tap floor or legs.)

Buenos días a todos aquí,
(Wave to everyone.)

A ti, a ti, y a mí.
(Wave to two specific people and wave to yourself.)

Translation note: *Buenos días a todos aquí a ti, a ti, y a mí means "Good morning to everyone, to you and you and me."*

E X T E N S I O N S

Reading With Story Boards

Create two song boards, one with the words to the song in English and the other with the words in Spanish. Make enough copies of the boards so each small group of students can work with them cooperatively.

> *Good morning to the _____.*
> *Good morning to the _____.*
> *Good morning to all the people in the*
> *_____.*
>
> *Let's take a _____ around.*
> *Buenos días al ____ , sí.*
> *Buenos días a la ___, sí.*
> *Buenos días a _____,*
> *a ti a ti, y a ____.*

Create two sets of cards to accompany the boards: one has the key words as pictures and the other set spells out the words. You'll need: *sky, ground, circle,* and *look.*

The Spanish cards should read: *cielo, tierra, todos aquí* (picture of a group), y *mí* (picture of one child pointing to self).

Students work in pairs or trios. First, use the picture cards. Ask the pairs to place the appropriate picture card in each blank space.

When they have done these successfully, use the words. Lead them step by step to help them study the cards and take turns placing them in the appropriate spaces.

Writing and Drawing

For preschool and kindergarten, begin with drawing. Say, "Draw who or what you want to say good morning to today." Then work with children to write the sentence, "Good morning to the _____," filling in with words to describe what their picture is about. For first grade and older, ask them to complete the sentence, "Good morning to _____."

Next, gather as a group to look at the drawings and writing. Sing what they express. Group four statements at a time to create a song unit. Don't worry about the length. For example:

> *Good morning to my cat Fluffer.*
> *Good morning to my cheerios.*
> *Good morning to my grandmother. She's leaving today.*
> *Good morning to the snow on the playground.*

Chinese Studies

Try singing the song in Chinese. Kathy Chang, who teaches Chinese at Brightwood Magnet School, provides this translation:

Zao lán tian tian tian
(Good morning blue sky sky sky)
Zao dà dì dì dì
(Good morning big ground, ground, ground)

Zao ni hao ni hao ni hao
(Good morning hello hello hello)
Sì bìan kàn yi kàn
(four sides look a look)

Here is how the words sound to my ears:
Zow lan tien, tien, tien.
Zow ta ti, ti, ti. (combine a "d" and "t" sound)
Zow nee how, nee how, nee how.
Zee bee-e-ne-kahn, ee, kahn

3 This Little Light of Mine

Children sing an important African-American traditional song.

● ●

Ages	All
When to Use	Gathering song, studying African-American traditional music, the Civil Rights movement, or peace-makers
Language	English
Location	Side 1, Song 3
Source	African-American Gospel song

OBJECTIVES

- to build classroom community
- to recognize one's own light within
- to connect to African-American music

PROCEDURE

1 Tell children about the history of the song. It was sung in African-American Christian churches, then took on additional historical importance during the civil rights movement of the 1960s when it was used to raise a powerful feeling of community. New verses were invented spontaneously to bring courage. When people sang, "Nobody can blow it out," this sent the message that nothing could stop the struggle for freedom.

2 Teach the chorus first. Note that—as in many traditional songs—there are different ways to sing the melody; children in your class may know a different variation of the tune. Follow their lead.

3 Help children think about the meaning of the verses as you share them. Here are traditional verses you can add:

- *Hide it under a bushel, no! I'm going to let it shine.*
- *Ain't gonna make it shine. Just gonna let it shine.*

4 Create verses that fit your class. Example: Singing to my friends, I'm gonna let it shine (3x). Or use the song as a zipper song. Here's a pattern that's traditionally used for this song: All around _____ I'm gonna let it shine.

Examples

> *All around my neighborhood, I'm gonna let it shine.*
> *All around this great big world, I'm gonna let it shine.*
> *All around my family, I'm gonna let it shine.*

Children enjoy supplying the words for ever-widening circles: all around our class, school, city, state, country, earth or solar system.

5 Here's how to sing the chorus in Spanish:

> *Esta luzesita mía la dejaré brillar. (3x)*
> *Brillará, brillará, brillará.*

Gathering

Bilingual second-grade teachers Marta Toro
and Luz Rodríguez at the Brightwood Magnet
School in Springfield, Massachusetts introduced this song as part of a peacemakers unit.
Now they sing it daily as a signal that it's time
for everyone to gather.

This Little Light of Mine

African American Gospel

This little light of mine,
I'm gonna let it shine.
This little light of mine,
I'm gonna let it shine.
This little light of mine,
I'm gonna let it shine.
Let it shine, let it shine, let it shine.

Everywhere I go,
I'm gonna let it shine. (3x)
Let it shine, let it shine, let it shine.

All around this room,
I'm gonna let it shine. (3x)
Let it shine, let it shine, let it shine.

Nobody can "pfoof" it out.
I'm gonna to let it shine. (3x)
Let it shine, let it shine, let it shine.
(Hold up your finger like a candle and
indicate blowing.)

I'm gonna take this light around the
world. I'm gonna let it shine. (3x)
Let it shine, let it shine, let it shine.

Discussion

Help make the abstract meaning of the song more concrete. Ask, "Do you know that feeling when you're happy or you know you're good at doing things? We call that shining your light. What does it feel like to shine your light?"

Convey that there's room for everyone in the class to shine their light at the same time. This is a foundational concept of the Peaceable Classroom. There's no competition when our inner light is concerned —there's room for each light. In a peaceable classroom each person shines his or her light and encourages all the others to do the same. Then continue, "How can we show other people that we want them to shine their lights brightly?" Sing the chorus again and ask children to show by their expressions that they encourage their classmates.

Group Drawing Activity: Circles of Peace

Place large sheets of paper on tables. In front of each chair, trace a circle with a marker using an aluminum pie plate as your guide. Each child will draw in one of the circles. Put cups of crayons or markers in easy reach.

RELATED SONGS
"I Want to Know Your Name" (Song 18)
"Grandmother Spider" (Song 19)

Ask the children to draw in their circles what they love—favorite activities, people, and places. Use pictures instead of words.

Give each child a chance to tell about one thing he or she drew.

Option:

> Zip their words into the song, fitting one or two items to a line. As you sing about each child's circle drawing, she feels affirmed.

Example:

> *We like dogs and water slides. We're gonna let it shine.*
>
> *We like racing bikes down the hill. We're gonna let it shine.*
>
> *We like Sunday dinner at grandma's. We're gonna let it shine.*
>
> *Let it shine. Let it shine. Let it shine.*

Have children look at the space between the circles. Ask them to find ways to connect their circles. Example: In one class, a child drew a bridge of musical instruments to other circles. Others made lines of color, rainbows, or a rope of leaves reaching out.

Ages 3 to 9

When to Use Gathering or sharing news

Language English

Location Side 1, Song 4

Source Sarah Pirtle

4 Come Join in the Circle

Children gather and sing a welcoming song.

●●●●●●●●●●●●●●●●●●●●●●●●●●●

OBJECTIVES

- to help children feel welcomed
- to build community
- to sing the news of the children
- to practice listening

PROCEDURE

1 Gather the children in a circle. Play the song, "Come Join in the Circle."

2 Ask the children to wave and look at each other when they hear the words, "Wave around the circle." As the song repeats, ask the children to invent the kind of wave they want to use: "How would you like to wave today?" You can expand their ideas by suggesting other parts of the body to use: "Let's try waving with our elbows."

3 Sing about the news and events of your class. The recording models how to ask children what is important in their lives. Ask, "Who has news to put in our song today?" Use their words to create a new verse for the first four lines of the song. Example:

> *Emma climbed to the top of the apple tree.*
> *Pavel helped his grandma make pierogi.*
> *Isabelle's cat's still missing.*
> *We hope your cat comes back.*

Note: *This is a good activity to use at the start of each day. The words ask the children to notice each other and help them all to feel seen and included.*

Singing their News

. . . .

First graders in Ashfield, Massachusetts, were restless during sharing time until their teacher asked them to echo back the events they shared. After Martin spoke, the teacher asked, "What can we sing about Martin's brother getting hurt?" His classmates supplied these words:

Your brother got hurt last night,
last night, last night.
Your brother got hurt last night
and we're sorry he got hurt.

METHOD

- Gather enough information to fit four lines.
- Use the exact words of the children. As shown on the recording, it's okay to squeeze many words to a line.
- Include whatever is important to the children—even if it's about upsetting events. What they have to share isn't always happy news.
- Ask the class to echo back each sentence as you present it.
- Add:

  We want to hear your news,
  We want to hear your news.
  Come tell us what happened.
  We'll sing it in the song.

SUPPORTING CHILDREN WHO HAVE DISTURBING NEWS

The unexpected may surface when you ask children for their news. If you hear about the illness or death of a family member or a pet, you'll need to take more time and acknowledge what this event means. Also, when young children tell you what is important in their lives, they don't censor it. You may learn that "The police came to our apartment" or "My Dad hit my Mommy." Respond appropriately and supportively. Let the child know you understand this must have been very upsetting and that you care about him or her.

Options

- Decide whether singing the news affirms the child or trivializes the event. Follow the child's lead. Check with him or her if you're unsure: "I'm glad that you let us know what happened. Would you also like us to sing about this?"
- Give more attention to the news. Gather information to add details and feelings. List everything the child or the group wants to say, and then create one or more verses just about this event. For example,

  Ramon's guinea pig died last night.
  He liked the way it sat in his lap.
  He never ever bit Ramon.
  We're very sorry he died.

- Change the melody to a slower and more serious mode. For instance, substitute the tune of a folk song you know, such as "Go Tell Aunt Rhody" or "Deep Blue Sea."
- End the song and talk with the child alone.

OTHER VARIATIONS

Another variation is to sing about what children did today in class. Ask, "Who'd like to put something into the song about what you did today?" This helps foster the ability to recall events. For example,

> *Caitlin built a rocket.*
> *Keno cut a snowflake.*
> *Jessie did the circle puzzle,*
> *and Reggie hummed a song.*

Or, create a verse about a special trip:

> *We took a trip to Boston,*
> *and we rode in the swan boats.*
> *We threw bread in the water,*
> *and the ducks gobbled it up.*

Or, invent a verse to welcome children back after they have been away from the group. For example,

> *We're glad to see you're back now.*
> *You're back now, you're back now.*
> *You were gone for eight long days.*
> *We'll read you the Big Book we made.*

Come Join in the Circle

©1997 Words and Music by Sarah Pirtle
Discovery Center Music, BMI

Come join in the circle,
Moon, Moon, the Moon and Sun.
Come join in the circle,
There's room for everyone.

I'm so glad you're here. (clap, clap)
I'm so glad you're here. (clap, clap)
Come join in the circle,
There's room for everyone.

Wave around the circle,
Moon, moon, the moon and sun.
Wave around the circle,
Wave to everyone.

Wave the way you like,
Wave the way you like.
Wave around the circle,
Wave to everyone.

E X T E N S I O N S

Dictation and Recall Activity

Ages: 3 to 6

Circulate among children while they are playing. Ask them to dictate what they are doing and write down their exact words. For example, "Kazu played house with a red hat. Kim climbed up the climber. Lee and Dominic painted together. Jocelyn jumped and jumped."

Sing their words during Circle Time as a guessing game.

> *Who played house with a red hat?*
> *Who climbed up the climber?*
> *Who painted together?*
> *Who jumped and jumped?*

Reading Preparation: Symbol Making

As children tell you what they want to put in the song, record their comments in words and symbols on chart paper. For example, if they say, "I played with the blocks," write the word "blocks" and make a sketch of blocks. Then, as you sing their contributions, point again to the words and symbols for each item. As a variation, have children make their own drawings.

RELATED SONGS
"Our Own Song" (Song 8)

Restatement and Listening Activity

Ages: 6 to 9

Develop listening skills by involving children in crafting a child's words into a new verse. This helps each child feel heard.

a. One student shares his news.

b. He selects someone to repeat what he said.

c. After the listener has restated, you help create a new verse. (e.g. Rita describes riding on her bicycle. She picks Lee to repeat what she said. The teacher sings Lee's description.)

Affirmation Activity

Write a verse to express genuine caring for your group. For example:

> *I like you in this circle,*
> *this circle, this circle.*
> *I like you in this circle.*
> *I'm glad to be with you.*
> *I'm so glad you're here. (2x)* (Point to everyone in the circle).
> *I like you in this circle.*
> *What will we do today?*

CHAPTER 3 Friendship Songs

Across the wide ocean
Across the wide ocean.
I hear you calling me, oh, my friend.
I hear you calling me, oh, my friend.
— from "Across the Wide Ocean" (Song 10)

Songs in this chapter explicitly talk about friendship and help children feel connected to each other. They encourage children to look at each other and respond to those around them. These songs give your students an opportunity not only to relate to children who they already know, but to interact with everyone. From these moments, friendships gradually develop.

When we tap our hands together in "Chocolate," (Song 5) we feel more unified as a group. We're having fun doing the same thing. Songs where we all move together are called unison songs. Children also need opportunities to move their own way. In "Across the Wide Ocean," (Song 10) children invent their own way of pantomining waves. A child moves his fingers like the little tiny waves splashing close to shore at low tide while another swoops her arms like waves crashing. Each is concentrating on what she or he uniquely enjoys.

As you use a song, think deliberately about where you want to place the emphasis: We move together or I explore my preferences. Within a song you can use both. For instance, in "Step by Step, Paso a Paso" (Song 13):

We walk together in a line during the slow part of the song.

I invent the way I will move my hands during the fast section.

In Kenya people say: "I am, because we are." They recognize that self-esteem develops, not in isolation, but within community through relationship and attachment. Building friendships involves navigating this rhythm of "I" and "we." This dynamic is explored in the "Creeping Mouse Game" (Song 9).

Singing friendship songs, children learn:
- I contact what I feel as I move my own way.
- I am part of a group.
- I notice that what I do impacts the people around me.
- I notice that other people around me have their own unique needs and interests.
- I want to communicate with these people and connect to them.

Building friendships also involves setting personal boundaries and respecting the boundaries of others. "My Space/Mi Espacio" (Song 6) explictly teaches how to establish your own personal space. "Sitting in the Soup" (Song 7) teaches how to respect clear boundaries such as stop and go, slow and fast. Song games provide a way to encounter each other within safe parameters.

Part of building friendships is also affirming and using other people's ideas. "Our Own Song" (Song 8) uses the words of classmates as children recall the activities they did that day. In "Jump, Jump, Jump" (Song 7) we sing each other's preferences, and in "Across the Wide Ocean," (Song 10) we mirror others' favorite movements.

You are invited to think deliberately about the songs in your Song Circle. Which song you use and the order in which you use them is part of the fun of creating your group's experience.

5 Chocolate

Children make hand movements as they sing in Spanish.

●●●●●●●●●●●●●●●●●●●●●●●●●●●●●

Ages	3 to 9
When to Use	Circle time or when studying Mexican and Mexican-American culture
Language	Spanish
Location	Side 1, Song 5
Source	Mexican rhyme set to music

OBJECTIVES

- to sing and count in Spanish
- to increase concentration and focus

PROCEDURE

1 Describe to the children the background of the song. In Mexico, chocolate (pronounced "cho-co-LA-tay") is a common beverage made of chocolate and hot milk. Traditionally, it is mixed using a carved wooden beater called a molinillo (in Mexico, pronounced as "mo-li-NEE-yo"). The molinillo is spun by rubbing the handle between your palms. To help children, José-Luis Orozco leads a pantomime of pouring in the milk and chocolate and then stirring the beverage using a molinillo. (Note that on the recording the words are pronounced as they are said in Puerto Rico.)

2 Teach motions to accompany the song. In Part I, begin by counting with your fingers—uno, dos, tres. Then, at each syllable—cho, co, la, te—tap one fist on top of the other.

During Part II, tap your fists as you sing "chocolate, chocolate." Then rub your palms together, like you're using the beater to stir the chocolate as you say, "Bate, bate, chocolate." (The recording says, "Rub your hands together like you're twirling the beater, the molinillo.")

3 Adapt the motions to fit the needs of your age group. Younger children may be most comfortable rubbing their palms together for all or most of the whole song, while older children enjoy the alternation of movements.

If children hit their hands hard, encourage them to treat themselves in a friendly way: "We can make the motion strong without hurting our hands."

Tip!

This song helps children become physically present. When the group needs a quick break or you want to help them become more centered, you can sing this song.

Note: *Children ages three to nine ask to sing this joyful song again and again. I first taught the words as a chant. After hearing Jose-Luis Orozco put this rhyme to music, I brought it to classrooms as a song. In the course of singing and experimenting with the tune, I've changed the melody he created and created my own, but this is inspired by his work. He points out that children enjoy singing the song faster and faster.*

Chocolate

Mexican Chant
Tune by Sarah Pirtle

Un-o, dos, tres CHO__ Un-o, dos, tres CO__ Un-o, dos, tres LA __ Un-o, dos, tres TE __

Cho - co - la - te, cho - co - la - te ba - te, ba - te, cho - co - la - te.

Cho - co - la - te, cho - co - la - te, ba - te, ba - te, cho - co - la - te.

Part I

Uno, dos, tres, CHO
Uno, dos, tres, CO
Uno, dos, tres, LA
Uno, dos, tres, TE

Part II

Chocolate, chocolate, bate, bate, chocolate.
Chocolate, chocolate, bate, bate, chocolate.

E X T E N S I O N S

Cooking

Prepare a chocolate drink by mixing carob or cocoa in milk.

Reading Practice

With first and second graders, Roberto Díaz likes to write the syllables—cho, co, la, te—on four separate sheets of paper. Four children come to the front of the class. Each takes one of the four sheets of paper and then stands in order of the correct spelling of chocolate. Roberto also likes to joke with the children and intentionally mix up their order: "Oh, you like to drink co-la-te-cho?" As they practice reading the scrambled order, as well as the correct order of syllables, their facility with reading increases.

Partner Game

Partners face each other and play a clapping game to the rhythm of the song. Select a clapping pattern for Part I that fits the abilities and interests of your students, or ask them to create a pattern. For example, students can tap their own legs on the numbers, "uno, dos, tres," and clap hands on the syllables, "cho, co, la, te." Then on Part II of the song, partners link up with each other. They can join hands and twirl, spin, or twist from side to side. Encourage them to invent their own way of connecting as they sing, "Chocolate, chocolate, bate, bate, chocolate." Say, "Pretend you are stirring up the chocolate together." Traditionally, children play rhythm games to this chant on playgrounds.

ADDITIONAL RESOURCES

These bilingual resources include the chant "Chocolate" and provide illustrations of how the molinillo is used:

De Colores and Other Latin-American Folk Songs for Children, selected, arranged, and translated by Jose-Luis Orozco, illustrated by Elisa Kleven. (New York: Dutton Children's Books, 1994). This outstanding resource of 27 songs, chants, and rhymes is highly recommended. Jose-Luis Orozco traveled as a boy with the Mexico City Children's Choir to 32 countries. Today he lives in California, presenting concerts and training teachers.

Tortillitas Para Mama and other Nursery Rhymes in Spanish and English, selected and translated by Margot Griego, Betsy Bucks, Sharon Gilbert, and Laurel Kimball, illustrated by Barbara Cooney. (New York: Henry Holt and Co., 1981). Place this excellent paperback in the book corner for children to enjoy the pictures or to read in Spanish or English.

Ages	4 to 9
When to Use	Circle Time, movement, or teaching conflict resolution concepts
Language	Bilingual
Location	Side 1, Song 6
Source	Sarah Pirtle

6 My Space/Mi Espacio

Children define and explore their own personal space.

OBJECTIVES

- to build self-esteem
- to explore the boundary of personal space
- to respect the space of others
- to help children express themselves by encouraging authentic movement

PROCEDURE

1 Become familiar with the basic pattern of the song in the language of your choice:

English
Here I am. Here I am.
I can _____ in my space.
I can _____ in my space.
There's no better place in the world for me.

Spanish
Este es mi espacio.
Yo puedo _____ (o yo me puedo _____).
Estoy aquí. Estoy aquí.
No hay mejor lugar en el mundo para mí.

2 Say, "Here's a way we can all feel safe as we move. We'll each move in our own space." Invite children to find a spot to stand in the room. Your first goal is to help children be in their own space. Observe them: Can they find the boundaries of their personal space? Explain: "Keep your feet in place. Move your arms in every direction to make sure you have enough room to stretch without bumping anyone else. Imagine you have a ball of air around you. Move your hands and trace the edges of that ball. This is your space bubble." In dance and physical education this "bubble of space" is referred to as our kinesphere. You can help them in this process by starting with motions that ask children to stay anchored in one spot. Ask them to keep their feet "glued" to the floor as they move the rest of their body.

Use the following verses to help students define their own space.

(From the recording)
- *I can twist in my space.*
  Yo me puedo torcer. Estoy aquí.

- *I can stretch in my space.*
  Yo me puedo estirar. Estoy aquí.

- *I make a circle with my arms.*
- *I touch the edges of my space.*

3 If two friends stay together in the same spot, invite them to find their own spaces, so that they can each discover their individuality.

4 After children have established their own space, lead motions to help them freely explore this space.

In order to encourage children to explore their space through movement, provide suggestions that encourage variety in movement. Provide an open-ended verse in which the children determine on their own how they'd like to move, such as:
- *I'll move my arms the way I want.*
- *I can move in my space.*
  Yo me puedo mover. Estoy aquí.

(From the recording)
- *I can dance in my space.*
  Yo puedo bailar. Estoy aquí.

- *I can bend in my space.*
  Yo me puedo doblar. Estoy aquí.

Model what it looks like to follow your own authentic movement.

5 As you watch the group, you will learn about their needs for movement, and you will see what motions they've discovered. Decide whether to:

a. Describe what you see individuals doing to make the next verse:
- *I stand on my tiptoes and wiggle my fingers.*
- *I'm lifting something heavy from the ground.*

b. Offer suggestions that open children to broader possibilities, especially if their movements seem stuck and static:
- *I can move high and low.*
- *I can move fast and slow.*

c. Keep an eye out to sense the needs of the group.
Is there a need for vigorous movement? This is a safe arena for strong stamping; sing:
- *I can stamp in my space.*

Is there a need for gentleness? If so, ask children to remember something very soft they've touched. Try:

- *I can smooth and pat my space.*

Do you want to add humor?

- *I can laugh in my space.*
  Yo me puedo reir. Estoy aquí.

Do you want them to move with increased concentration? Try:

- *I can explore in my space.*

Move your hands slowly as you explore all around.

d. Sing their movement suggestions to make new verses.
"How do you like to move in your space?"

- *I can move my arms like twirling spaghetti.*

 6 Choose one of these effective ways to end the song:

a. **Pantomime Painting**   Painting the space with a favorite color is an act of self-affirmation. Say: "Imagine you are holding a can of paint and it's your favorite color. See the color of the paint as you dip your brush. Paint all around your space high and low." Afterward, you can regroup and have the children describe what colors they chose.

- *This is me. I can paint my space. (3x)*
  There's no better place in the world for me.

- *Yo puedo pintar en este lugar. (3x)*
  No hay mejor lugar en el mundo para mí.

b. **A Growing Seed**   Help the group transition to the floor by singing "On the floor I can pat my space." Now ask the children to curl up like a seed. Stop the song and make up a story. "Once upon a time, seeds were resting in the ground. The sun began to warm them and they started to move. Slowly they reached out a shoot toward the sun. They began to grow." Return to the song and sing, "I can grow in my space." Then, after everyone is on their feet again, "I can open like a flower." This ends the activity with a feeling of calm.

c. **Sharing Space**   Having the children share their space helps the group reunite and gather slowly. Invite the group to start moving closer together and share their spaces, their "space bubbles," with each other.

- *This is me. I can share my space. (3x)*
  There's no better place in the world for us.
  Yo comparto mi espacio.
  Contigo, contigo, contigo tambien.

  (Point to others around you.)
  Seguro yo estoy de que no hay
  Otro hermoso lugar en el mundo para mí.

Lead a discussion with the children. Ask, "When you're waiting in line, playing outside, or riding on the bus, are there ways in which people enter your space that are not okay with you? What message can you give them?"

Tip!

How to Work with Children's Suggestions

Sometimes children suggest standard movements for this song from gymnastics or physical fitness like jumping jacks. After using their ideas, I follow that movement with a more open-ended suggestion like jumping. I'm also alert to make sure the suggestions do not set up a comparison of physical abilities, which can be divisive in this context. For instance, in a second-grade class in Bemidji, Minnesota, a boy suggested "push-ups" and many classmates reacted with groans. With his permission, I reframed and expanded on his idea. I asked him, "Can you think of another choice so people have two choices if they don't want to do push-ups? How about, 'I can go low in my space,' and everyone decides how they want to do that?" He agreed and the whole group felt that their needs had been taken into account. Likewise, when a girl chose to "do the splits," I rephrased the verse, with her permission, to "I can do something tricky in my space." Then everyone could choose whether they wanted to do the splits or their own favorite movement. As you hear a suggestion, ask yourself whether everyone can do it. How can you include the idea but expand on it so that everyone can participate and feel affirmed?

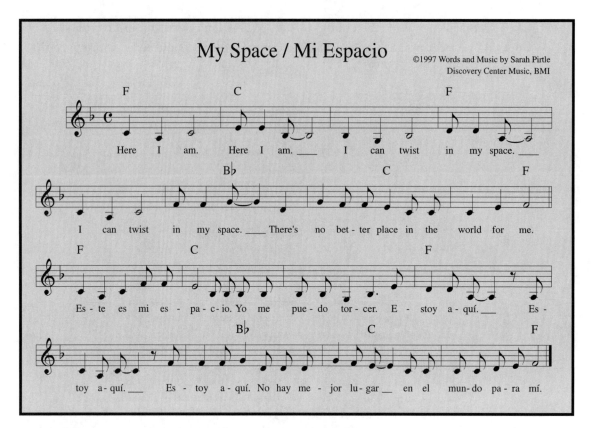

My Space / Mi Espacio

©1997 Words and Music by Sarah Pirtle
Discovery Center Music, BMI

English

Verse 1

Here I am. Here I am.

I can twist in my space.

I can twist in my space.

There's no better place in the world for me.

Verse 2

Here I am. Here I am.

I can dance in my space.

I can dance in my space.

There's no better place in the world for me.

Spanish

Verse 1

Este es mi espacio.

Yo me puedo torcer. Estoy aquí.

Estoy aquí. Estoy aquí.

No hay mejor lugar en el mundo para mí.

Verse 2

Este es mi espacio.

Yo puedo bailar. Estoy aquí.

Estoy aquí. Estoy aquí.

No hay mejor lugar en el mundo para mí.

Affirmation Lyrics

I stamp in my space, saying this is me! (3x)
I feel safe in my space.

Este es mi espacio,
Seguro yo estoy, en este lugar
Seguro yo estoy, en este lugar
No hay mejor lugar en el mundo para mí.

Affirmation Mirror

Ask, "Who'd like to show us a way you enjoy moving in your space?" Or say, "Let's move like Anna in our own space." When we mirror someone, we affirm her on a very basic level.

RELATED SONG

"When I say Stop, I Mean Stop" (Song 29).

Affirmation Drawing

Have paper ready on each desk before you sing the song. Pantomime painting your space as your last verse. Explain to the children: "We're going to walk silently to our desks to draw anything this game reminded us of. First, close your eyes for a moment and think about the feelings, colors, or motions you want to include in your drawing."

Ages	3 to 8
When to Use	Circle Time or for an energizing break
Language	English
Location	Side 1, Song 7
Source	Sarah Pirtle

7 Sitting in the Soup

Children pretend to be vegetables dancing in soup.

OBJECTIVES

- to move with self-control
- to follow a stop-and-go pattern
- to create movements

PROCEDURE

1 Start with the children seated together in a circle of chairs or on the rug. Or begin with the children sitting in small groups.

2 Review the instructions. The group stays seated as they sing the refrain, "Here we are sitting in the soup." Then, after the word "Now," they stand and dance in their "soup bowl"—the space created by their circles. The children return to their seats when the song calls them back and they need to be seated by the word "home." If the group needs more time returning, you can repeat the last line of the bridge: "Come back a-giggle on home."

3 You can change the word "Sunday" in the refrain to match the actual day of the week.

Example:

Here we are sitting in the soup on Monday.

Sitting in the Soup

©1997 Words and Music by Sarah Pirtle
Discovery Center Music, BMI

Refrain

Here we are sitting in the soup, sitting in the soup on Sunday.

(Group is seated)

Verse 1

NOW! Shake yourself like salt, shake yourself like salt.

Shake and shake, shake again, and shake yourself like salt.

And twist that pepper out, twist that pepper out.

Twist and twist and twist some more and twist that pepper out.

Bridge

The beans are jumping in the pot, pour more water from the water spout. Spin around, they all jump out, come back a-giggle on home.

Refrain

Here we are sitting in the soup, sitting in the soup on Sunday.

Verse 2

NOW! Do the wiggle walk, do the wiggle walk.
Soup is ready, serve it hot, do the wiggle walk.
Jump holding hands, jump holding hands,

bring that soup to a bouncing boil, keep on holding hands.

Bridge

The beans are jumping in the pot, pour more water from the water spout. Spin around, they all jump out, come back a- giggle on home. Come back a- giggle on home.

. . . .

E X T E N S I O N S

. . . .

Movement Exploration

A longer version of the song is on my recording, "The Wind is Telling Secrets." Here are the additional verses that provide other movement challenges:

> *Now, make a chain around the room.*
> *A chain around the room.*
> *The soup keeps falling off the spoon*
> *Make a chain around the room.*

> *Now, touch elbows with your friends.*
> *Touch elbows with your friends.*
> *Round about and back again,*
> *Touch elbows with your friends.*

> *Now, make a bridge and go on through.*
> *A bridge and go on through.*
> *Soup keeps bouncing back to you.*
> *Make a bridge and go on through.*

Select a verse and repeat it again if necessary to allow enough time for children to complete the action. For instance, if you are making bridges, assist half the class in forming bridges in pairs and repeat the verse while the others go under their hands. Then sing:

> *Now, new partners make a bridge,*
> *New partners make a bridge.*
> *And the rest of us go under,*
> *The rest of us go under.*

You can sing whatever instructions give clear directions for movement. Here's a sequence children enjoy because they switch from one interesting animal movement to another.

> *Now, be a monkey.*
> *Be a monkey around the room.*
> *Be a monkey swinging in branches.*
> *And get ready to switch.*

> *Now, be a worm.*
> *Be a worm curling around.*
> *Be a worm curling around.*
> *And get ready to switch.*

When children need a rest, use the bridge to bring them back to the circle.

Jump, Jump, Jump

This version of "Sitting in the Soup" adds words that affirm individual preferences and helps children learn to return to their places on time.

PROCEDURE

Begin with the group seated in chairs. Ask one child at a time, "What do you like today?" Use this zipper song pattern to sing the words they say:

Verse

Oh, I like _____ a lot.
I like _____ a lot.
You ask me what I like?
Oh, I like _____ a lot.

The recording models a verse about Emily's response:

Oh, I like strawberries a lot.
I like strawberries a lot.
You ask me what I like?
Oh, I like strawberries a lot.

Tip!

If you want a clear lesson plan for your group circle time, but don't want to make different plans each day, use "Jump, Jump, Jump" as the main activity. It allows enough variety that you can repeat it many times.

They can select anything: they can mention a food, say the names of friends, celebrate their new pet, or pick a different movement for the group to do.

I like my brother's birthday.
I like fruit roll-ups.
I like project time.

After singing one child's words, all children, not just the one who made up the verse, get up and jump while singing the bridge:

Bridge

NOW! Jump jump jump jump jump
jump jump jump jump jump
jump jump jump jump jump
and get back to your place.

We use the rule that if you aren't back in your chair by the word "place," you skip one turn and stay seated. You can decide whether or not to use such an agreement. For other age groups and situations, this rule might be too rigid and impede the fun of the game.

If you do make this agreement, reinforce it with a light approach. Comment each time on how they did; notice how the children chose to work with the rule. Then, go right into the next verse. For example, say, "Everyone got back. Rodney, what do you want to put into the song?" Or, "Dalia, you stood at your chair but didn't sit down. That means you skip one turn of jumping. Libby, what do you want to put into the song?" This gives children a chance to experiment with social boundaries without feeling judged.

A Class Tradition

This is the song that I led with my first-grade class every afternoon at the end of the school day for several months without them tiring of the game. It became a class tradition. Children jumped with glee, then dashed back to their chairs, or waited until the last second to plop down. The open framework provided freedom for them to express exactly how they felt at that moment.

E X T E N S I O N S

Vary the Movement

Instead of jumping, children may suggest a new activity. Sing their suggestion in the verse. For example:

Teacher: Zeke, how do you want us to move today?

Zeke: Be a chicken.

Teacher sings verse: I like to be a chicken. (Seated children act out the chicken with their hands).

For the movement section, teacher sings: Now be a chicken. (3x)

(All children stand up and pantomime chickens with Zeke).

Teacher: Now come back to your chicken house.

Pantomime Guessing Game

Sing the verse "I like juggling a lot," but change the second section to:

> *Juggle, juggle, juggle* instead of *jump, jump, jump.*

Each child pantomimes what he or she is juggling—realistic objects such as scarves or tennis balls, or unrealistic objects such as corn flakes. Watch three children at a time and guess what they are juggling—is it footballs, ping-pong balls, bowling balls?

Move the guessing along quickly by having three jugglers take turns picking one person to take one guess about what they did.

Ages	2 to 5, variations for 5 to 9
When to Use	Recall Time, Circle Time, or playtime
Language	English, Spanish optional
Location	Side 1, Song 8
Source	Sarah Pirtle

8 Our Own Song

Children hear their words sung by their teacher and classmates.

●●●●●●●●●●●●●●●●●●●●●●●●●●●

OBJECTIVES

- to build language skills
- to notice others
- to practice names

PROCEDURE

 From the following, select the method that works best for your group.

A. Dictation Method

1. During free choice time before your Song Circle, walk around the room with a paper and pencil and ask children, "Please tell me what you are doing so that I can put your words into the song." Then craft their words to create a guessing game. The sentences don't need to rhyme.

Don't worry about the length of each line. Sing exactly what they offer. The verse gives you room for three statements. Sing their words when you gather at Circle Time. Here's the basic pattern:

> *Who was_____?*
> *Who was_____?*
> *Who was_____?*
> *Our own song. Our own song.*

Examples:

> *Who was cutting playdough into little pieces?*
> *Who was making the hood pop open on the white truck?*
> *Who jumped off the climber and splatted on the pillows?*
> *Our own song. Our own song.*

Spanish text:

> *¿Quíen estaba jugando con_____? (3x)*
> *Esa nuestra cancíon.*

Tip!

"Our Own Song" makes a good starting or ending song because the tune is simple and lyrics can be created to express feelings of the moment. Keep the tune in mind also when you need to send a message like "Now it's time to clean up for lunch."

2. Pause after each line to let the children guess who is described in that line. Encourage children to learn each other's names. Note that the younger children, ages two to four, may not remember words they dictated a few minutes earlier because they're involved in what's immediate.

B. Recall Method

Divide the children into smaller groups. Three children at a time tell what they did during Choice Time, and everyone sings their words:

> *Lourdes made a Lego bridge.*
> *Anna balanced cars on a block.*
> *Curtis cut up pieces of paper.*
> *Our own song. Our own song.*

C. Method of Singing During the Play Activity

In order to develop language skills, ask children playing in a group to describe what they are doing. Use the same pattern as "The Spoony Song." (See the following extension.)

> *Put some _____ in the playdough song (e.g. pounding, cutting, rolling, stars).*
> *The playdough song, the playdough song. (Repeat)*

SNAPSHOT

I sat at a table of four-year-olds playing with Play-Doh™ at the Brightwood Magnet School in Springfield, Massachusetts. I asked them to tell me what they were doing with the Play-Doh™. We sang each child's response in a separate verse and this helped them become more aware of the people around them.

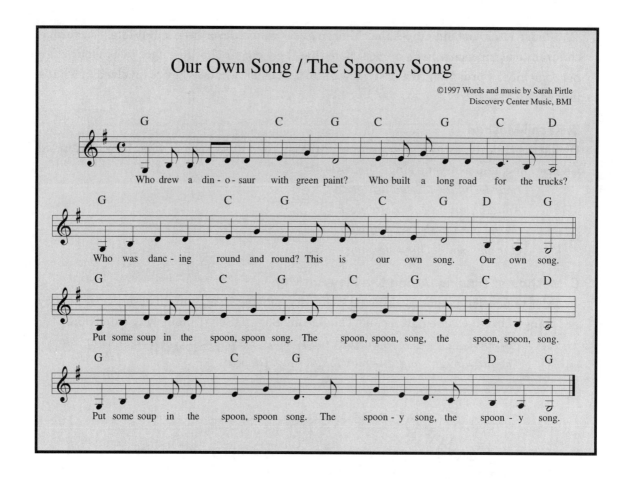

Our Own Song / The Spoony Song

©1997 Words and music by Sarah Pirtle
Discovery Center Music, BMI

Who drew a din-o-saur with green paint? Who built a long road for the trucks?

Who was danc-ing round and round? This is our own song. Our own song.

Put some soup in the spoon, spoon song. The spoon, spoon, song, the spoon, spoon, song.

Put some soup in the spoon, spoon song. The spoon-y song, the spoon-y song.

. . . .

E X T E N S I O N S

. . . .

The Spoony Song
. . . .

This variation of "Our Own Song" helps children develop language skills and affirms different food preferences. You can use this song during Circle Time with children ages three to six. Here's the basic pattern:

> *Put some _____ in the spoon, spoon song.*
> *The spoon, spoon song. The spoon, spoon song.*
> *Put some _____ in the spoon, spoon song.*
> *The spoony song. The spoony song.*

Have children suggest foods to zip into the song. The repetition of the "s" sound gives speech practice. The whole group can panto-mime that they are eating with a spoon, or you can use real spoons: *Put some cereal in the spoon, spoon song.*

Tip!

Use this song right before leading "Sitting in the Soup." Sing the verse, "Put some soup in the spoon, spoon song." These are the words that appear on the recording.

If you are using real spoons with children ages three to five, make an agreement not to use the spoons to hit before handing them out. If possible, bring spoons with a variety of colors and textures, such as spoons from Russia with painted flowers. Chant the word "spoon" while handing them out to help the group focus. When you are finished, sing *"Put your spoon in a teacher's hand"* to the same tune, while you are collecting spoons.

Affirming Foods

As a way to affirm the foods that the children eat in their families, ask, "What's a food you like to eat?" Sing about the favorite foods of each child. If children mention a food that others don't like or that is unfamiliar, make sure all feel supported by intervening and providing information as needed.

Teacher: Kazumi, what food do you want to put in the song?

Kazumi: Sushi.

BJ: Oooh. Yuck.

Teacher: I bet you haven't heard of sushi before. It's made with rice and vegetables wrapped up in seaweed. It's really good. It's important that we don't make fun of each other's favorite foods. Every family has their own favorites. What could we say when we hear a food and we don't know what it is?

Liela: Ask what it is.

Teacher: Like if I said tempeh burger and you'd never heard of it, what could you say, Liela?

Liela: I'd say—what's that?

The Anything Song

This pantomime game variation is suitable for ages five to nine. Place interesting objects in the center of the circle—kitchen utensils, rolling pins, fruits, paper tubes. Students take turns selecting one and making up a new identity for it. For example, Mayra picks up a banana and pretends she's talking on the telephone. Pantomime with her or pass the banana around and give everyone a turn. Sing:

> *Talk on the phone in the anything song.*
> *Talk on the phone in the anything song.*
> *Talk on the phone in the anything song.*
> *Mix it all around and make it new.*

Closing Song

Ask three children what they liked best about Song Circle today. Create a quick closing by singing their responses, and then orient them to what they will be doing next.

> *Jessie liked jumping, holding hands.*
> *Sharee liked stomping in her space.*
> *Lucas liked playing the soup game.*
> *And now it's time for us to eat snack.*

Or, for a closing, sing an affirmative statement.

> *I liked singing with you today (3x).*
> *Now it's time to end our group.*

Ages	3 to 7
When to Use	Circle Time
Language	English, Spanish optional
Location	Side 1, Song 9
Length	3 to 5 minutes as children act out the story
Source	Words and format by Sarah Pirtle

9 Creeping Mouse

Children greet each other and pat hands.

OBJECTIVES

- to increase awareness of others
- to build group unity
- to guide children in connecting with each other

PROCEDURE

1 Listen to the tape and notice the major action of the story: mice (children's hands) creep out from behind the mountains, they gently greet others (children pat one another's hands), then return to hide behind the mountains (children's backs). Work with the narrative and make sure the motions are clear to you.

2 Gather the children in a circle. Kneel on the floor instead of sitting. Provide guidelines: "In this story we're going to be leaning forward. Practice leaning forward as you kneel. Make sure you don't block the people on either side of you."

3 Start the recording and lead the children through the movements that are described.

Once upon a time there were mice.
Let your hands be the mice. Pantomime that both of your hands are mice talking to each other.

They lived behind the tall mountains.
Place your hands behind your back and continue to move them as if they are talking.

And they talked to each other: "I wonder if there are other mice behind the other mountains. There must be other mice in the world. Let's go look for them." And so they went:
> *Creep, creep, creeping mouse,*
> *Creep, creep, creeping mouse,*
> *Creep, creep, creeping mouse.*
> Very slowly, walk your fingers toward the center of the circle of children. At first go only a few inches from your knees.

They waved to each other. They were so glad to see the other mice.
Freeze, then look, and wave your fingers from where the mice are standing on the ground.

But then they heard a sound—Eeeh, Eeeh, Eeeh.
The eagle! They ran back and hid behind the mountains
again.
Hands return behind backs. Mice talk to each other behind the mountains.

"We have to be careful. I want to go back and see the other
mice. Let's go again." And so they went:
>   *Creep, creep, creeping mouse*
>   *Creep, creep, creeping mouse*
>   *Creep, creep, creeping mouse*

And when they saw those mice, they were so happy. Now,
try this first by patting your own hands: very gently they
began to pat the other mice. They patted and they patted.
Model gentle touching of your own hands in a patting gesture. Then everyone tries patting their hands. Lean forward and touch several hands close by. Make sure everyone is included and that no one is squished. Model respectful encounters. Look around for children sending a signal
that they don't want to be touched. Respect and acknowledge their message.

And then they heard that sound again:
Eeeh, Eeeh, Eeeh.
And they ran back and hid behind the mountains.
"I'm scared of that sound. But I miss the mice!"
"I'm scared of that sound. But I miss the mice!

Should we go again?" "Yes!" And so they went again.
>   *Creep, creep, creeping mouse*
>   *Creep, creep, creeping mouse*
>   *Creep, creep, creeping mouse.*

Oh, they saw the mice, and they began to pat them and
greeting all around and dancing and saying hello.
Greet and pat mice. Reach toward any child who is left out
or who hasn't yet tried touching.

Then they heard that sound again:
Eeeh! Eeeh! Eeeh!
They ran back behind the mountains.
I'm scared of that sound. But I miss the mice.
I'm scared of that sound. But I miss the mice.
Let's go again.
Feel free to repeat the sequence as many times as you
choose.

Facilitation Strategies for Teachers

• • • • • • • • • • • • • •

The story of Creeping Mouse
speaks to one of the developmental tasks of children at
this age. Just as the mice in
the story ask if there are
other mice in the world,
young children are learning
to integrate the reality of
other children. I've been
leading this song for 15 years
and in that time, only once
have children pounded or
hurt each other's hands. Yet
the encounter with other
children can stir up feelings.
How do you respond if
children aren't gentle with
each other?

a) Start by waving at the
other mice and progress no
further in the story than
having the two hands of the
children—the two "mice"—
gently greet their own hands.
Over a series of days build
up to the point of children
encountering other
children's hands.

b) Let your "mice" go first
and greet all the others. Then
ask for volunteers to be
greeters until safe touching
has been firmly established.

c) Make the eagle sound after
a short period of contact.

d) Have your mouse walk
next to an individual child's
mouse. Or, respectfully take a
child's hand in yours and
guide them in a slow, careful
touch.

e) Address a hurtful touch as
a child's request to be heard.
If children pound or hurt
hands, talk about it within the
framework of the story: "But

that day, some of the mice were hurt and so they decided to stand on their houses and look at each other. 'Ouch,' said one mouse. 'I don't like to be bopped on the head. How do you feel?'" Let the mice talk about the problem. Then ask, "Should we go back and hide behind the mountains? Or should we try again? What promises can we make so it will be safe for me and safe for all the mice here?"

Once during "Creeping Mouse," a four-year-old girl formed her hands like claws. A three-year-old boy in the same class began growling. I looked for a safe way to integrate the growling that needed expression with the movements in "Creeping Mouse." It became the seed for "The Anger Chant" (Song 28).

Sometimes I feel like growling. (claw hands stir without touching anyone)

And sometimes I run away. (hands hide behind your back)

And sometimes I go to my own little house. (palm up by waist)

And here's where I'm going to stay. (other hand jumps on palm).

Their teacher reports that the girl who initiated the clawing action asked for this song nearly every day for the next two months. If you have children in your class who are having trouble with anger, listen to "The Anger Chant," and use just the first verse. Replace the words on the recording with the words above.

To end the game, finish by saying:
> *So one more time they went:*
> *Creep, creep, creeping mouse*
> *Creep, creep, creeping mouse*
> *Creep, creep, creeping mouse*

And they visited the other mice, and they patted them and they patted them, and then they looked up in the sky. "Look at that! The eagle is flying away!" And so they stood at the front of their mountain and began to make themselves a little house right at the stomach of the mountain.

Put your hands in front of your body. One hand makes the house by creating a flat platform near your waist. The other hand is the mouse who stands on it.

And so they stood on their house, and all the mice waved to each other. "Good-bye!"

4 Learn to tell the story yourself without the recording. As the mice come out and greet each other, notice how long the group can sustain careful touch, then decide when to make the eagle call to signal a quick retreat.

5 Here is an abbreviated version of the story translated into Spanish:

El Juego de Los Ratoncitos

¿Dónde estan los ratoncitos?
Detrás de las montanas.
¿Dónde están los otros? Yo no sé.
(Creeping) Anda, anda, anda...
Pero el águila ....(eeh, eeh, eeh)
El aguila se fue.
Otra vez .....anda, anda, anda.
¡Hola! Con cuidado tocamos las manos.
Una vez más...anda, anda, anda.
Vieron al águila volar.
Hicieron una casita en frente de la montaña.

The Story of Creeping Mouse by Sarah Pirtle

Once upon a time there were mice. They lived behind the tall mountains. And they talked to each other: "I wonder if there are other mice behind the other mountains. There must be other mice in the world. Let's go look for them." And so they went:

> Creep, creep, creeping mouse,
> Creep, creep, creeping mouse,
> Creep, creep, creeping mouse.

They waved to each other. They were so glad to see the other mice.
But then they heard a sound— "Eeeh, Eeeh, Eeeh." The eagle! They ran back and hid behind the mountains again.
"We have to be careful, I want to go back and see the other mice.
Let's go again." And so they went:

> Creep, creep, creeping mouse
> Creep, creep, creeping mouse
> Creep, creep, creeping mouse

And when they saw those mice, they were so happy. Very gently, they began to pat the other mice. They patted and they patted.
And then they heard that sound again, "Eeeh, Eeeh, Eeeh."
And they ran back behind the mountains.
"I'm scared of that sound. But I miss the other mice!"
"I'm scared of that sound. But I miss the mice! Should we go again?"

"Yes!" And so they went.

> Creep, creep, creeping mouse
> Creep, creep, creeping mouse
> Creep, creep, creeping mouse.

And they saw the mice, and they began to pat them and greeting all around, dancing and saying, "Hello."
Then they heard that sound again. "Eeeh! Eeeh! Eeeh!"
They ran back behind the mountains.
"I'm scared of that sound. But I miss the mice."
"I'm scared of that sound. But I miss the mice."
"Let's go again."
So one more time they went:

> Creep, creep, creeping mouse
> Creep, creep, creeping mouse
> Creep, creep, creeping mouse

And they visited the other mice, "Hello! Hello!" And they patted them and they patted them, and then they looked up in the sky. "Look at that! The eagle is flying away!" And so they stood at the front of their mountain and they began to make themselves a little house right at the stomach of the mountain. And so they stood on their house, and all the mice waved to each other, "Good-bye!"

Mice and Eagle Dance

Dance teacher Janice Steinem, director of The Silver Birch/Shelburne Falls Center for Dance in western Massachusetts, involves children in dancing the Creeping Mouse story. Janice stands in the center of the room making mountain shapes. Children get into three groups. One group is eagles who roost in a hidden part of the room. The other two groups are mice who haven't met before. Each group of mice stands on a different side of the mountain. They creep from their spots, looking for more mice and encounter each other. As they are greeting one another, the eagles swoop down. The mice run and hide in their original loca-tions on their own side of the mountain, and then come out again. At the end, as the eagles fly away for good, the mice build one house together by the stomach of the mountain.

Tip!

You can use this game to lead into the next song. Children move like eagles, mice, or mountains as they sing, "Across the Wide Ocean."

SNAPSHOT

Bringing the Group Together

Members of a kindergarten class assemble for the morning circle time, but there is a disjointed feeling. I choose this game to help them regroup and become aware of each other. From the starting words "Once upon a time," eyes turn with interest. They are drawn in by the story. I notice each child joining in on the chant, "Creep, creep, creeping mouse;" they come closer and lean into the center. When the story asks them to pat the hands of the other mice, they are uniformly gentle. By the end of the game, the mood in the room has altered. The children are focused and ready to concentrate on the next activity.

10 Across The Wide Ocean/ A Través Del Inmenso Mar

Children create calming wave movements.

Ages 3 to 10

When to Use To focus and calm, for Circle Time, or with science units on whales, dolphins, and the ocean

Language Bilingual

Location Side 1, Song 10

Source Sarah Pirtle

OBJECTIVES

- to center children
- to explore movement
- to increase social awareness by mirroring other children
- to cooperate in a pair or small group

PROCEDURE

1 Form a seated or standing circle of children. Encourage each child to create wave motions his or her own way. "We're going to move together as we learn this song. Instead of doing the same motions I'm doing, discover the way that you like to move. What ways of making waves feel fun to you?"

2 If the children need encouragement to explore a wider variety of movements, offer suggestions:

- Try very large waves or very tiny waves.
- How many ways can you move your fingers?
- Try one arm high and the other arm low.
- Try doing two different things at the same time.

3 Move along with the group. Convey the attitude that you are not setting the standard for how to move. Instead, set a tone of interested exploration. Show that you are curious about the movements they invent.

Affirming a Child's Choice

· ·

On one occasion of using this song I watched as
one girl moved her right hand in a spiral shape
around her left hand with great concentration.
Usually, she was reluctant to be the focus of
attention; but I asked if we could all try her
movement. She agreed. I sensed her feeling of
pride as the whole class imitated the spiral
shape she had invented.

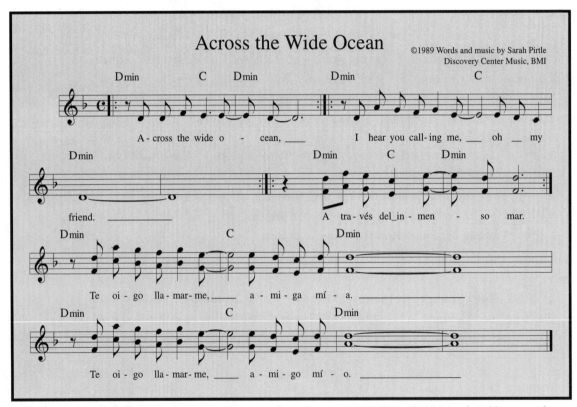

Across the Wide Ocean

©1989 Words and music by Sarah Pirtle
Discovery Center Music, BMI

Note: *I use this song more than any other because it is both calm and engaging and children of a wide range of ages enjoy it.*

Across the wide ocean.
Across the wide ocean.
I hear you calling me, oh, my friend.
I hear you calling me, oh, my friend.

A través del inmenso mar.
A través del inmenso mar.
Te oigo llamarme, amiga mía.
Te oigo llamarme, amigo mío.

Affirmation Mirroring

Ages: 3 to 10

Watch for children inventing motions that are clear and easy to follow. Think about who you particularly want to affirm at this moment. Based on these considerations, choose one individual and ask if she or he would be willing to lead the group in his or her own way of moving.

Introduce the process of mirroring. Encourage the group to keep their eyes on the leader and try to move exactly as the leader does. Go through the song once with each leader's movements. Catch the spirit of the motion. The goal is not to achieve accuracy, but to affirm each child by focusing the group's attention on him or her.

Each leader chooses the next child to lead. Make sure that children with all types of physical abilities have a chance.

If you want to verbally affirm the movements they invent, acknowledge the quality of the movements rather than comparing, evaluating, or praising.

For instance, say, "I noticed how high you reached." Or, "You moved fast with one hand and then slow with the other." Also affirm their awareness of others: "It looked like you noticed we couldn't keep up with you, and you slowed down to make it easier to follow you. You thought about us, didn't you?"

When you sense the group is restless, you may use this framework for closure: "Let's have two more turns today." If many children want a turn, you can divide into pairs and ask everyone to learn from and teach their partners.

Dolphin Game: Sending and Receiving Social Messages

Ages: 5 to 8

Children stand in facing lines: one group is the dolphins and the other the people on the shore. Establish two types of signals for the people to use: they beckon with their hands if they want the dolphins to come closer, and they cross their arms if they don't want the dolphins to touch them.

As everyone sings the song "Across the Wide Ocean," dolphins approach the humans. As they come near a child whose arms are crossed, they keep a respectful distance and investigate them without touching. If a child is beckoning to invite their presence, they gently touch their classmate's outstretched hands. At the end of the four lines of the song, add "and come back to the ocean." This calls the dolphins back to their line.

Discuss any problems or misunderstandings regarding the hand signals.

Change identities. Those who were dolphins are now people, and those who were people are now dolphins. To reinforce the switch, ask dolphins to press their palms together like a fin and undulate their spines to feel their flexible backs.

Cooperation in Small Groups

Ages: 5 to 10

Divide the whole class into smaller groups of two, three, or four. Each person takes a turn leading the small group using his or her motion while the others mirror it. Select a method for the order in which the children lead. Ask groups to create a collective dance using an idea from each member.

Take turns showing the dances. While the rest of the class sings the song, "Across the Wide Ocean," ask one, two, or three groups at a time to show what they created until every group has had a turn. Another option is for the whole class to try the movements from each small group.

Social Awareness as a Group

Form a circle. As you sing "Across the Wide Ocean," challenge the group to move closer and closer to the center but stop before anyone gets squished. Or, have the group move together so that all go high, then low, at the same time.

Discuss the awareness needed for this movement to work. Keep evaluating and practicing until the group feels successful. For example:

Teacher: How did it work when we moved closer? Did anyone get squished?

Student 1: There wasn't room for me.

Teacher: What can we do?

Student 2: We could notice if we're shoulder to shoulder with the person next to us.

Student 3: Some people are moving too fast.

Teacher: What can we do?

Student 1: We could watch each other and go the same speed.

Teacher: Let's try it again.

11 ¡Hola!/Hello

Children are greeted by name.

●●●●●●●●●●●●●●●●●●●●●●●●●●●●●

Ages 4 to 8
When to Use Starting song
Language Bilingual
Location Side 1, Song 11
Source Sarah Pirtle

OBJECTIVES

- to greet and welcome all class members
- to learn names

PROCEDURE

1 Sing the song sequencing six names at a time until you have greeted every person in the class. Encourage all class members to sing along. Use the language of your choice.

> *¡Hola! ¿Qué tal?*
> *¡Hola! ¿Qué tal?*
> *Hola, _____. Hola, _____.*
> *Hola, _____. Hola, _____.*
> *Hola, _____. Hola, _____.*
> *Hola, a todos aquí. ¡Sí¡*
>
> *Hello, my friends.*
> *Hello, my friends.*
> *Hi to _____. Hi to _____.*
> *Hi to _____. Hi to _____.*
> *Hi to _____. Hi to _____.*
> *Hi to everyone here. Yes!*

2 Wave to each person when you sing their name. Wave to the whole group on the first two lines.

3 To emphasize the greeting you can vary the pattern by going back and forth between just two children:

> *Hola, Juan. Hola, Luz.*
> *Hola, Juan. Hola, Luz.*
> *Hola, Juan. Hola, Luz.*
> *Hola a todos aquí. ¡Sí!*

4 If you want to give focused affirmation, such as if a new child has joined your class, repeat his or her name for the entire verse:

> *Hola, Noemi. Hola, Noemi.*
> *Hola, Noemi. Hola, Noemi.*
> *Hola, Noemi. Hola, Noemi.*
> *Hola a todos aquí. ¡Sí!*

¡Hola! / Hello

©1997 Words and Music by Sarah Pirtle
Discovery Center Music, BMI

¡Ho-la! ¿Que-tal? ¡Ho-la!¿Que-tal? Ho laRo - sa, Ho-la Step - a-nie, Ho-la Pe - dro, Ho-la An - tho-ny,

Ho-la May - ra, Ho la Yo- ki- ko, Ho-la Ru - by, Ho-la Ry - an, Ho-la to-dos a- quí. ¡Si!

Spanish

¡Hola! ¿Que tal? ¡Hola! ¿Que tal?
Hola Rosa, Hola Stephanie, Hola Pedro,
Hola Anthony, Hola Mayra, Hola Yokiko,
Hola Ruby, Hola Ryan, Hola a todos aquí.
¡Sí!

English

Hello, my friends. Hello, my friends.
Hi to Daniel. Hi Felicita. Hi Latisha. Hi
to Kuame. Hi to Lourdes.
Hi Ricardo.
Hi to everyone here. Yes!

SNAPSHOT

Becoming Part of the Group

. . . .

This morning seven-year-old Mercedita asks to sing each name by herself. Three weeks ago she was new to the class. As she goes around the circle with ease, not forgetting a single name, she signals that she's no longer "the new person." This event shows that she is fully one of the group.

Waving Game

As you sing a person's name, she creates her own kind of wave (e.g., with an elbow) and everyone mirrors her.

Learning Names

Listen to the names on the recording. Ask if any are unfamiliar. Discuss the cultural background of names, such as:

African American: Latisha, Kuame.

Latino/a: Rosa, Pedro, Mayra, Felicita, Lourdes, Ricardo.

Irish: Ryan

Japanese: Yokiko

Jewish/Hebrew: Daniel

Italian: Anthony

Greek: Stephanie

Ages 3 to 8

When to Use Circle Time

Language Bilingual

Location Side 1, Song 12

Source Mexican traditional

12 Pajarito/Little Bird

Children interact as birds.

OBJECTIVES

- to encourage cooperation
- to develop language

PROCEDURE

1 Start by teaching the song as a fingerplay.

2 Act out the song. The actions are structured to begin with quieter movements and then progress to hopping and flying. When the song ends you are back in the place you started. If you have more than one adult in the room, divide the group and meet in separate circles. Call the smaller circles "nests."

3 Feel free to zip in additional action words. For example, "besar" means "to kiss." Use a puppet or a hand shaped like a beak to kiss the cheek.

Pajarito, besas tu.

4 Ask students what other things the birds could be doing: splash in a puddle, build a nest, rest on a roof, peck the sunflowers, shake their wings, fly south for the winter, look out for cats, and act out the day of a bird.

Pajarito / Little Bird

Mexican Traditional Song

Pa - ja - ri - to, can - tas tú, can - tas tú, can tas tú.

Pa - ja - ri - to, can - tas tú, can - tas pa - ra mí.

1. **Spoken**: *Pajarito, ¿quieres cantar?*
   Do you want to sing?
   Sing: *Pajarito, cantas tú, cantas tú,*
   cantas tú.
   Pajarito, cantas tú, cantas para mí.

   English
   Little bird, sing, sing, sing. Sing, sing,
   sing. Sing, sing, sing.
   Little bird, sing, sing, sing. Come and
   sing to me.

2. **Spoken**: *Pajarito, ¿quieres comer? Do*
   you want to eat?
   Sing: *Pajarito, comes tú, comes tú,*
   comes tú.
   Pajarito, comes tú, comes para mí.

   English
   Little bird, have some food, have some
   food, have some food.
   Little bird, have some food, have some
   food for me.

3. **Spoken**: *Pajarito, ¿quieres trinar?*
   Do you want to whistle?
   Sing: *Pajarito, trinas tú, trinas tú,*
   trinas tú.
   Pajarito, trinas para mí.

   English
   Little bird, whistle now, whistle now.
   Little bird, whistle now with me.

4. **Spoken**: *Pajarito, ¿quieres escarbar?*
   Do you want to look for worms?
   Sing: *Pajarito, escarbas tú, escarbas*
   tú, escarbas tú.
   Pajarito, escarbas tú, escarbas para mí.

   English
   Little bird, look for worms, look for
   worms, look for worms.
   Little bird, look for worms, look for
   worms for me.

5. **Spoken**: *Pajarito, ¿quieres saltar? Do*
   you want to hop?
   Sing: *Pajarito, saltas tú, saltas tú,*
   saltas tú.
   Pajarito, saltas tú, saltas tú, para mí.

   English
   Little bird, hop around, hop around,
   hop around.
   Little bird, hop around, hop around for
   me.

6. **Spoken**: *Pajarito, ¿quieres volar? Do*
   you want to fly?
   Sing: *Pajarito, vuelas tú, vuelas tú,*
   vuelas tú.
   Pajarito, vuelas tú, vuelas tú para mí.

   English
   Little bird, fly around, fly around, fly
   around.
   Little bird fly around, fly around for
   me.

7. **Spoken**: *Pajarito, quieres dormir?*
   Do you want to sleep?
   Sing: *Pajarito, duermes tú, duermes
   tú, duermes tú.*
   Pajarito, duermes tú, duermes para mí.

English
*Little bird, go to sleep, go to sleep, go
to sleep.*
*Little bird, go to sleep, go to sleep for
me.*

E X T E N S I O N S

Eating interaction

In this fingerplay, one child is the bird. The
other children hold out their hands as if they
are holding corn. The child uses a bird puppet
or hand to eat the corn as they sing "Pajarito,
comes tú" until every child's hand is touched.
Switch and give everyone a turn as the bird.
This is most effective in small groups of five
to eight children.

Class Book

Pairs of students cooperate together to draw
birds doing one of the actions in the song or
other actions they have invented. Add captions
to the drawings and assemble them as a class
book to develop reading skills.

RELATED SONG
"Sleeping Birds/Los Pajaritos Duermen" (Song 23)

Hand puppet

Hold a bird puppet and talk to it as you introduce each verse. You can buy cloth finger puppets designed to look like bluebirds, robins,
and other birds for $5 each plus postage from
Lynn Swanson, The Toy Lady, 118 Rollingwood
Drive, North Kingston, RI 02852.

Partners

In pairs, children act out the song their own
way.

13 Step by Step/ Paso A Paso

Fast movements contrast with slow deliberate steps.

● ●

Ages 3 to 10
When to Use Movement game
Language Bilingual
Location Side 1, Song 13
Source Sarah Pirtle

OBJECTIVES

- to develop self-control
- to work with the opposites of slow and fast
- to develop bilingual language awareness
- to introduce the concept of one step at a time

PROCEDURE

1 Introduce the song as a fingerplay. On the refrain, two fingers of one hand walk step-by-step along your other arm as if it is a road. Start at your fingertips and walk up to your shoulder. To complete the sequence, on "*así, así*" the walking fingers jump onto your shoulder.

2 Vary the speed on the verse for a humorous effect. Sing "*muevan las manos*" slowly taking the whole phrase to move your hands to one side. Then speed up the English and shake your hands quickly in front of your face.

3 Next, sing the song standing in a circle. Ask the children what other body parts they want to include. Here are new verses:

> *Muevan la cabeza, muevan la cabeza.*
> *Move your head, move your head.*
>
> *Muevan la lengua, muevan la lengua.*
> *Move your tongue, move your tongue.*
>
> *Muevan la cintura, muevan la cintura.*
> *Move your middle, move your middle.*

Tip!

Lead into this song with "My Space/Mi Espacio" (Song 6) to learn about personal space.

Use the following verse to have children interact with others nearby. Their fingers creep close as in a tickle game but don't actually touch other children:

> *Muevan los dedos, muevan los dedos.*
> *Move your fingers, move your fingers.*

4   Progress to having the children travel on the refrain. Decide where and how they want to step. Will they walk in a circle, move anywhere in the room following a line leader, or walk randomly around each other? Let the movement feel like creeping. On the verses, children stay in place. Encourage them to stay in their "space bubble," i.e. personal space. Feel free to use these additional words for the fast section:

> *Den palmadas, den palmadas.*
> *Clap your hands, clap your hands.*
>
> *Estiren las manos, estiren las manos.*
> *Stretch your hands, stretch your hands.*
>
> *Salten alto, salten alto.*
> *Jump so high! Jump so high!*

5   Talk about what it means to take things one step at a time. If a child feels frustrated with a difficult task, use this song to remind her that she can accomplish it step by step.

Step By Step / Paso A Paso

©1997 Words and Music by Sarah Pirtle
Discovery Center Music, BMI

Refrain – SLOW

Step by step. Paso a paso, paso a paso. Así así.

Step by step. Paso a paso, paso a paso. Así así.

Verse 1 – FAST

Muevan las manos. Muevan las manos.

Move your hands. Move your hands.

Verse 2

Salten, salten. Salten, salten

Jump around, jump around.

Refrain – SLOW

Step by step. Paso a paso, paso a paso. Así, así.

Step by step. Paso a paso, paso a paso. Así, así.

14 En La Feria/At the Fair

Children pantomime musical instruments.

OBJECTIVES

- to follow the pattern of the song
- to develop language
- to learn pantomime

PROCEDURE

1 Play the recording to familiarize yourself with the repeating pattern of the song.

2 Use motions to teach the song. Pantomime each instrument. On the chorus, point to other people as you sing *you should go/vaya usted.* Then gesture with your thumb to the location of the fair behind you as you sing *to the fair/en la feria.* Children enjoy singing this song faster and faster.

SNAPSHOT

Vary the Words

First-grade teacher Marta Rodríguez from Brightwood Magnet School in Springfield, Massachusetts, created new words for "En La Feria." She used animals on a flannel board to sing each verse.

"En La Finca/At The Farm" por Marta Rodríguez

Verse 1
En la finca de Pepín yo encontré una ovejita, "bee,bee" una ovejita.
(At the farm of Pepín, I meet a sheep, baa, baa, a sheep.)

Chorus
A gozar y a reir en la finca de Pepín. (2x)
(We have fun and we laugh at the farm of Pepin).

Verse 2
En la finca de Pepín yo encontré un perrito, "jau, jau" el perrito. (At the farm of Pepín, I meet a dog, bark, bark, a dog.) Repeat the sounds and name of the animals that came before, ending with "una ovejita" (bee, bee).

Other animals on the farm and their sounds may include: pio, pio, un pollito (chicken); oinc, oinc, un cerdito (pig); muu, muu, una vaquita (cow); cuac, cuac, un patito (duck); miau, miau, un gatito (cat).

En La Feria / At The Fair

Puerto Rican Traditional

English

Verse: At the fair in San Juan
I play the guitar
tara, tara, tara the guitar
tara, tara, tara the guitar

Chorus: You should go, you should go
To the fair in San Juan.
You should go, you should go
to the fair in San Juan.

Spanish

Verse: *1) En la feria de San Juan*
yo compré la guitarra
tara, tara, tara la guitarra
tara, tara, tara la guitarra

Chorus: *Vaya usted, vaya usted*
a la feria de San Juan.

Vaya usted, vaya usted
a la feria de San Juan.

2) En la feria de San Juan
yo compré las maracas
chacas, chacas, chacas las maracas
chacas, chacas, chacas las maracas
tara, tara, tara la guitarra
tara, tara, tara la guitarra.

3) En la feria de San Juan
yo compré el tambor
bor, bor, bor el tambor
bor, bor, bor el tambor
chacas, chacas, chacas las maracas
chacas, chacas, chacas las maracas
tara, tara, tara la guitarra
tara, tara, tara la guitarra.

E X T E N S I O N S

Movement

Stand in a circle. On the chorus, march around with gusto. On the verses, stay in place and pantomime the instruments.

More instruments

Ask your class for new ideas for instruments, such as:

> *nete, nete, nete el clarinete*
> *lin, lin, el violín*
> *fon, fon, fon el saxofón*
> *iro, iro, iro el guiro*

Festivals

Ask children to describe street fairs, country fairs, or festivals they have gone to with their family. Draw a picture of a fair or festival.

ADDITIONAL RESOURCES

"En la Feria" is similar to the Mexican traditional song, "La Pulga De San Jose." Jose-Luis Orozco has a series of five outstanding cassettes entitled "Lirica Infantil, Hispanic Children's Folklore". "La Pulga de San Jose" is on the second of the series. Contact Arcoiris Children's Music, PO Box 7428, Berkeley CA 94707.

Libros Rodríguez Literatura Infantil is a monthly book order club for paperbacks in Spanish. Contact Mireya Rodríguez, P.O. Box 2854, Oxnard, CA 93034 Fax (805) 981-9504.

15 Llegó La Hora/ Now It's Time

Children sing to end Circle Time

●●●●●●●●●●●●●●●●●●●●●●●●

Ages 3 to 8

When to Use Transitions

Language Bilingual

Location Side 1, Song 15

Source Roberto Díaz

OBJECTIVES

- to end one activity and get ready for the next
- to develop a sense of time

PROCEDURE

1 Use this song to help with transitions. Sing it before clean up, to end Circle Time, to prepare for lunch, or before returning home. Play the tape or sing the words.

2 Use the underlined areas as a zipper song. Change the words to fit your needs.

Spanish

Es la hora de _____

English

Now is the time for _____

Tip!

Roberto Díaz created this song for his bilingual second-grade class. When it's time for a transition, he prepares his class by going to the piano and playing "Llegó la Hora."

Llego la Hora / Now's the Time

©1997 Words and Music by Roberto Díaz

Llegó la hora de, la hora de, la hora de,
Llegó la hora de, la hora de almorzar.
Now the time for lunch has come, for lunch has come,
for lunch has come. Now the time for lunch has come,
now is the time for lunch.

Llegó la hora de, la hora de, la hora de.
Llegó la hora de, la hora de ir al casa.
Now's the time for going home, going home, going home.
Now's the time for going home. Now it's time to go.

PART II

Songs for the
Social Skills Curriculum

* *

Speak up when something's not fair.
Speak up and show that you care.
Speak up when something's not right.
Speak up and follow your light.
— from "Speak Up" (Song 17)

Children develop social skills through direct experience. Song games and activities place children in an environment in which they can create new meaning and choose new behaviors. Here are tools that you can integrate throughout your day—as part of language arts, social studies, or for teaching social skills.

Although Affirming Diversity Songs (Chapter 4) and Conflict Resolution Songs (Chapter 5) are in separate chapters, it is helpful to think of them together. When we encourage children to cooperate or talk out their conflicts, we are also teaching them to embrace diversity, to experience their unity, and to promote fairness. Conflicts or bias can erupt during any moment of the day, including during a song. Children need assurance that the teacher will pay attention to both the overt problems that surface during song games such as pushing, and also the more subtle but important events, such as snickering, facial expressions or body language that signals exclusion, unfriendly teasing, or put-downs. These chapters also provide strategies for intervention.

The songs in Chapters 4 and 5 can be used:

- to make use of teachable moments
- to provide positive group-building experiences
- to raise important topics
- to teach skills directly
- to model recommended behavior
- to bring out thoughts and feelings
- to amplify social studies and language arts units

Here is a summary of what each chapter offers:

Chapter 4 Diversity Songs includes songs which:

- affirm differences
- emphasize our underlying unity
- encourage us to intervene when others are mistreated
- celebrate family and peacemakers
- provide an experience of inclusion
- model responsiveness

16. In the Very Middle
17. Speak Up
18. I Want to Know Your Name
19. Grandmother Spider
20. We Won't Leave Anyone Out
21. Sing About Us/Cantemos de Nosotros
22. Canción de la Nube/Song of the Cloud
23. Sleeping Birds/Los Pajaritos Duermen
24. Full Circle

Chapter 5, Conflict Resolution Songs, includes songs that help children:

- identify what makes a conflict worse or better
- choose the option of talking it out together
- model face-to-face communication
- address anger and identify why they are angry and what they need
- respond to the verbal and nonverbal messages their friends send them
- learn to brainstorm
- find words to describe what they want when they're in a conflict

25. How Can We Be Friends Again?/Amigos de Nuevo
26. Two in a Fight/Dos en Una Pelea
27. Heart to Heart/Corazón a Corazón
28. The Anger Chant
29. When I Say Stop/Cuando Digo Ya
30. There is Always Something You Can Do
31. ¡Dilo!/Talk to Me

CHAPTER 4

Appreciating Diversity

Sing about us. Tell me again.
You don't have to be just like me
to be my friend.
— from "Sing About Us/Cantemos de Nosotros" (Song 21)

Here's a story I heard from a mother. Two children were going up a climber in a public park in Connecticut. One was an African-American girl, three years old, and the other was a European-American boy, four years old. They'd never met before. We've seen children who are strangers freely play together, but the mother of the girl related how, to her shock, the boy suddenly stopped, looked at her daughter and said, "There are too many black people on this climber."

Every day children encounter bias. Every day children are mistreated on the basis of who they are. Bias is learned behavior that informs our interactions and our power relationships. By age three and maybe earlier, children "show signs of being influenced by societal norms and biases and may exhibit pre-prejudice toward others on the basis of gender, race, and physical abilities," according to the landmark book for early childhood educators, *Anti-Bias Curriculum: Tools for Empowering Young Children* by Louise Derman-Sparks and the A.B.C. Task Force (NAEYC, 1989).

From many sources in our culture, such as watching television, playing with prescripted toys and video games, and hearing adult conversations and opinions, children take in false and unhelpful messages that encourage bias. False messages of inferiority are received by girls, children of color, children with disabilities, and others, such as children whose religion or economic class is not the norm in their group, while those in the dominant groups receive false messages of superiority.

How do we as teachers change these messages? Humans are not born biased; we are born curious about our diversity. We take our social cues from the people who form our most important relationships. A teacher can interrupt bias to re-direct learning, can give accurate information about differences, and can help students explore similarities and differences in a child-centered way. From these experiences children learn about our fundamental interconnection, our individual diversity, and our underlying unity.

One way children learn this truth of our unity is by talking about the differences they see. I remember when Wes, a new student at my son's preschool, arrived in a van. A ramp came down from the van, upon which Wes rode down on a motorized wheelchair. The children peppered Wes with questions—How do you make that move? Why can't you walk?—while the teachers comfortably promoted dialogue. If the teachers had shushed the children, they would have sent a very different message—that we needed to hide Wes' reality of being in a wheelchair. Instead, a bevy followed Wes closely as he began his new day.

Another way we help children construct meaning is to re-frame a situation after pre-prejudice has been expressed so that children can encounter each other apart from bias. Take the moment of the children on the climber. If this had happened in your school playground, as a teacher or another parent, what could you have said? Imagine going up to the children to offer a new outlook:

> You're both on this climber, aren't you, and you have different colors of skin. You haven't met each other before, have you? Well, today you have. That's great. Today you're both on this climber. Can you show each other some of the things you like to do on the climber? Both of you are going to have lots of chances to play with children who have skin or hair or eyes different than yours. So, what could you do together today?

ADDRESSING BIAS THROUGH MUSIC

How do songs address bias? A song can also provide a bias-free framework that children are invited to enter. For example, singing "In the very middle you're a lot like me" (Song 16) palm to palm with another child, can help children make a physical connection to their basic underlying unity. Also, a child learns from the way a teacher presents the reality of our diversity. For instance, as a teacher helps children sing about their differences in the song "Sing About Us" (Song 21) the message is conveyed that I am comfortable with and interested in differences and you can be, too.

In offering this collection of songs, I don't want to minimize the reality of institutional, cultural, and individual racism, sexism, classism, and other oppressions. Music alone can't change these conditions. As educators we need to examine our curriculum, literature, bulletin boards, how parents are welcomed into the classroom, and how we intervene when pre-prejudice is expressed. But music has an important role to play. Songs are powerful resources, especially when combined with interactive activities that help build children's understanding.

Here are five ways music can help you teach bias awareness and respect for diversity:

1. Song activities can allow children to explore differences in a child-centered way.
   Sing About Us (Song 21)
   The Colors of Earth (Song 1)

2. Songs provide a bias-free framework.
   In the Very Middle (Song 16)
   Grandmother Spider (Song 19)

3. Songs model intervening when bias, unfairness, or injustice occur.
   Speak Up (Song 17)
   I Want to Know Your Name (Song 18)

4. Songs affirm caring, responsiveness, and inclusiveness.
   We Won't Leave Anyone Out (Song 20)
   Sleeping Birds/Los Pajaritos Duermen (Song 23)

5. Songs bring a direct experience of many cultures.
   En la Feria (Song 14)
   Night Critters Game (Song 34)

Intervening in Bias

As teachers we send a powerful message when we intervene during moments of bias. But how do you intervene effectively in a way that promotes learning?

Tip!

What music has meaning for the children in your classroom and their families? Ask parents to help you enrich your room with music that affirms all cultures represented.

SNAPSHOT

Los Amigos Hoy

Northampton, MA, Head Start. Four-year-old bilingual class (Spanish and English). I came into the class as a music teacher in residence.

SP: This game we've made up together is fun. We've been singing it in English, but I know that lots of children here speak Spanish. I'd like to sing the song in Spanish, too. (I turn to a teacher who is bilingual). We've been singing, "Friends Today." How can we say this in Spanish?

T: Los amigos hoy.

SP: Los amigos hoy. (Most of the group begins to sing.)

Keri: (Turns away) Hoy, toy, foy.

Keri uses a mocking tone; her body language and voice tone suggest uneasiness and perhaps disapproval of the Spanish words. Other children freeze and are unsure how to react.

SP: Are the Spanish words new for you?

Keri: (Frowns) I don't like it.

SP: I really like Spanish. I'll go over the words so that you can learn them, too. Does anyone in your home speak Spanish?

Keri: No.

SP: My family doesn't speak Spanish either, but I like learning it because then I can talk to more of my friends in the language they know best. I want to get better at speaking Spanish. Let's say the words together: "Los amigos hoy." (Slowly)

Group: Los amigos hoy.

Keri listens with growing interest.

SP: Every language is a good language. It's important that we don't make fun of Spanish because that's making fun of our friends. (Turning to the group) Who knows Spanish?

Carmen and Angela nod.

SP: That's great. Let's say the words again. Will you help lead us?

Group: Los amigos hoy.

Carmen and Angela take the lead; Keri joins in.

SP: Why don't we all join hands and play the game again.

Key Ideas

1. *Everyone is affected when anyone of us is hurt.* I still remember that moment Keri said, "hoy, toy, foy." It was as if something felt torn in the group. I believe that all the children present, whether or not they were Spanish speakers, were affected. If anyone of us is allowed to be hurt for any reason, then none of us are secure and safe.

2. *As teachers our intentions are more important than our words.* Let your intentions guide you to the right words. This moment happened so suddenly that one might not see it or decide to let it go by. What did I think about as I made the quick decision to intervene? I didn't have any magic words, but I had a sensation inside me. I wanted to build a bridge. I wanted to re-tie the broken strand. Keri, Carmen, Angela, and all the members of the group who had created the game stayed as we continued to play it, alternating in Spanish and English. That told me my efforts to respect each person were holding firm.

3. *Children want to know that a teacher will intervene if they are targeted.* I stepped in to offer affirmation of the targeted children. I also continued to affirm Keri herself in my tone and body language. I also added information. What information was I trying to convey to the group?

   That Spanish is valued in our world. That we can help each other learn. That learning new languages is for all of us; it's not just incumbent upon Spanish speakers to accommodate to English. That making fun of the culture of others is hurtful and unfair.

USING A GUIDANCE APPROACH

When a child is targeted or pre-prejudice is expressed, we can again offer a guidance approach:

Information + Affirmation

1. Focus on the situation
2. Promote dialogue and respect all children
3. Provide information or correct misinformation
4. Support children who are targeted
5. Help build a bridge

This time I'll take us step by step through an invented example of how I'd handle a situation of pre-prejudice based on gender.

Example

Four- and five-year-olds are playing a collaboration game in small groups to the song, "My Roots Go Down" (Song 33). They act out each verse — becoming horses and then frogs. The child who is the next leader wants everyone to be in a rocket ship. Following his lead, we sing his words:

> *We're in a rocket ship going to the moon.*

As we start the song, most groups are huddling together and making rocket ship sounds. One group, of two boys and a girl named Greta, however, have stopped working together. Greta sits down and covers her face.

1. Focus

   Help the children stop and think. I approach the group and sit down next to Greta.

   > *SP*: I see some children upset here. Let's talk about it.

2. Promote dialogue

   If appropriate, ask for more information.

   > *Liam*: She can't dance with us. She's a girl.

   > *SP*: Why do you say she can't dance?

   > *Liam*: Rockets aren't for girls.

   Reflect back their words or describe what seems to be occurring.

   > *SP*: So you're saying that girls can't dance the rocket ship dance because rockets aren't for girls. It looks like you feel some things are just for boys. Is that what you're thinking?

3. Provide information or correct misinformation

   Refer to the agreements that you have made with the children.

   > *SP*: We've agreed that we won't leave anyone out. You're leaving Greta out of the rocket ship dance.

   > *Liam*: Boys like rockets.

   > *SP*: Rockets are something both girls and boys can work on when they grow up. Women are scientists who build rockets, and women are astronauts. We have a book that shows a picture of Sally Ride who was an astronaut. You and Greta and all the children here get to decide what you like to do. Being a girl or being a boy isn't how you decide what you like. Every girl and every boy can make up their own mind of what they like.

4. Support the children who are targeted

   > *SP*: (Turning to Greta) It doesn't feel fair when someone says you can't do something because you are a girl.

   Indicate also that she's seen as a unique person and not just a member of a group.

   > *SP*: Greta, I see how much you like to do dancing and how high you jump and all the ideas you bring to your dancing group.

5. Help build a bridge

   > *SP*: (To the group) So how can all three of you be part of the rocket ship dance?"

"Make it a firm rule—a person's identity is never an acceptable reason for teasing or rejecting them."

—from the *Anti-Bias Curriculum* by Louise Derman-Sparks

16 In The Very Middle

Children explore their basic unity and diversity.

Ages	4 to 10
When to Use	Game with pairs, teaching about diversity
Language	English
Location	Side 1, Song 16
Source	Words and music by Carol Johnson, © 1982 Noeldner Music BMI

OBJECTIVES

- to affirm diversity
- to affirm the unity underlying diversity

PROCEDURE

1 Gather the children and teach them the song.

2 Provide a method to help the students form pairs. If you ask children to pair up by themselves, some may be left out and experience exclusion. Try one of the following methods for pairing: (a) consider which children could benefit by thinking about each other's similarities and differences, (b) draw names randomly, or (c) ask children sitting near each other to work together.

3 Teach the children the hand movements described below. Encourage the children to modify the movements while singing the song.

> *In the very middle you're a lot like me.*
> (Face your partner and touch palm to palm.)

> *A shining personality.*
> (Shake your palms around your partner, tracing an invisible circle from your partner's feet to the top of your partner's head.)

> *The clothes and the skin are just the covering.*
> (Touch your own shoulders and then your face.)

> *In the very middle you're a lot like me.*
> (Clap palms with your partner.)

Use this song every day for a week culminating in making partner books or a bulletin board display. If you wish to create books, keep the same partners all week. If you plan on a bulletin board display, choose new partners each day.

Monday: Learn the song in pairs with hand motions.

Tuesday: Review the song. Do a similarities search in pairs. Then partners begin writing and drawing about one similarity.

Wednesday: Do a differences search in pairs or make lists of types of differences. Partners select one kind of difference between them and create a second section of their book or make a drawing about this difference.

Thursday: Discuss the meaning of middle. Partners work on the third section of the book, write a poem, or create a drawing in response to one aspect of how they are alike in the middle.

Friday: Complete books and share them with the class, or post drawings on the bulletin board display and ask each person to read and describe one drawing they made in the display. End with the song sung in a circle.

See the Partner Books extension.

In the very middle you're a lot like me.
A shining personality.
The clothes and the skin are just the covering.
In the very middle you're a lot like me.

Partner Game: Similarities and Differences Search

To introduce the game, ask one child to be your partner and have that child stand next to you. Ask the class: "How are the two of us alike? How are we different?" Usually children begin with visible aspects like age, height, hair, skin color, gender, or whether glasses are worn. Next, model how to use questions to find more similarities and differences:

> Do you have a sister?
>
> Where were you born?
>
> Do you like to play soccer?

Help the group divide into pairs. Give partners about three minutes to ask each other questions and come up with ways that they are similar. Come back together as a whole group and ask several partners to say one similarity they discovered in their search.

Have partners explore ways that they are different. Again, have them share their examples.

To end, partners sing the song to each other palm to palm. Ask the children, as they are singing, to think about how they discovered they are both alike and different from each other.

Variation

Focus on just one aspect—similarities or differences—whichever will best serve your group.

Discussion Activity: The Meaning Of Middle

A key culmination to this activity is to discuss what "in the very middle" really means. Here are sample responses children have made:

> We all have blood in the very middle.
>
> We have bones.
>
> We breathe air.
>
> We all have hearts.
>
> We all have spirits.
>
> We all care.

This discussion has led to poignant reflections.

Poetry

Provide a line to start a poem that the children finish. For example:

- I'm like you in the middle. I _____.
- If you look in the middle of me, you'll find _____.
- What is in the middle of you and me?

Partner Books: "We Are the Same and We Are Different"

Prepare little books by placing one piece of paper folded in half inside another. In this way, create a book that has a front and back cover and six pages (front and back) inside. Partners will record what they discovered in their discussion of similarities and differences through writing or drawing in these books.

a. The Cover: Together partners write their names and the title on the cover. One child writes "We Are The Same" and the other child adds "We Are Different."

b. The first two pages: The interior of the book has six sides. Have the partners start by using just the first two pages of their books. Ask, "What is one way you are the same that you want to put in your book?" Provide the sentence starter:

> We both _____.

Ask the partners to work together on a drawing that illustrates their similarity. They can add more than one statement, but remind the partners only to use the first two pages.

c. The middle two pages: Ask, "What is a way you are different that you'd like to mention?" Use the next two facing pages for a statement from each person on the this topic. Each person uses one page. Offer examples to help them decide what topic they wish to use, such as:

- I am from Jamaica. And I am from Thailand.
- I have curly black hair. And I have short straight red hair.
- I live with my mother and my uncle and my baby brother.
- And I live with my mother and my cat.

Each person adds a picture on the same page as their sentence.

d. The last two pages: For the final two pages of the book, ask partners to complete this sentence starter:

In the very middle _____.

Tell partners, "Work together to make a drawing to end your book."

Cooperative List-Making on Diversity

Tell the class, "Let's think of all the many ways we can be different." (Examples include eye color, number of teeth, languages we speak.) With second graders and older students, create written lists. Ask partners to meet together and write as many types of differences as they can. Each pair meets with another pair. Combine all class lists. Notice how the list got longer. This provides a chance to see the power of group cooperation and collaboration.

Bulletin Board

Instead of making a book, partners make drawings to post in a display. Unlike the book, separate drawings can be made with different partners on any or all of these topics: similarities, differences, or their understanding of "in the very middle." Use sentence starters to encourage students to add words to their drawings.

Round Singing

Carol Johnson wrote "In the Very Middle" to work as a four-part round. Start by dividing the class in half. Sing the song in two parts. The second half enters the song after the first line is done. If you like, then break into four groups and try it as a four-part round.

RELATED SONG

Sing "The Colors of Earth" (Song 1). Partners make hand tracings to add to the bulletin board.

ADDITIONAL RESOURCES

"In the Very Middle" is a song by Carol Johnson from her recording *Isn't It Good to Know*. Since the 1970's, Carol has written meaningful songs for children, including "Love Grows One by One." You can order her recordings by writing her at P.O. Box 6351, Grand Rapids, MI 49516.

Ages	4 to 12
When to Use	Bias awareness and empowerment
Language	English
Location	Side 1, Song 17
Source	Sarah Pirtle

17 Speak Up

Children are encouraged to speak about what matters to them.

•••••••••••••••••••••••••••••••••

OBJECTIVES

- to help children communicate their concerns
- to learn how to be an advocate for fairness
- to develop an awareness of bias

PROCEDURE

1 Gather the children together and teach them the song. Ask the children what the song means to them.

2 Provide an example of a time a person spoke up in the class and notice together how it was helpful. For example, "Remember the time I was handing out snacks and I left out Geraldo by mistake? T.J., you spoke up because you didn't want him to be left out. That really helped."

3 Customize the verses so that the words fit your group. The line "we need your voice in our world" can be sung differently. Here are options to zip in:

> *We need your voice in our circle.*
> *We need your voice in our class.*
> *We need your voice in our school.*

Or:

> *Speak up, we want to hear (2x)*
> *Speak up, we want to hear what you feel.*

Variation: Sing "speak out" instead of "speak up."

Speak Up

©1997 Words and Music by Sarah Pirtle
Discovery Center Music, BMI

Verse 1

Speak up, we need your voice.
Speak up, we need your voice.
Speak up, we need your voice
in our world.

Chorus

Speak up when something's not fair.
Speak up and show that you care.

Speak up when something's not right.
Speak up and follow your light.

Verse 2

Speak up, we need your voice. (3x)
ringing strong... Speak up!

. . . .

E X T E N S I O N S

. . . .

You'll find that many of these extensions are useful to promote productive classroom communication. This short song provides an opportunity to help children give voice to the things they feel. It asks:

- How can we express ourselves when we feel upset or mistreated?

- How can we help when we see someone else mistreated?

- How do we become more alert to unfairness?

Friends Speak Up

. . . .

Materials: 2 Puppets

Play the song on the recording. Take out two puppets and give them names. Point to the one that will be Puppet B in the skit below. Say, "Watch the way this puppet speaks up when he/she is upset." With this skit, teach the concept that if someone is pushing, teasing or bothering you, you can tell them you don't like it and ask them to stop.

Puppet A tickles Puppet B.

Puppet B retracts.

Puppet A continues.

Puppet B: I don't want to be tickled.

Puppet A: You don't?

Puppet B: No, it's not fun for me.

Puppet A: I thought it was fun.

Puppet B: I want games to be fun for both of us.

Puppet A: What else could we do?

Puppet B: Play blocks.

Puppet A: Yes, I like blocks. I want to play with you.

Discuss the way that Puppet B spoke up. Although the words and concepts are more complex than many young children might actually say, they illustrate an important process that they can learn. At any point, you can stop the drama and ask the children to suggest what the puppets could say. Close the lesson by repeating the song.

Puppets Uncover Children's Hidden Concerns

Materials: 1 Puppet

Use the song to give permission for children to reveal school problems that have been troubling them. After playing the song, have a puppet say or sing:

> *I don't want to go to school today.*
> *And I don't want to tell you why.*
> *If the same thing happens to me today,*
> *I think I'm going to cry.*

Ask the children what might have happened to the puppet and then explore with them what the puppet could do next.

Speak Up Time

Use the song to introduce group meeting time when children and adults have a chance to bring up concerns in a constructive way. Set ground rules:

1. As we talk about a problem, we'll name the situation without naming the people in it.

2. As we talk and listen, we'll make sure everyone is respected.

3. We'll remember that we all make mistakes, and we all can learn.

When Do You Speak Up?

Use the song to explore the difference between tattling and speaking up. A puppet explains a situation she has witnessed, and the children decide if they think the puppet should speak up, who she should tell, and what she could say. Examples:

- I just saw someone punch my friend and my friend is really hurt.

- We have a new person in our class and some of the kids are making fun of his clothes.

- One of my friends is walking in puddles and the teacher said that wasn't a good idea because your feet will get wet and uncomfortable.

- One person won't let another person use their swing, and they've had it a long time.

Standing Up For Fairness

Materials: 1 Puppet

Designate one puppet to be the "Learning Puppet." This is a puppet who can make mistakes or exhibit bias, and he will get help from the children in the class.

The puppet takes on the role of a person who is saying unfair things, but at the end of each scenario, with help from the children, he will make new realizations and grow.

The children practice finding helpful words to use as they speak up.

Ask for a team of volunteers—two to four children—to come up together and speak to the puppet. Provide a situation where the puppet needs more information. The children practice interrupting bias/unfairness by finding helpful and informative words to say.

Remind the group that people can change. Tell the children:

- Help the puppet stop and think about the situation.

- Talk to him in a way that indicates that you know he is not a bad person and that you are not making fun of him.

- Teach him what he doesn't yet understand in a friendly way.

Four Situations of Bias that Children Can Interrupt

Materials: 1 Puppet

Making Fun Of Names
Pretend a new child joins the class and he has a name that the puppet has never heard before. The puppet says, "I don't like that name."

Example of responses that have been made by third graders:

"Just because he has a different name doesn't mean he's a bad person."

"It doesn't hurt to be different."

Misunderstanding Disabilities
Pretend children are going to play kickball and one member of the group is in a wheelchair. The puppet says, "How can she play? I don't understand."

Example of a response made by a first grader:
"Sure, everyone who wants to gets to play. Watch. She kicks the ball with her chair and she wheels around the bases."

Religious Differences
Pretend it's December and children are talking about the holidays they will be celebrating with their families. The puppet says, "I don't see why everyone doesn't celebrate Christmas. It's the best holiday."

Example of a response made by a second grader:
"It's the best holiday for your family but other people do different things."

Sex-Role Stereotyping and Gender Bias
The puppet says, "I asked my friend to play basketball and he said he was tired and didn't want to. He's a sissy. He's a girl."

Example of a response made by a third grader:
"He wants to do something different. That's okay. But I don't like to hear anyone use the word "girl" as a put-down. That's not fair to girls."

When a child calls another child "sissy," "queer," or "gay," it is important that we step in and address the roots of the incident in a child-centered manner. Often what is occurring is that a child is using what they consider powerful words to try to put down or intimidate another.

Variation
Instead of using a puppet, it is very effective to have an adult take the role of the person who is making a mistake. When I take this role, I encourage the interrupters, "Stay connected with me and don't put me down for my mistake. Help me learn."

I name the things they are doing that help me learn from them. "When you looked right at me in that calm way, I really wanted to pay

Addressing Gender Bias

A second-grade teacher in Harrisburg, Pennsylvania, asked me to help her class with the problem of boys calling other boys "girls." I did the whole sequence of four scenarios and put this one last. Instead of using a puppet, I took the role of the person making the statements. Those who took the role of interrupting said "That's not fair. He doesn't have to play basketball if he doesn't want to play," but they didn't know how to directly deal with the gender bias in the name calling.

During our discussion I conveyed this central point: the word "girl" isn't ever meant to be a put-down. That would not be fair to girls and women. Also, you are you no matter what you do. I presented examples of girls and women, boys and men stepping out of stereotypes. When my friend Margie works as a carpenter, does that mean she's stopped being a woman? When my friend Gavin dances ballet, does that mean he's stopped being a man? To each question I posed, they heartily answered "No." A boy in the class who took dance class perked up and told about being teased for dancing. It was a long, lively discussion. Afterward, a girl came up to me and showed me words she'd written down. "This is the song I wrote," she beamed. "Whatever you do, you're still you."

attention to you." During the role play, they see me reacting, nodding, learning from what they say. At the end I make it clear that they have helped me think and change. I tell them, "I understand this differently now."

INTERRUPTING BIAS PRACTICE: ADDITIONAL SITUATIONS

These poems can be read, said by a puppet, or set to a simple tune:

Waiting in line for the bus,
two kids tease her everyday.
Others do nothing and look away.
What can I do? What can I say?

Some kids have been best friends since kindergarten.
Anna is new and she wants to join in.
She watches the games but she feels left out.
How can I help her enter in?

Most kids are white in our class.
Maya is African American.
When we make a circle, kids moved away.
They said your skin is dirty. I won't take your hand.

ADDITIONAL RESOURCES

Bully Proof: A Teacher's Guide on Teasing and Bullying for Use With Fourth- and Fifth-Grade Students by Nan Stein, Emily Gaberman, and Lisa Sjostrom (Center for Research on Women, Wellesley College, 106 Central St., Wellesley, Massachusetts 02180). Teachers of younger grades will also get excellent suggestions from this book.

"Walls and Bridges" by Sarah Pirtle. Students in grades 2 and up can listen to the song and discuss the story it tells of prejudice and the effort to change it by building bridges instead of walls. At the start of the song two girls are becoming best friends, but one mother objects because, as she puts it, "She's black and you're white." Intended to show the struggle involved in changing bias, by the end of the song we see the families succeed in building bridges. This song is based on true stories of teenagers. The song is recorded on *Magical Earth*, on cassette or CD and can be ordered from The Discovery Center, P.O. Box 58, Shelburne Falls, Massachusetts 01370.

Teaching Young Children in Violent Times by Diane E. Levin, Ph.D. (Educators for Social Responsibility, 23 Garden St., Cambridge, Massachusetts 02138). An excellent, detailed resource on group meetings and other important components of the Peaceable Classroom.

Ages 5 to adult

When to Use Social studies,
family events

Language English

Location Side 1, Song 18

Source Sarah Pirtle

18 I Want to Know Your Name

Children honor significant people in their families, neighborhoods, and in the wider world.

● ●

OBJECTIVES

- to learn more about the lives of family and community members
- to learn about and feel connected to people in history
- to learn about peacemakers

PROCEDURE

1 Familiarize yourself with the three parts of the song and the melodies by listening to the recording.

2 Use the example on the recording to introduce the song. Next, show how to put the name of any person you'd like to honor into the song. Prepare an illustration in advance to extend the song in a way that will be meaningful for your students. Make up a group echo to present to them and ask them to join in on the chorus. Here are three methods.

• Sing about the school community:

"Let's sing about somebody who has helped our class." Honor a person whom the children will recognize, such as a teacher, crossing guard, cafeteria cook, or principal. Use as many phrases as you need to create the echo section of the song. Children echo back each line:

Mrs. Sandini our bus driver,
you greet us with a smile
you ask us how we're doing.
I want to know your name.

Sing the words you have prepared as an illustration, then ask students, "Who else do you want to put into the song?"

• Sing about families:

"Let's sing the name of someone in our family. I'll show you how. I'm going to choose my _____ (for example: mother). Then let's sing about people in your family." Here's a group echo about the grandfather of a child in the class named Aaron.

> *Jacob Perlman,*
> Echo: *Jacob Perlman.*
> *Grandfather of Aaron,*
> Echo: *Grandfather of Aaron.*
> *I want to know your name.*
> Together: *I want to know your name.*

• Sing about classmates.

Start a group echo about each person in the class. (See the extension "Singing About All the Children in the Class.")

3 Talk about the meaning of the words in the chorus, "links on a chain." Bring in necklaces with pendants or other kinds of chains. Show the children what a "link" means and talk about the way the links work together. Next, stand in a circle and link arms so that you are making a chain. Look for images of the power of combined effort. For example, the United Mine Workers Union song says, "Drops of water turn a mill, singly none."

Create an awareness of how the people in one generation pass on help, skills, and knowledge to the next generation. Speak about older people helping younger people.

SNAPSHOT

A Tribute to Anti-Racism Crusaders

• •

The elementary school in the small rural town of Ashfield, Massachusetts, launched a year-long effort to help children learn about bias and respecting diversity after a Jewish town official received a death threat. The town mobilized with a variety of responses. When they invited me to present a program of music, I wanted to find a way to help the children meet people in history and the unsung people alive today who work to make the world a peaceful place where everyone feels safe. I wrote "I Want to Know Your Name" and brought it to the assembly using names of people in the tradition of anti-racism. I sang:

> Morris Dees,
>
> You started the Southern Poverty Law Center,
>
> You put the spotlight on the hate groups,
>
> You send schools "Teaching Tolerance" magazine.
>
> I want to know your name.

I Want To Know Your Name

©1997 Words and Music by Sarah Pirtle
Discovery Center Music, BMI

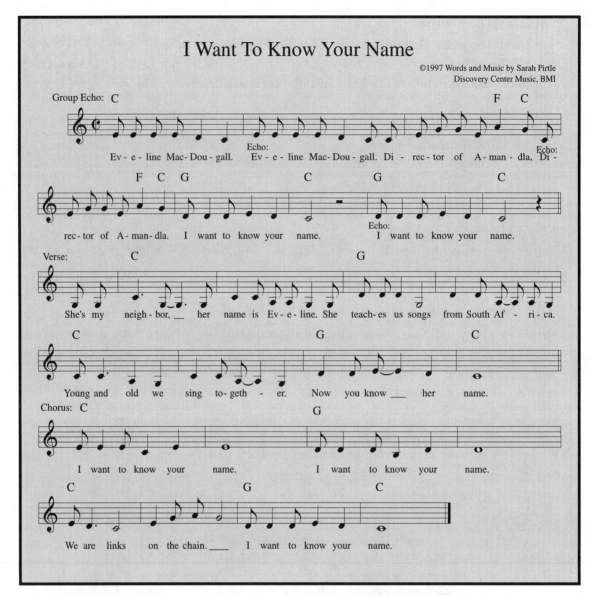

Group Echo

Eveline MacDougall,
Eveline MacDougall.
Director of Amandla,
Director of Amandla.
I want to know your name.
I want to know your name.

Verse

She's my neighbor,
her name is Eveline.

She teaches us songs
from South Africa.
Young and old we sing together.
Now you know her name.

Chorus

I want to know your name.
I want to know your name.
We are links on the chain.
I want to know your name.

Songwriter's Note: *I chose Eveline MacDougall as an example of a peacemaker who helps our community in western Massachusetts. She directs a community chorus of forty people called Amandla. They sing songs for freedom and justice in the languages of South Africa: Zulu, Xhosa, and Sotho. Eveline also directed the children who sing on this recording.*

E X T E N S I O N S

This song can complement your curriculum:

- as part of a family unit, make verses about the children's families;

- focus on people featured in biographies in the school library.

Identify the people you want to illuminate. Here are examples:

- Women in history;

- People in your community who are peacemakers;

- Latino writers and leaders of the 20th century.

Singing About All the Children in the Class

Ask each child, "Do you want to decide the words we sing about you, or do you want us to think about you and suggest some words?" Use the group echo pattern. For instance:

> *Maisie Sibbison-Alves*
> *likes to make up plays with her friends.*
> *I want to know your name.*

Variation: Affirmation Interview

Pairs ask each other questions and then make up verses about each other.

Honoring Families

Respect each child's unique family by giving the group this general assignment: "Select one person in your family to write about. Gather information by interviewing that person. If you can't talk to him or her directly, ask other people in your family questions about that person. Then pick two things you learned and put them into the verse."

Here are examples of verses that could be written by my son, Ryan:

> *There's my grandma, her name is Lucy.*
> *She likes to paint, great big paintings.*
> *She started to paint when she was 40 years old.*
> *Now you know her name.*

> *She's my godmother, her name is Paula Green.*
> *Her work is to teach nonviolence.*
> *She's worked in twelve countries.*
> *Now you know her name.*

Note: *If you limit the assignment to grandparents, mothers or fathers, not every child will be able to participate. Also, some may prefer to write about a person who is part of the "family of their heart" but not a relative. Respect the family constellation of every child. Also, let them choose more than one person if they wish so they don't have to leave out anyone significant.*

Singing About Community Members

Help children learn about the vast web of people who help things go well in their community and make positive contributions. For example, a sixth-grade boy at Brightwood Magnet School in Springfield, Massachusetts, created these words for the group echo:

> *Maria in my neighborhood*
> *stops the fights.*
> *People trust her.*
> *I want to know your name.*

Singing About Peacemakers

This song can highlight and help us discover names of contemporary people and people in history who have worked for social justice. Children are invited to think of themselves as new "links on the chain" and to feel connected to this legacy. The song can tell children about an important hero—such as Cesar Chavez—and convey respect.

It's difficult to summarize whole lifetimes in a few phrases. It helps to be clear about your objective. Let the summary lead to further interest in reading about the person's life. After each section, add the refrain "I want to know your name." Below are some examples.

Objective: to recognize African-American inventors.

> *Garrett Morgan,*
> *Every stoplight sings your genius.*
> *Lewis Latimer,*
> *You lit buildings with electricity.*

Objective: to feature contemporary African-American women.

> *bell hooks,*
> *You speak out across the country.*
> *Your books move people to action.*
>
> *Toni Morrison,*
> *You won the Noble Prize for literature*
> *For your fifth novel called* Beloved.
>
> *Marian Wright Edelman,*
> *You give voice to children.*
> *You started the Children's Defense Fund.*

Objective: to reveal the legacy of white people who worked against racism so that white children can see themselves as part of this tradition.

> *Laura Haviland,*
> *Quaker woman ending slavery,*
> *Underground Railroad conductor.*
>
> *Levi Coffin,*
> *At seven years old you turned against slavery.*
> *You helped hundreds of people to freedom.*
>
> *Anne Dudley,*
> *You founded Black schools and colleges.*
> *You let no one stop you.*

Bringing Biographies to Life

Students in grades 3 and older who are studying biographies can use this pattern to summarize their reading.

> **Group Echo**
> *We want to honor*
> _____ (Write the name of the person you studied.)
> _____ (Tell one thing that is important about what he or she did.)
> *I want to know your name.*

Example:
> *We want to honor*
> *Elizabeth Cady Stanton.*
> *She worked for women to vote.*
> *I want to know your name.*

Illuminating Unsung People

Ages: 7 and up

Help your students understand that there are millions of people whose names we don't know who do important things. Select a book about the lives of everyday people whom you would like your students to meet. Write short phrases to introduce their story.

- *It's Our World, Too!—Stories of Young People Who Are Making A Difference* by Phillip Hoose (Boston: Little, Brown and Co., 1993). This book details significant actions taken by young people.
  > *Children in New Mexico*
  > *wanted to build a peace statue.*
  > *They got help from all around the world.*
  > *They worked for five years until they did it.*
  > *I want to know your names.*

- *Many Thousand Gone* by Virginia Hamilton (New York: Knopf, 1993). Here is a resource about African-Americans and African-Canadians. The lives of these individuals span the years 1745 - 1850.

Olaudah Equina,
kidnapped by slave traders,
wrote a book to end slavery.
I want to know your name.

- *Her Story: Women Who Changed the World* edited by Ruth Ashby and Deborah Gore Ohrn (New York: Viking, 1995). This contains readable, informative descriptions of over 100 women.

  Rigoberta Menchu,
  Noble Peace Prize winner.
  You protect your people of Guatemala.
  I want to know your name.

- *The Book of Women: 300 Notable Women History Passed* by Lynn Griffin and Kelly MacCann (Holbrook, Massachusetts: Adams Publications, 1995). A paperback reference book.

  Jackie Mitchell,
  you were a great baseball player.
  You even struck out Babe Ruth.
  I want to know your name.

- *Wisdom Keepers: Meetings with Native American Spiritual Elders* by Steve Wall and Harvey Arden (Hillsboro, Oregon: Beyond Words Publishing, 1990). Pages 24-27 are about Audrey Shenandoah.

  Audrey Shenandoah, clan mother
  of Onondoga nation.
  You spoke at the United Nations.
  I want to know your name.

Audrey Shenandoah represents the Haudenosaunee (Hoo-de-na-show-nee) of the Six Nation Iroquois Confederacy, which goes back a thousand years. This confederacy is the first United Nations. The Onondoga and five other nations came together under the leadership of the Peacemaker and learned ways of peace. In the 1700's the founders of the United States went to learn from the Haudenosaunee and put their ideas into the structure of the U.S. Government. In 1990 Audrey Shenandoah spoke in Moscow at the Global Forum, asking that respect for the earth and for all peoples be a beacon for the United Nations of today.

Stones of Honor

Identify people you would like to honor—family members, community members, or people in history. Assemble enough stones so there is one for each child or one for each name. Look for stones large enough to cover a child's palm. Use rubber cement to attach squares of paper on stones with the names of the significant people you have chosen. If you want a more permanent collection, coat the stone in shellac and allow the stones to dry.

A Classroom Ceremony as the Culmination of a Unit on Families

Assemble in a circle with a candle in the center. Children bring the verses they have created as described in "Honoring Families." In advance, write the names of each person they have chosen on a stone. Place the stones around the lit candle. Children take turns holding the stone, reading the name of the family member, and then reading or leading the class in singing the verse or group echo they have written.

Tip!

Use this song in combination with "Carry the Candle" to honor family members at a Family Day.

Ages	4 to adult
When to Use	To build unity, to start or end Circle Time, for Native American studies, or a spider unit
Language	Native American
Location	Side 1, Song 19
Source	Native American song taught by Rainbow Weaver with addition by Sarah Pirtle

19 Grandmother Spider

Children explore the connections between all creatures.

OBJECTIVES

- to value all members of the group
- to experience a caring community

PROCEDURE

1 Gather the children together and form a circle. Introduce the spider web image. Here are two ways to do this:

a) Ask the children to imagine there's a spider who travels all around the world. She weaves a web that connects every person.

b) Ask the children to imagine that a friendly spider travels all around our class to help us remember to think about each other.

2 Teach these movements that I learned from Rainbow Weaver to accompany the song.

Hey-la
Stretch your hand out from your heart, palm down.

Hey-ooo
Hand touches the opposite shoulder then moves horizontally.

Hey-la, Hey-ooo
Repeat.

Ah-dow-wee
Palm out, make a small circle as if tracing a flat vertical web in front of your face.

Sing
Draw one thread and bring it to your heart.

3 I invented these words to explain the meaning of the song and to help reinforce the movements.

Grandmother Spider travels far.
Stretch your hand out from your heart, palm down.

Grandmother Spider travels wide.
Hand touches the opposite shoulder then moves horizontally.

She weaves a web with everybody in the world.
Palm out, make a small circle as if tracing a flat vertical web in front of your face.

And she makes sure you are not forgotten.
Draw one thread and bring it to your heart.

4   On the additional words "I care about you," guide children to stretch their fingers out, palm down, and sweep their hands horizontally while they look at each person's face. Reverse directions and sing "You care about me." Repeat in each direction, "I care about you. You care about me."

5   Let the song help you build unity in the classroom. Articulate the attitude it conveys: "This time as we sing 'Grandmother Spider,' let's think about how much we want to send good wishes to everyone in our class. We want them to do their best." Sing the song together again. This song helps to convey a building block of peace through mutual regard.

6   Say to the children, "One of the most powerful things we can do at any moment is give respect to the person with us. This doesn't mean we have to agree with everything that person says or does. This doesn't mean we are best friends. But we say with our eyes, the expression on our face, our attitude, and our heart, 'I greet you. I see you. I hear you. I welcome you.'"

You can add, "There may be places where it's not safe to show this attitude. In those places you might need to convey, 'Don't mess with me.' It's important to be aware of where you are. In this class we make a place where we're carrying the attitude of 'Grandmother Spider'— that everyone here deserves a chance to be welcomed, encouraged, and feel that they belong."

Responding to the Unexpected

· ·

As I taught "Grandmother Spider" to a second-grade class, one boy drew his hand back to his forehead instead of his heart on the last line, "Ah-dow-wee sing." He was very engaged in the song, not mocking it or defying the movement pattern. I stopped and responded: "Robert, I notice what you're doing. That's really interesting to me. Tell me about it."

"My head means I'm thinking," he said.

I turned to the group, "As you draw your hand back next time, you decide where you want to bring your hand. It could be to your forehead like Robert or your heart, or use any other idea you have."

That day the class was more focused and thoughtful for the rest of Circle Time than usual, and I think that moment was the reason. By affirming his contribution rather than censoring him for deviating from the prescribed movements, I tried to live the Grandmother Spider attitude and say, "This group belongs to all of us."

Grandmother Spider

Native American Traditional

Hey __ la, Hey- ooo Hey __ la, Hey-ooo Ah - dow __ wee sing

I care a - bout you, you care a - bout me.

Hey-la, Hey-ooo
Hey-la, Hey-ooo
Ah-dow-wee sing

I care about you, You care about me.
I care about you, You care about me.

Note: *I met a Native American woman named Rainbow Weaver at the Rowe Conference Center in Rowe, Massachusetts. She taught this song and said it came from many Native American nations, not just one tradition. She told me that I was welcome to share it with others.*

. . . .

E X T E N S I O N S

. . . .

Friendship Discussion

We can help children understand the complexities of friendship using the model of "Grandmother Spider." We can also teach mutual regard rather than the model of scarcity and competition. Ask, "If I like one person, does it mean that I don't like others?" Allow children time to pause and consider this. "No, we can like more than one person. What about if I'm just playing with one person? Do I still like the other people?"

Sample discussion

Gina: Lily's not playing with me. She's with Maria.

Teacher: You and Lily played together all morning, didn't you?

Gina: Yes, and I want to play with her now. I want to be in the tree house with her.

Teacher: Lily and Maria have chosen the tree house, and it has just enough room for two people. It's one of the places in the playground where we say two at a time.

Gina: But Lily's supposed to play only with me.

Teacher: When friends play with other people, they still like you. Lily will want to play with you again. She likes you as much as she did this morning. Right now she's taking a turn playing with Maria. What else would you like to do now?

Spider Web Game

Materials: a ball of yarn

Form a circle with the children. The person who starts the web calls the name of a person across the circle and tosses the yarn to her while keeping hold of the end of the yarn. Repeat so that each child receives the yarn. As the yarn crisscrosses back and forth, the strand extends. Each person still holds onto her section of yarn so that a web is formed.

Variation: One child goes underneath the web and becomes an animal in the center of the circle. The child in the middle announces what animal she is and the class sings to her using a verse from "My Roots Go Down" (Song 33), such as "I am a turtle looking all around." Encourage the child in the center to dance.

Name Echo

Materials: a special object such as a rock, a spoon, or a ball

Gather the children in a circle. Have the children pass the object around the circle. Each person takes a turn holding the object and saying her name. Then, the group echoes back each name while keeping in mind the thought, "I welcome you. I send you good wishes." Since the tendency is for the person receiving the group's focus to rush this moment, ask the children to pause and breathe in the good wishes before handing the special object to the next person.

ADDITIONAL RESOURCES

Keepers of the Animals: Native American Stories and Wildlife Activities for Children by Michael Caduto and Joseph Bruchac (Fulcrum Publishing, 1991). This contains the Hopi story "How Grandmother Spider Named the Clans" and the Osage story "How the Spider Symbol Came to the People," as well as scientific information and activities about spiders.

"Spin Spider Spin," by Patty Zeitlin, is a positive song about spiders. It is included in a collection of songs for ages two to eight on feelings, nature, self-esteem and nonsexist roles called *A Song Is A Rainbow*. It is available in cassette, songbook and teacher's text. Contact Patty Zeitlin at 12233 Ashworth Ave., N. #40, Seattle, WA 98133.

Ages	3 to 9
When to Use	For passing objects during sharing, as a game at Circle Time, before recess, or to reinforce social values
Language	English
Location	Side 1, Song 20
Source	Sarah Pirtle

20 We Won't Leave Anyone Out

Children celebrate inclusion.

● ●

OBJECTIVES

- to act inclusively
- to notice others

PROCEDURE

1 Gather the children together, teach them the song, and ask them what the words mean to them.

2 Add motions to the chorus such as clapping or tapping your legs with your hands.

3 Start a discussion on inclusion. "Let's look at the agreements in our classroom. Do we like the idea of promising 'We won't leave anyone out?'"

Responding to the Unexpected

● ●

The first class to try the game of "Back and Forth" was a second-grade class at Brightwood Magnet School in Springfield, Massachusetts on a day when we were specifically practicing noticing others and thinking about the whole group. One boy held up a beanbag he called a "hornet," and he asked if we could use it in a game. I asked him whether he wanted to start off as the first traveler, and instead he thought it was more fitting for his friend to go first since that boy's mother had sewed the beanbag for him. He set a tone of thinking about others.

As the first traveler completed the circle, he noticed that he'd omitted the two children and aide who were working in a corner of the room and went over to include them. We noticed with excitement that it was working: we weren't leaving anyone out. After we played the game two times through, all the children had their hands up asking to have the next turn as the traveler. I paused and asked them, "Do you think this game would be fun if we played it a hundred times?" They shook their heads. "How many more times could we play it and it would still be fun?" One girl responded wisely, "Two more times." That's what we did.

We were excited about the close connection we'd built. We played "Let's Get Together," and the experience of collaboration continued. When it was time to end, I asked which closing song they thought would fit. They chose *Across the Wide Ocean* (Song 10), and we sang, "I hear you calling me, oh my friend."

4 Generate ideas for ways to be more inclusive. Encourage children to think about situations, such as kickball or playing in the block corner, where people can be left out. Encourage children to speak generally rather than naming individuals who they feel are being exclusive. Address just one situation during a particular meeting. An excellent resource for facilitating this kind of meeting is *Teaching Young Children in Violent Times* by Diane Levin (Cambridge, MA: Educators for Social Responsibility, 1995).

We Won't Leave Anyone Out

©1997 Words and music by Sarah Pirtle
Discovery Center Music, BMI

Verse 1

We won't leave anyone out. (2x)
This is what it's all about.
We won't leave anyone out.

Chorus

With a click and a clack and a zoom, zoom, zoom.
A click and a clack and a zoom, zoom, zoom.
A click and a clack and a zoom, zoom, zoom.
Click, clack, zoom, zoom, zoom.

Verse 2

When we're together we're strong. (2x)
Here's a place we all belong.
When we're together we're strong.

Tip!

Sing this song before recess to remind children to be aware of each other. At the end of recess, discuss how the class did at keeping this agreement.

Passing Games

This song can be used with various passing games—where an object is passed around the circle. Decide whether you want to pass during the whole song or just during the chorus. One method is to sing just the first verse, and then repeat the chorus as many times as you need to bring that round of the activity to a close.

Everyone At Once
Materials: objects such as shells, buttons, acorns, or stones.

Give each child a shell, button, acorn, or stone to hold. Pass these around in the same direction, allowing a satisfying length of time to hold each object. For example, sing two lines and then call, "Pass!" Keep singing and passing until you have the same object you started with so that each child has the opportunity to hold all objects.

Pass It On

Use the same method to share special objects that are interesting to explore. The words reinforce the fact that everyone will get a turn holding them. If you have a regular sharing time where children bring in things that they would like others to look at, you can use this song to help increase their attention for sharing.

Table Groups
Grades One and Up

If children sit with desks pushed together or at tables, use these groups for the game. Each group plays with its own object and passes just to the children within its own table or desk area. This works best if each table has a different object, such as a special shell or rock.

Switch items with other tables until all groups have explored each one. Before you start, ask children to model the length of a turn so that the passing feels fair.

Travel Around The Circle

Back and Forth
Materials: Use a soft ball, bean bag, or stuffed toy.

While the rest of the group is seated, a "traveler" goes around to each child in the circle, tossing the object to the child then receiving it back.

Have Some Food
The traveler holds a stuffed animal toy, and the others hold out their hands as if offering food. The traveler makes the stuffed toy nibble at the outstretched hands.

Tap Hands
The traveler goes around from person to person and repeats a motion such as clapping hands with each person. This gives a chance for the traveler to control her or his movements so that no one's hands are hit hard and the game stays fun for everyone. Travelers can select which movement they will do. If a child doesn't want to be tapped, he can hold his hands back to indicate that he is passing.

As the first person finishes, another child takes the role of the traveler. Notice how many rounds can occur before the group loses interest. Set a framework such as, "Let's play this four times through today." Or instead of playing this game in one big circle, make lots of smaller circles in different parts of the room so that everyone can have a turn being the traveler in small groups.

GROUP MEETING CHECK-IN

At a group meeting ask, Was there a time today we left somebody out by mistake? Was there a game or other activity that we could plan better so that everyone can play?

GROUP MEETING PROBLEM SOLVING

Model how to plan an activity inclusively. This doesn't mean necessarily treating everyone the same, but thinking about each person and taking the variety of needs into account. Examples:

- Some children have said that they want to go hiking and pick up fall leaves. We need to find a trail that's accessible to all of us. Wheelchairs can't go on the bumpy trails. We also need to figure out how the members of our class who can't pick up leaves can also enjoy them. Let's talk about this. How could we use partners to make sure everyone is included?

- We're going to make cookies tomorrow and I know that some people are allergic to wheat. How can we make sure that everyone has something good to eat? Sample solution: Let's make one batch of cookies made with spelt and oat flour and another with wheat.

ADDITIONAL RESOURCES

Vivian Gussin Paley's *You Can't Say You Can't Play* (Cambridge, MA: Harvard University Press, 1992).

Ages 4 to 12

When to Use Exploration of unity and diversity, or for songwriting to affirm differences

Language Bilingual

Location Side 1, Song 21

Source Sarah Pirtle

21 Sing About Us/ Cantemos De Nosotros

Children identify and celebrate differences through song writing.

● ●

OBJECTIVES

- to think inclusively
- to explore differences that interest the children
- to affirm each person's uniqueness

PROCEDURE

1 Preview the song to familiarize yourself with the music, lyrics, and the pattern of the song.

2 This is a "zipper" song—new verses can be created using a whole-language approach. The words that the children contribute don't need to rhyme. The ending words "too" and "you" provide enough of a rhyme to carry the verse.

3 Think about the purpose of the song-writing. As children contribute to the song, they articulate their identities. As they sing each other's words, they affirm each person's uniqueness. Select a topic that fits your age group or ask the children what they want to write about. Children in kindergarten and below understand the pattern of the song best when they begin with preferences, like favorite foods, and first graders and older can begin with identity issues, such as "who's in your family?"

Tip!

Help children understand that we like the food in our family because it represents the heart and love of our family. Other people can like different foods, or say, "No thanks. That's not for me."

4 Make a group agreement at the outset: "We won't make fun of what other people say. If what they are saying isn't familiar, we can ask questions about it." For example: if the class is exploring food, one child might say he likes calamari. Another child might make a face and say, "Yuck." Stop and discuss it: "It's

Note: *This song was first created for Angela DeLeon and the "A World of Difference Program" and dedicated to her second-grade class at Putnam Valley School in New York.*

fine for us to like different things. It can feel unfriendly when someone turns away from something we like, so let's find out more. Calamari is seafood, isn't it? It's cooked squid. How can you cook it at home? Oh, you fry it. And it looks like tiny circles and is very crispy like potato chips. I'm glad to know more about it."

Take the time to process any judgment or disapproval of others' contributions to the song in a way that feels non-punitive and still keeps the exploration fun.

5 Go around the room involving everyone—all children and all adults including yourself—in the song creation. Ask each person for words to put into the song. Give people the option to pass.

6 Group together three responses at a time to form a verse. If you are working out loud rather than writing down their words, ask the whole class to help memorize the three responses, and then help yourself to remember by repeating each phrase before you sing the verse.

7 Sing the words the children say, no matter how long. For example, when you're exploring family diversity, if a child says, "Grandmother Betty Jean lives with us," then use her exact words in the song.

In my family Grandmother Betty Jean lives with us.

Establish that it's okay to use another person's idea. This doesn't mean someone is "copying." Each person is saying what's true for herself.

When you pose a new topic for the class, make sure it's phrased so that everyone can make a contribution. For example, instead of asking, "Name a pet you have," ask, "Name an animal you wish you could have as a pet, a pet you used to have, or a pet you have right now." And instead of asking "Name one of the countries your ancestors come from," ask, "Name a place that has meaning for you. Maybe your family is from there, or maybe you wish you could visit that place."

Sing the song for a week. Each day select a different topic to explore.

TOPICS FOR NEW VERSES
Affirming Our Preferences

a. What food do you enjoy? Is there a food you like that you think maybe other people here haven't tried?

> *We like brussel sprouts with butter.*
> *We like sushi wrapped in seaweed.*
> *We like hot peppers, too.*
> *We all belong. You're with me and I'm with you.*

b. What instrument would you like to play?

c. What animal would you be if you could be any animal for a day? Why? What would you like to do?

Affirming Our Physical Identity

Ask for descriptions of hair, eye color, or skin color.

> *My friends have curly hair.*
> *My friends have dark straight hair.*
> *Some is short, and some long, too.*
> *You don't have to look just like me to be my friend.*

Affirming Our Cultural and Family Identities

Create a verse about the racial and ethnic diversity in your classroom.
For example:

> *My friends are Filipino.*
> *My friends are French Canadian.*
> *My friends are Armenian, too.*
> *We all belong. You're with me and I'm with you.*

You can use the same method to sing about religious diversity in your school.

Here are some guidelines to follow when exploring cultural and family identities:

- Keep making more verses until everyone's identity is represented.
- Create an affirming discussion, letting the children take the lead.
- Alter the verse pattern as needed to say what you want to say.
- Include all children in the way they want to be included.
- If some part of a child's identity is not known by every child, make sure that the parents and child want that information to be shared.
- Establish that there's no reason anyone should be put down for their identity.

Honoring Each Individual in the Class

Ask children to pick three things about themselves to make a new verse:

> *Sing about Mora. She is Jewish.*
> *Sing about Mora. She has curly hair.*
> *Sing about Mora. She's left-handed, too.*
> *You don't have to be just like me to be my friend.*

During the period of a week, give a fifth of your class a turn each day to be the focus of an individual verse. Pick names randomly and invite children to bring any special objects from home to show on the day that the song is about them.

Tip!

Add hand motions! If you're singing about foods, pretend to eat them. If you're singing about instruments, pantomime flute, drums, guitar, or whatever instruments children select. If you're singing about animals, stay seated and act out the animal using your hands.

Singing About Family Diversity

The third verse on the recording can kick off your discussion about family diversity. Create more verses to honor each child's family the way that they want to be described.

Here are key ideas to communicate:

- Love makes a family.
- Every family is a good family.
- We make families different ways.

Each class will have its own way of writing family verses. Also, you can ask parents to help write the verse. Plan a week ahead and ask parents what feature of their family they would like added to the song.

Here are some guidelines for affirming the family diversity present in your classroom:

• **Learn the feelings of children and parents**. Ask parents and legal guardians directly for input. Example: "I know you're Rita's foster Mom. We're studying families. In our family song I've planned to include the words 'Some of our families are foster families.' How does that sound to you? Should I check this with Rita?"

• **Be open to dialogue**. "We're studying the families in our classroom. I read your letter to the editor in the newspaper last year, and I know that you feel that the word 'family' should only be used to describe a family with a father and a mother. In our classroom, I'd say that about half of the families in the class have a different make-up than that. I want to tell you what activities I'm going to be doing as part of the unit. My intent as a teacher is to affirm each child in the class. I plan to teach that every family is a good family. I also want to respect the opinions of your family. What questions or concerns do you have?"

• **Be democratic and affirming**. Here's one example of a verse created for an all-day kindergarten class in Massachusetts to represent every family constellation in the room. While the children were at lunch, the teacher and parents who were visiting gave input for the words. One of the mothers who taught at the local day care center said it was important to her that her son's family not be omitted. She suggested that it be expressed this way: "We have two Moms." This is the description of the family diversity in their class:

> *In some families we live with our grandparents.*
> *In some families we live with our Mom and Dad.*
> *In some families we have two homes.*
> *You know, love makes a family.*
> *In some families we live with our Mom.*
> *In some families we have two Moms.*
> *In some families we have a foster Mom.*
> *Every family is a good family.*

Note that I built a longer verse and didn't stop to sing the chorus until everyone was mentioned. When I sang the words for the class, I observed at some points visible signs that children felt proud when their family composition was sung about and included. Sometimes students stopped the song so they could talk about it. Two boys reacted with recognition when I sang, "We have two Moms." The son of the Mom who had requested the words smiled. Another child spoke up: "I have two Moms. And I have two homes. There's my Mom and my step-Mom." By not omitting divorced families that are pejoratively called "broken families," or a foster family, or the family with lesbian parents, we made sure that all families felt supported.

Sing About Us

©1997 Words and Music by Sarah Pirtle
Discovery Center Music, BMI

English

Chorus:

Sing about us.
Tell me again. You don't have to be just
like me to be my friend,
be my friend.
You don't have to be just like me to be my
friend.

Verses:

1. (Food preferences)

My friends like to eat spaghetti.
My friends like to eat burritos.
My friends like fried tofu, too.
We belong. You're with me
and I'm with you.

140 L I N K I N G   U P !

2. (Identity: race and ethnicity)
My friends are Puerto Rican.
My friends are African American.
My friends are Irish, too.
We belong. You're with me
and I'm with you.

3. (Identity: family make-up)
My friends live in different families.
Some are families with one child.
Some have sisters, or brothers, too.
We belong. You're with me
and I'm with you.

Spanish
Coro:
Cantemos acerca de nosotros.
Dímelo otra vez
Cantemos acerca de nosotros.
No tienes que ser igual que yo
para ser mi amigo.

Verso:
A mis amigos les gusta _____ (3x)
No tienes que ser igual que yo
para ser mi amigo.

E X T E N S I O N S

Affirmation Family Drawings

Children draw the members of their family or extended family, putting in grandparents, other relatives, godparents, partners, neighbors, pets.

Affirmation Movement Game

Invent movements to add to the chorus. Collaborate as a whole class or in small groups.

SNAPSHOT

Improvising

A group of fifth-grade boys at Edward Smith Elementary School in Syracuse, New York, spontaneously began to put their arms around each other's shoulders as they learned the chorus of the song. Inspired by their example, I asked everyone in the class to get into groups of four to six people. They had five minutes to invent motions or a dance that fit the meaning of the chorus. Each group showed their ideas, and with much laughter, the whole group tried each creation.

ADDITIONAL RESOURCES

Under One Sky by Ruth Pelham is one of the most meaningful songs for children I know. The song affirms, "We're all a family under one sky." To order the cassette or CD contact: Ruth Pelham Music, P.O. Box 6024, Albany, NY, 12206.

22 Canción De La Nube/ Song of the Cloud

Children hear a story in two languages about a sympathetic cloud helping a dying flower.

● ●

Ages	5 to 12
When to Use	Weather and ecology studies, language development
Language	Bilingual
Location	Side 1, Song 22
Source	Words by Adrián Ramírez Flores of Guatemala Music by Roberto Díaz English text by Sarah Pirtle

OBJECTIVES

- to increase empathy and responsiveness
- to learn how to act out a story cooperatively
- to hear the words of a Guatemalan poet

PROCEDURE

 1 Listen to the recording and ask children to imagine the story.

 2 Check to make sure that the story is clear to everyone by reviewing what happened step by step.

 **3** Clarify that the words tell the same story in Spanish and English.

SNAPSHOT

School Assembly

● ● ● ● ● ● ● ● ● ● ● ● ● ●

Roberto Díaz worked with a classroom of second-grade students at Brightwood Magnet School to choreograph this song for a spring assembly. Students made costumes, created a backdrop, and painted paper clouds.

Canción de la Nube/ Song of the Cloud

Words by Adrían Ramírez Flores
Music by Roberto Díaz

A una nu-be blan-ca __ nu-be de_al-go-dón __ le do-lía __mu-cho __ mu-cho el co-ra-zón __

por-que allá en_el bos-que __ una __ po-bre flor se_es-ta-ba mu-rien-do __ de tan-to__ ca-lor.

Spanish

A una nube blanca nube de algodón
le dolía mucho, mucho el corazón
porque allá en el bosque una pobre flor
se estaba muriendo de tanto calor.

English

Why are you so sad, white cloud in the
sky?
Oh, I never want that flower below to die.
See how it is thirsty, see how it is dry.
I cannot forget. I won't pass on by.

Spanish

El amigo viento la llevó hasta el río
y la nube blanca se bebió el rocío.
Con la fresca lluvia se bañó la flor
y la nube blanca se sonrió de amor.

English

Oh, my friend the wind, take me to the
river.
I'll drink up the water so I can rain and
sprinkle.
When that tiny flower feels the rain above
I'll be smiling back my smile of love.

Translation Note: *The Spanish lyrics are in the past tense. In English they have been translated into the future tense in order to make the English lyrics more poetic. Here is an accurate translation of the second verse:*

> *Oh, my friend the wind, took me to the river.*
> *I drank up the water so I could rain and sprinkle.*
> *When that tiny flower felt the rain above.*
> *I smiled back my smile of love.*

Hand Movements

Younger children can follow the story more easily if they use their hands to narrate it. Pretend one hand is the flower. Make your fingers droop and show that it is thirsty. Now let your other hand be the cloud. Pantomime the cloud filling with water and then dropping the water on the flower.

Two Lines

One line of children who are flowers face another line of children several steps away who are the clouds. (Each flower faces a partner who is a cloud.) Act out the story together, then switch parts. If either Spanish or English is not familiar to the class, indicate motions that the children can do in place while they are listening to words they don't understand, such as swaying from side to side during the first verse, and pointing to their partners during the second verse.

Create a Play

Children select the part they want to play—cloud, wind, flower, or river. Allow each child to be the role of her choice even if this means having several flowers or clouds. Any part not selected—such as the river—by a member of the group can be imagined.

Next, children establish the location for each part. Ask them one question at a time, and let them solve it: Where are the flowers standing? Where is the cloud in the beginning of the song? From what direction does the wind come? Where is the river?

Before you try acting the story out to the recording, allow them to act out each stage of the events:

1. A flower (or flowers) droops over because it is thirsty.

2. The cloud notices the thirsty flower and feels concern.

3. The cloud gets an idea and asks the wind for help.

4. The wind carries the cloud to the river.

5. The cloud drinks up the water and gets bigger.

6. The cloud travels to the flower and provides rain.

7. The flower drinks in the rain, and becomes healthy and tall again.

8. The cloud sees the flower and feels happy.

Now play the recording while the group acts out the story.

Variation: After portraying the story with the whole class, small groups of 3 to 5 children can act it out themselves. Help them discuss who will take which part and redesign it according to the characters they choose to be.

Cooperative Art

Small groups draw the episodes in the song. Divide the class into small groups and let children talk about what part of the story they'd like to draw. Next, help the groups discuss what things they want to put in the drawing and who will do which part.

Link to Guatemala

The poet who wrote this story, Adrián Ramírez Flores, lives in Guatemala. (Show pictures of Guatemala.) Very likely, he is suggesting that people should act like that cloud and think about the needs of the poor who can be compared to withering flowers. One way to make this story meaningful is to use a book such as *Journey for Peace: The Story of Rigoberta Menchu*, by Marlene Brill. Ages 7 – 10. (Dutton Rainbow Biography Series 1996). This book discusses the life of this Guatemalan Noble Peace Prize winner.

Feelings of Empathy

Can we be like that cloud? When we notice another person, can we sense what they are feeling and what they might need? You can work on building empathy in a number of ways:

- Hold up pictures that convey the feelings of children and discuss them.

- At the beginning of the day announce that you will all be noticing other people and seeing if you can guess their feelings. Later,

RELATED SONG

"Heart to Heart/Corazón a Corazón" (Song 27)

discuss what you noticed and check if it was accurate.

- Assign children a person to watch and think about during the day.

If a child notices that the person he is watching needs help—like putting on his coat—he can assist. Children can also ask each other for help.

Empathy Project

Ask the children, "Let's think about projects that people are doing in our community that we could help with." Example: Whately Elementary School in western Massachusetts collected coats children had outgrown and passed them on to other families.

Ages	3 to 6
When to Use	Circle time or before resting
Language	English, Spanish optional
Location	Side 1, Song 23
Source	© 1997 music and English text by Sarah Pirtle
	Spanish text by Roberto Díaz and Sarah Pirtle

23 Sleeping Birds/Los Pajaritos Duermen

Children take turns pretending to be sleeping birds and gently patting each other on the back.

● ●

OBJECTIVES

- to learn to give and receive gentle touch
- to be part of a caring community
- to rest and feel soothed

PROCEDURE

1 Preview the song to familiarize yourself with the music and lyrics.

2 Select a place where children can lie down. Place a rug or blanket on the floor to make it comfortable.

Tip!

This is a good activity to use before a rest period.

3 Play the song so that the children can learn it. As children learn the song, have them gently pat their own hands. Ask them to pat their hands as softly as they would pat a kitten.

4 Help each child decide which role he wants to play—a sleeping bird or a person who pats. Even if there are many more of one role than the other, let the children decide which part they will take. As the teacher, you will be one of the back-patters each time. Point out which part of the body is the back.

5 Now ask the children to take the roles they have chosen. Ask the birds to lie down and get ready. Play or sing the song and have the children who are patting backs travel around from child to child. Make sure everyone lying down is patted at least once.

6 Repeat the activity asking, "Who wants to be a sleeping bird this time? And who will help pat their backs?" Let each child make her own new selection during each round of the song. Keep watch that the patting stays gentle.

Note: *If you are playing the cassette, this song has been positioned to make it easier to locate. Fast forward toward the end of side one, and you'll find it is the second to the last song on that side.*

BILINGUAL OPTION

You can sing this song in Spanish, English, or both. The recording offers two times through in each language. Translation note: "Mimar" is a Spanish word that doesn't have an exact English equivalent. It means to fuss over or cuddle.

English

We see the birds sleeping.
We see the birds sleeping.
We'll pat you, we'll help you,
feel safe in your nest.
Safe in your nest, safe in your nest.
We'll pat you, we'll help you
feel safe in your nest.
Spoken: *Wake up birds.*

Spanish

Los pajaritos duermen,
quietos en sus nidos
Acariciarlos los hace dormir.
Seguro estarán, seguro estarán.
Me gusta mimarlos, hacerlos dormir.
Spoken: *Despierten pajaritos.*

Ages	5 to 12
When to Use	To begin Circle Time, to study community or life cycles
Language	English
Location	Side 1, Song 24
Source	Sarah Pirtle

24 Full Circle

Children sing about their connection
to nature and each other.

●●●●●●●●●●●●●●●●●●●●●●●●●●●●

OBJECTIVES

- to experience the classroom community as a village
- to learn that each person has equal value

PROCEDURE

1 Gather the children together and teach them the song.

2 During the chorus have the children circle their arms outward and upward, moving their arms away from their bodies and then returning them back to their sides. Invent movements for the refrain. To underscore a connection with other children, use this sequence:

between (touch your heart with one hand)
you (extend the other hand to point to other children)
and I (return the extended hand to touch the hand on your heart)

3 With children kindergarten age and up, ask, "Why do people meet in circles? How are we like members of a village?"

4 If you are playing an instrument to accompany the song, you may prefer to use easier chords than the ones listed in the transcription. The song is recorded and transcribed in the key of E flat. You can sing it instead in the key of C. Play these chords:

Verse

C   F C
When we join the circle we join a village.

C   F C
When we join a village we join the sky.

C   F C
When we join the sky now we're in the branches

C   F C
and down through the roots now back to you and I.

Chorus

G FC G C G FC FG F GC
Full circle, full circle. Full circle between you and I.

Building Unity

Carrying a circular woven basket, I entered a second-grade classroom where the children were having trouble feeling unified as a group. I held up the basket for all to see and asked them to rearrange their chairs in the same shape—in a circle. The room was small. We had to leave desks in the middle to have enough space. I told them, "This song will explain why it's important for me that we all sit together in one circle." I placed the basket in the middle and began Full Circle. It set just the tone I was looking for. At the end I asked them, "Why do you think I like a circle shape?" "We can see each other," they responded, and "We feel more like a group." Here is the whole sequence I used to build unity and group awareness:

1. Full Circle (Song 24)
2. Grandmother Spider (Song 19)
3. Don't Leave Anyone Out (Song 20)
4. Let's Get Together (Song 40)
5. Across the Wide Ocean (Song 10)

Making a Circle

When shall we make a circle? I like thinking about the features offered by different spatial arrangements, and I like to make a deliberate choice about how to arrange the group. When I work on social skills, I usually arrange the group in a circle so that all children are equally visible to me and to each other. This is not to say that we can't have valuable music experiences with desks in rows. Many songs work well in that format, and some classrooms don't have enough room to rearrange the furniture easily. For example, presenting conflict resolution skills and setting up role plays is often effective from the front of a room. When the room is cramped, another option is to end the session by standing together in a circle around the desks and chairs singing "Full Circle" or "Grandmother Spider." A circle indicates without words that each person is important and we can learn from each other.

Full Circle

©1997 Words and Music by Sarah Pirtle
Discovery Center Music, BMI

When we join the cir-cle we join a vil-lage. When we join a vil-lage we join the sky. When we join the sky now we're in the branch-es. And down through the roots now back to you and I.

Full cir-cle, full cir-cle. Full cir-cle, be-tween ___ you and I.

Verses

When we join the circle
we join a village.
When we join a village
we join the sky.

When we join the sky now
we're in the branches

And down through the roots now
back to you and I.

Chorus

Full circle, full circle.
Full circle, between you and I.
Full circle, full circle.
Full circle, between you and I.

Note: *This song was written for Full Circle School in Bernardston, Massachusetts. Five of the children you hear on the recording are from this school community.*

. . . .

E X T E N S I O N S

. . . .

Circle Study

Collect circular objects such as marbles to accompany this song. Post pictures of circles in nature, such as sunflowers or planets and post pictures of people in circles.

Circles in Science

Talk about life cycles and explain what it means to come "full circle." Examples:

- A seed grows into a tiny plant, then into a mature plant. It produces seeds, and those seeds give rise to more plants.

- An egg hatches into a chick, the chick grows up into a hen and lays more eggs.

5 Conflict Resolution Songs

Talk to me!
I know it's not easy.
Talk to me!
Don't give up now.
Talk to me!
It's really important.
I want to be friends.
— from "¡Dilo!/Talk to Me" (Song 31)

Conflict is a normal part of human experience. In fact, conflicts are an opportunity for communication. They can have a positive outcome. What determines the outcome is how we handle the situation. The activities and song games in this chapter help children build their own understanding of how to handle conflict effectively. Rather than fight or run away when faced with a conflict, children can be assisted in learning how to resolve their conflicts constructively.

Heling to Talk It Out Together

Helping to Talk It Out Together

Noah, a four-year-old boy, runs up to Lois Bascom at Mohawk Nursery School, in Shelburne Falls, Massachusetts. He says, "Molly kicked me." To his surprise, his teacher tells him, "There's something we can do about this. I can help you talk this out with Molly."

Lois sits down calmly with both children.

"Molly, Noah said you kicked him. What did you want to tell him?"

"Sorry," say Molly.

"Sorry is nice," Lois responds, "but I think you have a problem here and we need to talk about it. What did you want Noah to know about what you were doing?"

As they talk about the situation, Lois realizes that Molly wanted to play alone. When Noah came over to join her, she didn't know that she could say "no" to him. All she could think to do was kick him to send him away. Lois helped her see her choices: "Molly, next time instead of kicking Noah you could say 'I don't want to share. I want to play by myself.'"

Noticing that the children seem calmer and satisfied with the resolution, Lois asks them both, "Can you be friends again?" They nod yes.

> To underscore the closure, Lois offers, "You just made an agreement. Would you like to shake hands?"
>
> Noah felt so relieved that he had received help that he gave Lois a big hug and said, "Thank you."

Teaching Young Children How to Talk it Out Together

What do young children need when during a conflict they are flooded with feelings and can't find their words? They need:

- to feel safe.
- to have their feelings accepted and understood.
- a concrete framework for problem solving (it's not enough to say, "use your words.")
- help communicating within their present skills.

How to Help Children Talk it Out: Two Tools*

The following two tools can be used to help children with anger, conflicts, and problem solving.

Tool 1: What to Do When You're Upset

1. Stop.
2. Go to the Peace Place.
3. Cool down.
4. Take time for feelings.

Spanish: Que Harías Cuando Estás Enfadado

1. Para.
2. Vete al Lugar de Paz.
3. Cálmate.
4. Toma tiempo para conocer tus emociones.

Tool 2: How to Talk it Out Together

1. Get together.
2. Take turns talking and listening.
3. What will help?
4. Choose a plan.
5. Let's do it.

Spanish: Como Podemos Hablarlo Juntos

1. Júntense
2. Hablen y escuchen por turnos.
3. ¿Qué nos ayudaría?
4. Escojan un plan.
5. Hagámoslo.

* *This model was developed though the collaboration of ESR's Early Childhood training team: Lisa M. Cureton, Maryland; Chris Gerzon, Massachusetts; Rebecca Johns, Montana; Kim D. Jones, New York; William J. Kreidler, Massachusetts; Carol Miller Lieber, Massachusetts; Sarah Pirtle, Massachusetts; Sandy Tsubokawa Whittall, Colorado.*

How to Talk it Out Together

⁙1 Get together.

⁙2 Take turns talking and listening.

⁙3 What will help?

⁙4 Choose a plan.

⁙5 Let's do it.

SPANISH: Como Podemos Hablarlo Juntos

⁙1 Júntense.

⁙2 Hablen y escuchen por turnos.

⁙3 ¿Qué nos ayudaría?

⁙4 Escojan un plan.

⁙5 Hagámoslo.

Getting Started

To implement these two tools in your classroom, you'll need to provide:

- A Calming Corner (a designated area for children to calm down).
- Concrete materials to help children implement Cool Down strategies.
- A Peace Place (a designated area for children to problem solve together).
- An illustrated Talk it Out Together Chart as a reference for children, staff, and parents.
- Concrete materials such as talking bears, puppets, or sticks, to help facilitate talking and listening.

[Some classrooms combine the Peace Place and Calming Corner.]

Your Calming Corner

You'll want to provide children with a safe space to cool down from anger. Include soft pillows, stuffed animals, or other props to help children feel comfortable. Consider adding paper and markers so that children can scribble or draw to express and release their anger.

Cool Down Strategies

Talk with your class about the activities that you recommend children do when they are upset. These might include curling up with a soft blanket, listening to calming music, vigorous movements like jumping jacks or jogging in place, or self-expression activities such as doing an anger drawing. Some children like to release upset feelings through tearing paper, popping bubble wrap, or even sorting buttons.

Your Peace Place

Providing a place for children to sit while "Talking it Out Together," such as a table, will help children enter the framework of constructive communication. Children can then indicate their willingness to participate peacefully in the problem-solving process by placing their hands on the table. (This action also help relax children by dropping their shoulders.) Decorate your Peace Place with your Talk it Out Together Chart and other props that help facilitate the process (see "Strategies for Helping Children Talk and Listen" for more ideas).

You can also provide a movable Peace Place by using a small rug or Talk-It-Out Bears that can be used anywhere in the classroom.

Make a Talk-It-Out Together Chart

Here is how I worked with a class of three- to five-year-olds to create a Talk It Out Together chart with photographs. The chart can then be posted and used as a reference when children are in a conflict.

1. I introduced two stuffed toys hidden in a covered basket to use as the Talk-it-Out bears. I said that children can hold these while they are talking out a problem.

2. I brought in a camera and enough film for 36 pictures. I told the group that we would make a chart of pictures showing children talking out a problem. We used the photographs two ways—to create a wall chart and a book.

3. To introduce the topic I started by showing the bears talking out a problem, and then I sang, "How Can We Be Friends Again?" (Song 25) The children provided words for the song to show what makes a conflict worse and what makes it better.

4. Lois (the other teacher) and I modeled the Talk it Out Together process. We paused at each step to pantomime the stages while a third adult took photographs:

   a. We were mad (we made angry faces).

   b. We decided to talk and brought chairs close to each other (we said, "We will meet face to face").

   c. We got the bears and each held one. (We modeled one person talking and the other person listening.)

   d. We showed ourselves thinking as we worked on the next step. (What will help?)

   e. We selected a plan we both liked (we held up our thumbs and did "thumbs up").

   f. We did the plan (we shook hands).

5. I asked if any of the children would like to sit in the chairs so that I could take their photograph while they Talked it Out Together. Two children sat down, held the bears, and practiced some of the same stages Lois and I had modeled. The group had enough interest to watch three series of pairs, and then we ended this session by singing, "Two in the Fight" (Song 26).

6. While the rest of the class had a free choice period of play, I continued to work with interested pairs of children. Three more sets of pairs worked with me. Working with just two children at a time, we practiced the Talk it Out Together process with pretend conflicts. Some wanted to do other motions with the stuffed toys like having them jump. In these cases, I alternated between taking photos of problem-solving and watching the children simply explore the bears.

Tip!

Take some photographs of two children holding a toy or block that they both want to use. Later you can make up a story about a particular conflict over that toy to put in your Talk it Out Together book.

7. We met again as a whole group. We practiced putting our thumbs up to show that something is okay with us. Some children invented their own idea for showing agreement when you're talking things out: they touched thumbs.

8. After the photographs were developed, I made a chart of the Talking it Out Together steps. I then illustrated that chart with selected photos for each stage that could represent any conflict. The chart showed five pictures:

   a. The children are mad and turning their backs.

   b. The children decide to Talk it Out Together. They sit down facing each other with the covered basket between them.

   c. The children take the bears out, hold them in their laps, and take turns talking.

   d. The children put their thumbs up when they both like a plan.

   e. The children shake hands after they tried the plan.

When we presented the chart, we made it clear that using thumbs up or shaking hands is not necessary—it's an option to use to help mark the resolution stage. It's important to include children's ideas as you go. As Lois commented, "The chart was meaningful because the children made it."

9. We also made a book that told the story of a specific conflict. All the photos showed the same two children handling a problem (they both wanted the same tractor.)

10. Some of the extra photos not used for the wall chart or book were posted on a bulletin board. The other photos were available for the children to hold, talk about, and use to make their own books.

Tip!

Place five or six photos of the same pair of children, each representing a different stage of their conflict, on a tray or table. Ask children to look at the series and place them in the order that they think they happened.

Strategies for Helping Children Talk and Listen

Since young children are concrete learners, it is helpful to provide concrete materials to make the problem solving process more accessible.

Peace Objects: Designate special spoons, shells, or sticks for children to hold when working out a problem. I have also used stuffed toys or puppets. This helps both the speaker and listener feel comforted during the process. Often children will pretend that is the animal who is talking or listening.

Talking Sticks: In many native American traditions a special stick called a Talking Stick is passed around, conferring the right to speak on the person holding it. You can use a Talking Stick to help focus communication and prevent the designated speaker from being interrupted.

Implementing Tool 1: Calming Down

Calming down helps a child learn to listen to the message of their emotions. Calming down doesn't mean ignoring feelings or sweeping them under the rug. It means releasing upset emotions so that talking and thinking are possible. Some children become aggressive when they are upset because they have only learned that method of handling their emotions. But we can teach children alternatives—constructive steps to take when they become upset.

Talk with your class about the variety of ways children cool down and ask them to identify what they think would help them most. Supply as many options for children as you can in your Calming Corner.

Cool Down Strategies

- Sometimes children need deep breathing.
  Supply birthday candles for children to hold and pretend they are blowing out a candle flame.
- Sometimes children need to be alone in a comforting place.
  Provide soft animals, blanket, pillows, as well as a cassette player with earphones and tape of relaxing music.

- Sometimes children need to do strong actions.

  Provide paper for scribbling or drawing or bubble wrap to pop. Post a picture of a child doing jumping jacks. Be aware, however, that vigorous motions register throughout the whole room. Designate when and where you want the actions done.
- Sometimes children need to switch their focus.

  Provide books, buttons to sort, something to squeeze, or something to smell.
- Sometimes children need comforting from the teacher.

  You will find more information about anger management in the activities for the Anger Chant (Song 28).

The Calming Down Process

1. **Stop**

   Help a child recognize that he is upset. Signal that you accept his feelings by approaching with open body language. Suggest he do one of the Cool Down Strategies. Listen to him. If the disruption is serious, use a nonpunitive intervention stategy such as holding the child until he calms down.

2. **Go to the Peace Place or Calming Corner** (or follow another plan to help the child cool down).

3. **Cool Down**

   The child cools down with the teacher or alone.

4. **Take Time for Feelings**

   Encourage expressions of feelings, i.e say "I see you're upset" Do not request an explanation until the child is ready. Reframe hurtful language. For example, if the child says, "I hate Melissa" reframe as "I see you are really upset with Melissa."

Implementing Tool 2: Talk It Out Together

Talk it Out Together is a simple phrase that identifies the problem-solving process that you want children to use:

> "Rosita and Misha, why don't you try a Talk-It-Out together."

> "Gerald, can I help you Talk-It-Out with Lee?"

> "I see you're both upset. Let's try a Talk-It-Out."

As they hear these words, children develop a mental picture of what they can expect when they agree to talk it out. Each year they can increase their ability to internalize this framework.

1. **Get Together**

   Say: Let's meet face to face.
   - Help children come together and feel safe.
   - Hold children or put a hand on their shoulder if they need support.
   - Put aside or hang onto objects that are part of the conflict.

2. **Take Turns Talking and Listening**

Ask: What's the problem? Let's hear each other's feelings.

- Start with the child who has the greatest need to be heard first and assure all participants that everyone will get a turn.
- Begin by responding to their feelings. Draw them out with statements that open communication like:
  - You look upset.
  - Tell me more.
  - I'd like to hear about it.
  - I'm listening to you.

- Next, gather information until you have a fuller picture of the problem:
  - What happened?
  - What's your side of the story?
  - What's the problem?
  - What do you need to know?

- Help children choose to talk constructively. If needed and age-appropriate, you can add agreements like:
  - Let's agree to stay here until the problem is solved.
  - Let's agree to take turns talking.
  - To help us talk, let's agree no hitting or yelling or calling names.

3. **What will help?**

With the children brainstorm some solutions to the problem.

- Start by paraphrasing what the problem is. If the problem has several parts, mention them and help the children address each issue one at a time.
- Choose one of these questions to ask:
  - What will help make this problem better?
  - What do you want to have happen next?
  - What's another way this could be solved?
  - Next time, how do you want to play together?
  - Or, say: let's brainstorm together how to solve this.

- Help the children to be specific and concrete in their plan. For example, if they say "share" help them spell out what sharing could look like.

4. **Choose a plan.**

- Help children think about the ideas presented. Ask, "How would that work?" so that children can imagine whether it can be carried out.
- Help the children be specific.
- Guide them to choose an idea that helps everyone (a win-win solution.)
- As much as possible, allow the choice to be theirs.

5. **Let's do it.**

   Help children describe the first step of their plan they will do together. Provide closure to the Talk It Out Together process in any of these ways:

   - Say to them in recognition, "You talked this out."
   - Shake their hands.
   - Invite them to shake hands if they like.
   - Repeat the first step of their plan.
   - Provide any supplies they will need to carry out their plan.

Here's how the Talk it Out Together process can be applied to a situation in a block corner where two four-year-olds, a boy named Jeb and a girl named Lee, are pulling on the same block as their teacher comes over to provide assistance.

Get Together

The teacher enters the situation using open body language. "I want to come over and sit with you and help you talk this out." She recognizes the children's feelings: "I see you're both upset."

She intervenes and sets boundaries to promote safety. Jeb grabs angrily for the block and the children tug on it some more. The teacher reaches for the block. "I'll hold this block while you talk. It looks like it's important to both of you." Jeb hits Lee and the teacher intervenes while recognizing feelings. "Jeb, you're really angry. But hitting won't tell Lee what you want. Hitting hurts. We can figure this problem out together. Come sit next to me."

Take Turns Talking and Listening

The teacher sees that Jeb isn't ready to express himself in words. "How about if you each show me where you'd like to put the block and then give it right back to me." Jeb puts the block in an arch like a bridge and runs a toy car over it. "So you want this curved block to be your bridge for cars to go over?" He nods. "Now we know what you're thinking, Jeb. Next I'll take the block back. Let's let Lee show me where she would like to put the block."

Lee places the block within a line of blocks. She says, "It's my road. I had it and then Jeb took it." The teacher repeats back what Lee said so that she feels understood. "You want the block to be a road?" Lee answers, "Yes."

Then the teacher tries to make the problem very clear: "I see there's only one curved block like this in the block corner. Lee, you found that it made a curved road. You were using it. Then Jeb, you looked for it to make a bridge. There's only one curved block and you both want to use it now."

What Will Help?

The teacher asks, "What would help?" Lee says, "What if it's a road and Jeb puts his cars on the road?" Jeb responds loudly, "No."

"What else could you do?" asks the teacher. "Share," says Lee. The teacher draws her out, "How would that work?" Lee answers, "First it's a road and then it's a bridge."

Choose a Plan

The teacher restates the solution with more detail. "You have two ideas. You could put the games together so that the cars go on the road, or you could each have a different game and take turns with the block." Lee is familiar with the timer in the classroom and she points to it. The teacher articulates, "The timer could let you know when one turn is over and then the other person gets the block." She allows them to make the decision. "Which idea do you want to do—make one game together or take turns with the block?"

Jeb points to the timer.

"You want to take turns with the timer, Jeb?"

"Yes," says Jeb.

Lee nods, "Okay."

Let's Do It.

The teacher gives them acknowledgment for solving the problem. "You talked out this problem." She makes the assessment that it will be a big step for Jeb to work with the structure of the timer, and more realistic for Lee to hold the timer first. The teacher checks with Lee. "How about Lee, if you hold the timer while Jeb uses the block for his bridge. When it rings, you switch. Then Jeb, you hold the timer while Lee uses the block." She waits to see if Lee wants to negotiate further and use the block first but she agrees to this format. The teacher hands the block to Jeb while Lee gets the timer from the shelf. Then the teacher anticipates another potential problem spot. She watches at a distance as they carry out their plan, and waits until Jeb's turn with the block is over. She notices that he is able to hand the block to Lee when the timer rings. He gives Lee a turn with the block. She comes over to affirm them. "You took turns with the timer just the way you planned. Do you want to use the timer again?" "No," they answer and leave the block area to play a different activity.

Helping Young Children with Thinking and Feeling

- Children need to express their upset feelings before they can think about the problem and what they need. They are not ready to answer the question, "What's the problem?" First, we need to receive and validate their feelings and reactions. The experience of being heard and understood shifts a conflict.

- Certain questions—like "Why are you angry?"—may seem helpful to draw out feelings but actually can stop the flow of the feelings by requiring children to stop and identify them. "How do you feel?" is a question requiring thought, and when a child is embedded in his or her feelings, it's difficult to answer.

- Instead, assist children with what they are feeling by witnessing the feelings, reflecting them back, and staying connected with them. Use open, affirmative body language and questions or statements that encourage conversation, such as "You look upset." Open body language indicates "I hear you" and "I accept you."

- Adults may underestimate the ability of young children to be able to come up with their own solutions. Yet once children see how brainstorming is done, they do contribute their own ideas. In fact, other children not involved in the problem often like to enter the discussion and offer the options they can think of. It's useful to teach the skill of brainstorming when not in the heat of the conflict. The song, "There's Always Something You Can Do" (Song 30) will assist you in explaining the process.

Guidelines for Teachers of 3-to 5-Year Olds

Expect that you will give extra assistance to three- to five-year-olds through the Talk it Out Together process.

- When children have limited verbal skills, provide the words they need, while checking with them to make sure you are accurate, e.g. "Is the problem with the truck?" or "Do you want a turn with the truck?"
- Take children clearly through the stages, e.g. "It looks like the problem is ____ (give a summary). Let's think about how it could be solved."
- Read children's non-verbal messages, e.g. "I see you frowning. It looks like the idea of both of you playing with the marble game won't work for you."
- Keep asking questions, giving opportunity for children to respond, e.g. "Do you have an idea of what would help?"
- Give children non-verbal options for responding, e.g. "Put your thumb up if you like that idea."

Reinforcing the Talk It Out Together Process

Would a fingerplay help your students internalize the sequence for Talk It Out Together? What about a puppet play? Or a series of drawings that show each step? Or an active movement song that reviews the procedure? Children need lots of repetitions in concrete forms. You can use all of these methods to help them learn the Talk It Out Together problem-solving process.

1. Talk It Out Together Song* (to the tune of "The More We Get Together")
   You can use this song to help staff and children learn the Talk it Out Together process.

   > *Let's talk it out together, together, together.*
   > *Let's talk it out together and be friends again.*
   > *We'll talk and we'll listen, we'll talk and we'll listen.*
   > *Let's talk it out together and be friends again.*
   > (Use American Sign Language for "together." T is made by fists with thumbs poking out between pointing and middle finger. Move "T" hands around in a circle.)

   > *What will help our problem, our problem, our problem?*
   > *What will help our problem? Let's be friends again.*
   > *Do you like this plan, or should we do that plan?*
   > *We'll choose a plan together and be friends again.*
   > (Pantomime thinking. Then use thumbs up on do you like this plan. Close by shaking hands all around.)

*   *By Sarah Pirtle, Sandy Whittall, and ESR's Early Childhood Training Team.*

(Join hands for verse three.)
We'll do our plan together, together, together.
We'll do our plan together and be friends again.
We talked and we listened, we talked and we listened.
We talked it out together, and we're friends again.

2. True Stories about Talking it Out

Actual stories of the process really carry weight with children. They like to know what other people their age can do. Use the extension activity, "How Anna Talked Out a Problem," in "Two in the Fight" (Song 26) to provide a true story of how a second grader negotiated a problem of rough play at recess.

Record and collect examples of real life moments of Talk It Out Together, then act a story out with puppets to share it with your students.

3. Use Your Words! But What Words?

Guide children to practice helpful phrases they can use as an alternative to hitting, pushing, or using force to solve a problem.

Examples:

Stop.

I don't like that.

Watch out.

Wait.

Will you talk to me?

The short version of "When I Say Stop, I Mean Stop" (Song 32) is a good companion to "Two in the Fight"(Song 26) because it provides that simple word: "Stop!"

When I say stop, I mean stop.

When I say no, I mean no.

I want you to hear me.

Listen to my words.

4. Basic Negotiation

Turn to the actitivies in this chapter for communication and conflict resolution practice. For example, use the puppet role plays to help children find the words to negotiate constructively.

5. Talk-It-Out Together Practice

In addition to the many activities in Chapter Five, here are three other ways to make the Talk-It-Out Together Process more concrete.

The Talk it Out Together Hokey Pokey

by Sarah Pirtle

to the tune of "The Hokey Pokey"

Sing the song standing. Invent dance motions to fit the words. Divide into pairs; one partner moves alone on verse 2 and the other on verse 3.

1. I'm gonna talk with you. We'll try to understand.
   We start face to face, and we open up our hands.
   We Talk it Out Together, gonna change some things around.
   Our feet are on the ground.

2. Well, one person starts and they say how they feel.
   They say what they want and they make it really real.
   The other one is listening and they don't scream or shout.
   Cuz that's what it's all about.

3. Now the next one talks and they take a turn to go.
   They tell what they feel and what makes that problem grow.
   The other one is listening and they never scream or shout.
   Cuz that's what it's all about.

4. Then we shake our brains, and we think what to do.
   That brainstorm is happening. Got a lot of choices, too.
   We Talk it Out Together, gonna change some things around.
   Our feet are on the ground.

5. Well, we make a choice, yes, we make a plan.
   And we start out to do it like the leaders of a band.
   We Talked it Out Together and we changed some things around,
   Yes, we Talked it Out Together and you know that we were grand.
   Come on now, shake hands.

Talk-It-Out Together Fingerplay

To practice the steps of negotiation, children can follow along with their fingers. Lead them in holding up the index finger of each hand.

1. Fingers face each other from a distance. "We're going to talk this out together." They're ready to begin.

2. They take turns sharing their feelings and what they think the problem is. Act this out by giving each finger a chance to twirl in a circle, first one and then the other, giving each finger as many turns as it needs.

3. Now the fingers reach toward each other, with less of a distance between them. "Our problem is about ____. Let's think together." They come up with different solutions and point to several, visualized in this fingerplay as if they are written in the air. "We could do this, or this, or this."

4. "Hm," the fingers pause and think. They ask each other, "What do you want to do?" and "What do you want to do?" Finally, they both point in the same direction: "Let's do this one." They have made a plan.

5. Next they get ready to carry it out. The fingers link as if shaking hands: "We talked it out."

Talk it Out Together Puppets or Stuffed Animals

1. If possible, get identical stuffed animals or bean bags. If they are different, clarify that it won't work if they fight over which animal they hold. Keep the stuffed animals or bean bags in a cloth bag, covered basket, or box so that they can be stored out of sight. To help the process go smoothly, say, "Put the basket between you and when you open it, take the one that is nearest to you."

2. Set guidelines for how the stuffed animals or bean bags will be used in the classroom, such as:
   - We don't have to use them all the time.
   - When a problem erupts and the teacher needs to give immediate assistance because children are upset, then children talk without the stuffed animals.
   - Clarify that the bears can't hit each other, just as children in the class are asked not to hit each other.

3. One person in the conflict can help get the stuffed animal as a way to help him or her cool down.

4. Children use the stuffed animals in a variety of ways—to hold for comfort, to have them do the talking, to express their anger. However, at times they can become a distraction. When this happens, ask to hold the bears yourself. The bears are particularly useful in acting out Talk it Out Together techniques during circle time.

Teachable Moments: Using Song Games to Intervene in Conflict

Here is an unexpected conflict that arose as I prepared to teach a conflict resolution lesson with first graders I'd never met before and how I used it to teach a skill.

A line of first graders enter the cafeteria for a program on conflict resolution and move onto a cafeteria bench. Geri is the first child; she sits down on the end. As the next children sit on the bench, they move closer to the one next to them. Suddenly, Geri turns and hits Mia, the girl next to her.

Actions and Dialogue	Commentary
Teacher moves close to Geri to help her down and think about what is going on.	Teacher provides structure.
Teacher: Geri, you must have been really angry. You just hit Mia. (talking quietly and privately)	Acknowledges feelings and the social situation—hitting.
Geri doesn't speak.	

Teacher: What did you want to say to Mia?	Teacher identifies that Geri needs to find alternatives to hitting in order to express herself.
Geri doesn't answer or look at the teacher.	This response tells the teacher that Geri doesn't know how to find the words she needs.
Teacher: Did you feel like you were going to get pushed off the bench?	Acknowledges feelings more precisely. Affirms Geri by helping her articulate her feelings.
Geri looks at the teacher.	This look informs the teacher that she has accurately connected with Geri's feelings.
Teacher: Try saying "Stop."	Direct guidance in the new skill.
Geri turns to Mia: "Stop."	

During this interaction, I learned that verbalization was hard for Geri. If I'd asked her to say, "Stop pushing," this probably would have been more than she could do. Geri needed a short, basic method of setting boundaries. My goal was to help her replace the act of hitting with an easy-to-remember word that she could say.

I moved from this real-life dilemma to lead the whole class in a collaborative learning experience where we practiced this same skill. I taught the group "When I Say Stop" (Song 29) in its shortest version:

> *When I say stop, I mean stop.*
> *When I say no, I mean no.*
> *I want you to hear me.*
> *Listen to my words.*

I asked volunteers to do a role play with me using a monkey puppet. I pretended that the monkey was teasing the children. They addressed the monkey with the stop hand signal and said words that worked for them such as "Stop," "Please stop," or "I don't like that."

Then I taught a game in pairs called "Cloud Hands" (Song 38) to help children practice interacting with one other person. The game provides a very concrete way to connect through eye contact. I intentionally paired up Geri and Mia to give them a chance to repair their friendship. The game gave them a way to reconnect.

We ended the session with "Heart to Heart" (Song 27) to reinforce the friendly interaction. When they sang, "Sometimes I feel very angry, but I won't hit and I won't shout," I felt pleased to see that they giggled and sang strongly to each other. The framework of the songs helped Geri and Mia jump right back into enjoying each other.

This is the Song Sequence that developed out of that moment. I recommend it to you as an effective sequence for K-1 students:

1. When I Say Stop (Song 29)
2. Role Play: Practice saying "Stop."
3. Cloud Hands (Song 38)—mirror game with partners
4. Heart to Heart (Song 27)—with the same partners

For second and third graders replace "Heart to Heart" with "¡Dilo!/Talk to Me" (Song 31).

Mistaken Behavior

Let's reflect on Mia's easy forgiveness of her friend Geri. Maybe Mia understood that Geri hadn't hit because she didn't like her or was trying to hurt her, but rather was trying to communicate her needs in the first way she thought of.

Daniel Gartrell, author of *A Guidance Approach for the Encouraging Classroom* (New York: Delmar, 1998) reorients early childhood teachers from thinking in terms of misbehavior to thinking in terms of mistaken behavior. Gartrell suggest that teachers need to evaluate the level mistake the child is making in order to respond appropriately.

Why did Geri choose hitting as her mode of expression? Here are three different explanations corresponding to the three levels from Gartrell.

Level One: Mistaken behavior while experimenting

Geri hit because she is still learning what to do when a social situation feels out of control and she is flooded with feelings. In this case, she is panicked that she'll be pushed off the bench. In this new situation she is trying to figure out what to do to feel safe. Her mistaken behavior was a result of experimentation.

Level Two: Mistaken behavior from social influence

Geri hit because her older sister Lola hits her whenever Lola doesn't like something Geri is doing. Geri has learned that hitting is the first thing to resort to when she wants someone to change what they are doing.

Level Three: Mistaken behavior that expresses strong needs

Geri hits frequently due to her general feeling of panic caused by recent events in her home. She is expressing the lack of stability she feels. Her experience is that she doesn't have control over key aspects of her life.

MISTAKEN BEHAVIOR: INTERVENING EFFECTIVELY

Situation: Song game "Let's Get Together" (Song 40). Children are in small groups of four. They are making shapes together like a wheel, a roof, and a flower as they sing "Let's Get Together."

Level One: Mistaken Behavior while Experimenting

Emilie starts to twirl her arms far up while gripping onto her friends' hands resulting in the others' hands getting pinched.

Analysis

Observing Emilie I discern that this is a mistake that comes from experimenting. She is so involved in the fun of twisting that she doesn't perceive the effect she is having on others.

Teacher Guidance

My job is to help Emilie notice her effect on others, without overreacting.

Not recommended

"Emilie, what in the world are you doing!"

Recommended

    a. Describe. "When you twirl, the others' hands are feeling pinched."

    b. Remind about agreements. "Can you keep it fun for everyone?"

    c. Teach. "Can you twirl a little but not so far?"

Level Two: Mistaken behavior from social influence.

Jason's small group is making a wheel together. As they reach their hands into the center, Jason slaps his friend's hands hard and they sting.

Analysis

This behavior doesn't look like experimentation. It looks imitative. Perhaps at home, Jason's brother likes to say "give me five" and slaps his hands very hard while Jason has to withstand the pain.

Teacher Guidance

By being both friendly and firm, the teacher helps the child rejoin the group's agreements instead of imitating behavior that isn't okay in the group.

Not recommended

"Oh well, I'll ignore this."

Recommended

    a. Describe. "That looks like that really hurt."

    b. Remind with firmness. "That's too hard a tap."

    c. Teach. "Find a way to join your hands so that no one gets hurt again."

Level Three: Mistaken behavior that expresses strong needs.

As the children in her group make the shape of a wheel, Carly won't hold hands. Instead she sits down in the middle of the circle and growls at the other children. They ask her to get up, and she growls back at them.

Analysis

As I watch this, I think how difficult it is for Carly to be near other children. From past experience, I don't think staying on the floor or growling will help her. I want to acknowledge what's happening while connecting to her.

Teacher Guidance

Enforce limits, protect general safety, and build a helping relationship with the child.

Not recommended

"Carly, get off the floor right now."

Recommended

a. Describe. "Carly, it's hard for people to dance while you're on the floor."
b. Build connection while setting limits. "I don't want you to be stepped on."
c. Provide two choices. "Carly, would you like to come over and play the drum with me during this song or do you want to stay and stand a way you like?"

The attitude we have toward children when conflicts arise is crucial. When we use threats, coercion, or criticism, we cut off the possibility for learning from the situation. When we use a friendly instructive attitude that is clear and compassionate, children have room to change.

WHEN A CHILD HAS BEEN MISTREATED:
Implications for Educators

In our classrooms we meet children whose primary life experience is that people have not respected their boundaries. They expect hurtful situations to reoccur and are ready to defend themselves in the ways they have learned. These are brave children. It is of great value to them when we provide a stable classroom environment and a trustworthy relationship. We give them new models of what it feels like to be respected by a dependable person who provides safety.

Violence means intent to harm. Whether this violation is emotional, physical, or sexual, the searing affect is felt by the child. He or she hears the message and knows, "At this moment I am not respected by this important person in my life," be it an older sibling, parent, relative, classmate, teacher, bus driver, or neighbor. The child starts to create belief systems about why this has happened and constructs strategies to prevent further violation. Many people in our nation are traumatized by experiences of violence. For young children this affects confidence in school work, skillfulness in social interactions, and general self-esteem.

In the last twenty years our nation has started to look at issues of childhood abuse with courage and new insights for healing. In my experience working with hurt children there are things we can do as teachers and conflict resolution trainers that are helpful and important. One step is to view the victims of mistreatment with more respect, less silence, and less distancing.

Here are insights for how we look at children:

- We need to think of children who are labeled "problem children" as children who *have* a problem and need our assistance. They are doing their best to take care of themselves. A chronically upset, aggressive, or withdrawn child is showing us the tenor of her world and is making a cry for help. Children's defenses come from their drive to respect themselves.

- Children who are stuck in aggressive behaviors are in effect re-enacting trauma from their own experience, this time by taking the role of aggressor, rather than victim. They aren't children who "like" to fight. They are children who have been taught more about aggressive than nurturing behavior. The fact that they are fighting means that they still have a sense of self, but they need to have the hurtful behaviors that they are doing stopped, and then they need guidance to break out of the cycle and find safety in new ways.

- Still other children re-enact their trauma by goading other children into hurting them so that they are once again the victim. It is not compassionate to dismiss them by saying, "that child is asking for it." What's really going on is that that they are creating a re-enactment of hurt as their own strategy for coping with what has happened to them. They are also asking for help.

- Not every abused child is visible to our eyes. Some "well-behaved" children are coping with hurt by withdrawing. Although there are many reasons for shyness, one of the many causes is that the child has suffered abuse. As we watch children who draw back from classmates or adults, or who are very upset when they drop things, or make a mistake, we gather information about whether they are enduring mistreatment.

We can change the distorted pictures they've been given of who they are and help them see themselves through our caring eyes. Unfortunately, safety is not guaranteed in every school today. In fact, schools can be the place where students are mistreated on the playground, in the lunch room, on the bus, or in the classroom.

Here is what hurt children need from teachers for safety. This advice covers a wide-range of causes and trauma:

- They need teachers to be responsible to make sure that no child in the classroom or in the larger school environment is allowed to harm them physically or emotionally.

- They need to hear — "I'm in charge of your safety. I'm working with you to help you learn how to take care of yourself. I'm looking out for you, but if I don't see what's happening, come and tell me when you need help."

- For those children who have decided that adults aren't safe and their help comes from peers, they may be afraid to tattle on a friend because they are following an "inborn code of honor." We can show them how to ask for help when a problem with a friend is escalating. Here's a way to explain: "You don't have to tattle on Billy. When things are getting out of hand with Billy, you can come and tell me that you'd like help figuring it out. Then you're not getting him in trouble. You're getting the help you need."

- They need teachers to notice their signals and inquire whether there is something upsetting happening at school or in the home that's affecting their school work. "I've noticed you have been upset, and I'd like to think about it with you and give you help. Let's think together about what we can do." Use questions that help open the topic and feel appropriate. These might include: Is there any time of day at school that's upsetting to you? "Is there anyone you feel afraid of at school?"

- Hurt children may have a hard time distinguishing whether given situations are safe or not. Provide a reality check. When appropriate and true, indicate—"you are safe now."

    e.g. "Yesterday Jenny did bite someone when she was upset. I can understand that you'd like to play with a different child today. I'm helping Jenny learn not to bite. Right now we're having snack in our chairs. Come and join us. The empty chair is next to Jenny. I want to let you know that it's safe right now to sit next to Jenny to have snack."

    e.g. "Yes, David moves his arms a lot, and I can see how that feels surprising. David's body doesn't have control over his arms. He's really fun to play with and he doesn't want to hurt you or anyone else. Let's play a game with him now. I'll help you get to know David."

- They need to know that the adults at school can truly be counted on for safety. If there is any adult in the school who is inappropriate in his or her method of guidance—habitually screaming, belittling, or using or threatening physical force—the school administration needs to intervene.

  This is a new area for some schools. Even though staff are aware of teachers who are inappropriate, the social agreements aren't necessarily in place to firmly and compassionately insist these behaviors are not acceptable. One factor is a denial of the impact this has on children. Instead, children are unfairly asked to tolerate stressful conditions. This gives the message that the adults can't truly be counted upon to protect them.

- Children need to be able to tell adults if another adult, perhaps a bus driver or parent volunteer, is doing something they find upsetting or confusing so that the teacher can carefully and responsibly check it out.

These are further implications on working with children who have been mistreated for our conflict resolution work:

Distinguish whether a situation should be negotiated by the children themselves or by older peer mediators or whether an adult needs to step in. When children are negotiating a conflict it is usually appropriate to help each child share responsibility for the problem. However, if there is a power imbalance, if one is chronically in the role of aggressor and the other is in the role of victim, they do not share responsibility in the same manner, and what is needed is for *the adult to remedy the situation*. It is then the role of the teacher to stop the one who is doing the mistreatment, and protect the one who is receiving the mistreatment.

Children who are acting out need to have compassionate and meaningful consequences. To tell the child, for example—you have lost your recess—is not enough. A teacher needs to indicate this is unacceptable and cannot go on. Seek help from a professional for the child. This person can teach him how to recognize the signals in his body that indicate his early warning system has been triggered. When a child is re-enacting aggression, feelings can overwhelm them like a locomotive with no breaks.

Researchers on trauma indicate that when a child feels that her survival is threatened, she may identify with the one who is mistreating her and take on the behaviors that person does and the beliefs that person holds. This identification is their effort to manage and gain control over the trauma. This is why abused children may grow up to be abusing parents. It's important to remember that not all abused children grow up to be abusive. An individual child's response to trauma is based on their own individual resources; a generalization or prediction cannot be made because hurt children can become responsible adults. Children in their courage call on their internal and external strengths. A caring, compassionate teacher is a key external resource.

Jungian psychologist Edith Sullwold comments that all children, including those who have known mistreatment, carry a deep structure for social harmony. They carry the "inner template" of what friendship means, what justice means, what archetypal figures like the good king and good queen or the good parent act like. They draw upon these resources.

Even as children are struggling with identification with the one who has mistreated them, they carry strong reserves. Guide them to explore in their play or in their artwork the archetypes of protectors like guardian angels, or a good king or queen, or a dragon. Provide play figures that can represent forces of safety and examples of wisdom.

Recommended practices to help strengthen children's internal support:

- Children need to be able to connect to feelings of being safe and being centered. Experiences with the expressive arts can be sources of comfort and sustenance. Also, connection to nature and animals is helpful. Movement and music have particular value because they help wrap children in a safe place. For those who feel dislocated by abuse, to be able to initiate movement in a secure classroom atmosphere is integrating and helps them feel their center.

- They need us to tell them what they are doing well—how we like their sense of humor, how we enjoy their drawings. We can describe children with their strengths. We can show them we see their value. Be a positive mirror for the hurt child. Write out a list of what these children are doing, and reflect back specific things they do as you affirm them daily. Let them know—"I see the good person you are."

- Children are working hard to stay connected to other people, and they are taking care of themselves in the best way they know how. Notice their efforts to make friends and join playmates, and give them a positive framework to understand the way they are reaching out in the world, e.g. "I saw you go over to Krista to play with her. You walked over to a friend you'd like to be with."

- Help children learn that their self-worth doesn't fluctuate. It doesn't depend upon the people around them and how they feel. Their worth is solid and unchanging.

- Provide time for working with art materials in a self-directed manner. When children can let their inner movement and imagery emerge and follow it's stream, this is an integrating force. There is no need for analysis or interpretation. The work itself allows important inner contact.

- If children have grown up in a chaotic environment, they haven't gotten the help they needed as a baby and young child to organize their nervous system. They may be hyper-vigilant or very disorganized. Transitions, even moving furniture in the room, may make them uneasy. Help them anticipate changes and give them extra support when the routine changes. Use clear charts to show how the day is organized. The whole class benefits from help with transitions, particularly those with learning disabilities such as sensory processing problems. If a child seems to be a "troublemaker" when transitions occur, gather data about exactly when the outbursts happen and meet with the school psychologist to solve the puzzle. Perhaps the behavior is from a low blood sugar crisis if the child is hypoglycemic. Find out what will assist.

- Some children may need to have five or ten minutes of undivided time with their teacher at the start of the school day to bond together. This can be a time when the child takes the lead in suggesting what they will do. This helps calm and orient particular children.

- Children need help creating boundaries. They need to learn they have a right to set limits and decide how they want playmates to play with them. If they don't want to play-fight, or be teased, or if they want to play alone, they need help finding words to say, and gaining permission to avoid a person or situation. Assist them to come in closer contact with themselves and learn how to identify safe places, people, and events.

- Staff can help those children who use only play-fighting as a way to interact to learn a wider range of behaviors. Kindergarten, first, and second graders are ready to learn kickball and other games, but sometimes get stuck in play-fighting. Enlist older children to teach younger children group games.

- Acknowledge and validate all feelings—not just the good ones—but also sadness, grief, fear, and anger. This tells the child that "all of you is okay." Empathetic statements signal that a teacher understands, such as, "I see you're really angry. If my glasses broke and I couldn't play my favorite game, I'd be really upset, too." Books and songs can also be used to give the message that are feelings all a healthy part of us.

In teachable moments we offer children a new direction. One day when I was working with young children using rhythm instruments, I noticed that a four-year-old girl had an instrument that looked like it was working but was really broken. To my surprise, she handled her frustration by hitting the instrument hard. I wanted to model a different response. I picked up the instrument, which was in the shape of a chicken, and began to pat it. I said, "When someone's having a hard time, we can give them help." Then she took the instrument and patted it. We were saying together that when there are upset feelings, we can respond with gentleness rather than letting the feelings escalate. As if to honor and accept this instrument the way it was, she didn't get a new instrument to replace this one. Instead, she continued to hold and pat the broken one.

In all these ways we are able to make a tremendous impact in the lives of young children. We tell children the "good" things we see them doing and recognize the efforts they are making. As we provide nurturing experiences such as hearing a story in a small group, interacting in a game, or being part of the warmth of group music, we hold them and give them new skills. We create a lifeline of safety, tenderness, and nurturing.

ADDITIONAL RESOURCES ON CONFLICT RESOLUTION

Creative Conflict Resolution: More Than 200 Activities for Keeping Peace in the Classroom, by William Kreidler, Glenview, Ill: Scott, Foresman, 1984.

Discovery Time for Cooperation and Conflict Resolution. by Sarah Pirtle, Nyack, NY: Children's Creative Response to Conflict, 1998.

Early Childhood Adventures in Peacemaking: A Conflict Resolution and Violence Prevention Activity Guide by William J. Kreidler with Nan Doty, Laura Parker Roerden, Sheryl Rainier, and Carol Wintle, Cambridge, MA: Educators for Social Responsibility, 1997.

Elementary Perspectives, by William Kreidler, Cambridge, MA: Educators for Social Responsibility, 1990.

Magical Earth, recording by Sarah Pirtle, available from A Gentle Wind and the Discovery Center. Among the fourteen songs are three that are relevant: "Talk It Out" is a cajun-style song about conflict resolution, "Walls and Bridges" is about overcoming racism, and "Paz Y Libertad/ Peace and Liberty" is by Jose-Luis Orozco.

School-Age Adventures in Peacemaking: A Conflict Resolution and Violence Prevention Activity Guide by William Kreidler and Lisa Furlong, Cambridge, MA: Educators for Social Responsibility, 1995.

Talk It Out: Conflict Resolution in the Elementary Classroom by Barbara Porro, ASCD, Asso. for Supervision and Curriculum Development, 1996.

Teaching Conflict Resolution Through Children's Literature by William Kreidler, New York: Scholastic Professional Books, 1994.

Teaching Young Children in Violent Times by Diane Levin, Cambridge, MA: Educators for Social Responsibility, 1994.

25 How Can We Be Friends Again?/Amigos De Nuevo

Children explore what makes a conflict worse and what makes it better.

●●●●●●●●●●●●●●●●●●●●●●●●●●

Ages 4 to 10

When to Use Conflict resolution skills development

Language Bilingual

Location Side 2, Song 25

Source Sarah Pirtle; Spanish text by Roberto Díaz and other teachers from Brightwood Magnet School in Springfield, Massachusetts

OBJECTIVES

- to explore what causes conflicts to escalate
- to explore what helps to resolve conflicts
- to think about friendship

PROCEDURE

1 Gather the children together. Teach them the song, working in the language that is "home base" for your children, either English or Spanish.

2 Draw a picture of a squiggle on a blackboard or on large newsprint. Ask the children, "What actions make problems between people become worse?" Each time they suggest something, such as hitting or punching, write the suggestion down then make the squiggle gradually expand into the shape of a tornado. Use the children's suggestions to make additional verses for the song. Group three items together to form a verse using the following song pattern:

> *If I _____, that makes it worse.*
> *If I _____, that makes it worse.*
> *If I _____, that makes it worse.*
> *I'll admit that makes it worse.*
>
> *Si yo _____, eso es peor.*
> *Si yo _____, eso es peor.*
> *Si yo _____, eso es peor.*
> *Entonces empeora la situación.*

3 Ask the children, "What actions make a problem better?" Draw a small squiggle that looks like a seed. Each time they suggest something, write the suggestion in words, then add something to the drawing of the seed to create a flower. Add a stem and roots, then leaves from the stem, and finally a flower. Group their suggestions in threes and use them to create new verses (in the language of your choice):

> *If I _____, that will help. (3x)*
> *That will help. It can help a lot.*

> *Si yo _____, eso es mejor. (3x)*
> *Así mejora la situación.*

4   To give closure to the song, end with this final chorus:
> *Yes, we can be friends again.*
> *Yes, we can be friends again.*

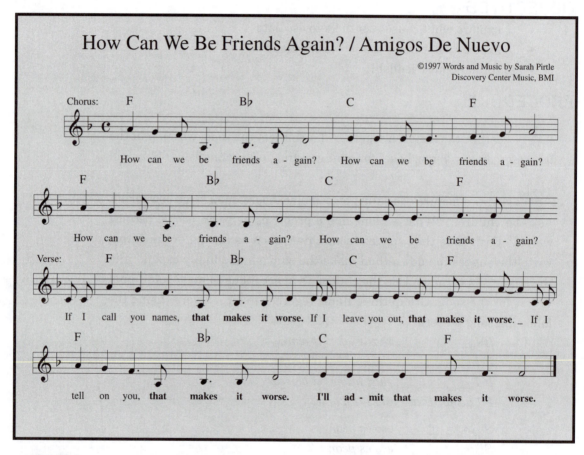

English

Chorus

How can we be friends again? (4x)

Verse 1

If I call you names, that makes it worse.
If I leave you out, that makes it worse.
If I tell on you, that makes it worse.
I'll admit that makes it worse.

Verse 2

If I meet you on the swing, that will help.
If I ask what you're thinking, that will help.
If I tell you the things that bother me, that will help.
It can help a lot.

Spanish

Coro

¿Cómo podemos ser amigos de nuevo?
(4x)

Verso 1

Si yo te hablo malo eso es peor.
Si yo te rechazo eso es peor.
Si me quejo mucho eso es peor.
Entonces empeora la situación.

Verso 2

Si yo te respeto eso es mejor.
Si yo te acepto eso es mejor.
Si te invito a jugar eso es mejor.
Así mejora la situación.

Transition

Make up your own words for this song.
What will help you get along?

Note: *The first verse in Spanish is a translation of the first verse in English. However, the second Spanish verse extends the second English verse.*

Translation of Verso 2

If I respect you, that will help.
If I accept you, that will help.
If I ask you to play, that will help.
This will improve the situation.

Note: *For easier chords, use the key of C. Change the F chord to C. Change the B♭ chord to F. Change the C chord to G.*

. . . .

E X T E N S I O N S

. . . .

Changing Worse To Better

As a class, choose an item from your list of "what makes conflicts worse." Make a group agreement that you will not engage in that behavior. A third-grade class at St. Phillips School in Bemidji, Minnesota picked a certain put-down that they wanted to stop: "No more calling anyone stupid." They were able to successfully eliminate that from their classroom community.

Changing To A Kangaroo*

Ages: 7 to 8

If you haven't already done so, prepare a written list of what makes conflicts better and worse and keep the list posted. Ask, "What helps? What opens communication?" (Examples: looking at the person, describing how you are feeling, asking a question, explaining something you need.) Then ask the children,

"What makes it worse? What closes communication?" (Examples: name-calling, blaming or accusing, yelling, pointing your finger.)

Tell the children, "When you are in a conflict there are several ways you can act. You can act like a shark by dominating, being aggressive, and scaring people. You can act like a turtle and retreat into your shell and avoid the problem. Or you can act like a kangaroo and jump in confidently to work together to find a solution."

Ask for two volunteers to role play a conflict. Suggest a conflict that is common in your classroom or ask the children to suggest one. Have each volunteer decide whether he or she will respond to the conflict as a shark or a turtle. (There can be two sharks or two turtles.) In this way, the volunteers will purposefully choose ineffective behaviors. It's up to the audience to help them change into kangaroos.

Tell the observers, "When you see either person in the role play doing a behavior that is making the conflict worse, call out FREEZE. After calling FREEZE, name the behavior that isn't working and suggest a different behavior." For example:

> "Freeze. You're turning your back. Look at her."

> "Freeze. You're teasing. Say what you are feeling."

> "Freeze. You're making a fist. Put your arm down and say what you think the problem is."

After a behavior is named and a suggestion is made, have the children in the role play use the suggestion.

* *Developed from theater methods used by Lynn Fisher, Metro ESR*

How This Song was Born

. . . .

"I don't want to write a song about conflicts. I want to talk about the fight I just had with my friend," said a first grader at Westminster West School in Vermont. "Okay," I responded. "Let's talk about that and maybe it will also lead to a song. When you're having a problem with a friend, what doesn't help?" I recorded all their answers, and these became the first verse. Then I asked, "What could help?" As the song took form, one girl thought it needed more of an ending. You can use her words as you sing the song. She added:

Here's an idea that we thought up.

Treat your friends like you treat yourself.

After the song was created, I reflected on how these simple words get to the core of transforming conflicts. Choosing to help make a problem better involves unlearning social messages. My experience is that we habitually respond to anger, fear, hatred, and hostility with more of the same. The way of the peacemaker is to respond from a different place, to use clear boundaries and compassion, to care and set limits, instead of adding fuel to the flame.

Two in a Fight/
Dos en una Pelea

Introduce conflict resolution with
a humorous finger play.

●●●●●●●●●●●●●●●●●●●●●●●●

Ages	4 to 10
When to Use	Introduce communication skills, remind children in a conflict of their options
Language	Bilingual
Location	Side 2, Song 26
Source	Tune traditional, lyrics by Sarah Pirtle and students. Spanish text by Roberto Díaz

OBJECTIVES

- to validate the experience of anger
- to work on expressing anger constructively
- to choose to talk out problems

PROCEDURE

1   Explain the story as a finger play, using the index finger of each hand, like two people are talking to each other. Show that there are two friends who have a problem and are upset. They are both angry, but they handle their anger in different ways. Indicate that "the little one" wants to talk out the problem, but the other is afraid and runs away. The little one says, "Come on back, we can figure this out." She wants to hear why her friend is upset. When her friend expresses her anger, she doesn't run away but listens so that they can figure out how to solve the problem together.

2   Now as you play the recording or sing the song, use your fingers to act out this story. Move the finger that is "speaking." As one finger runs away, the other finger who is taking the part of the "little one" beckons this "person" to return.

   On *"Come on back,"* use finger to beckon.
   On *"We can figure this out,"* show other finger coming closer.

Illustrate talking it out as a back and forth motion. On the recording, you'll hear us clicking our fingers to fill in the space where talking occurs. Don't click; instead act out what problem-solving looks like. One finger goes forward as it speaks while the other goes back as it listens. At the last, *"We can figure this out,"* end by linking index fingers.

3   Talk about the meaning of the song. Start with an open-ended question such as "What do you think about as you hear this song?"
Then ask, "What do children fight about at school?"

Add this ground rule: Let's not say the names of people in our class, but let's say the things children argue about.

4 Discuss the concepts introduced by the song. Say: One of the children didn't want to talk it out at first. What are some of the reasons a person might want to run away and not talk it out? (You might suggest that some people might need to "cool down" before discussing the problem.)

5 Discuss what it means to talk things out. Find out what their current understanding is. Ask: When people in the story song talked out the problem, what do you think they did? How did they make the problem better?

See if members of your class already have pictures in their minds of what occurs. Examples: The children listened, they took turns, they looked at each other, they didn't shout.

Two in the Fight

©1997 Words by Sarah Pirtle
Music Traditional

There were two in the fight and the lit-tle one said, "I'm an-gry, I'm an-gry." But the

oth-er one start-ed to run a-way. "Come back and hear what I have to say."___ Keep

talk-ing, keep talk-ing. Come on back, (snap) come on back. (snap) We can

fig-ure this out. "Come on back, (snap) come on back. (snap) We can fig-ure this out.

Traditional folk tune, "There were Two in the Bed," with new lyrics by Sarah Pirtle and second graders of Central Elementary School in Bellow Falls, Vermont

English

There were two in the fight
and the little one said,
"I'm angry, I'm angry."
But the other one started to run away.
"Come back and hear what I have to say."
Keep talking, keep talking.
Come on back, come on back.
We can figure this out.
Come on back, come on back
We can figure this out.

There were two in the fight
and the other one said,
"I'm angry, I'm angry."
But the little one did not run away.
"Tell me what you have to say."
Keep talking, keep talking.
Talk it out, talk it out.
We can figure this out.
Talk it out, talk it out.
We can figure this out!

Spanish: Dos en una pelea

Hay dos niños peleando
y el pequeño dice,
"Tengo coraje, tengo coraje."
Pero el otro se quiere echar atrás,
"Ven acá, tú y yo podemos hablar."
Hablemos, hablemos.
Ven acá, ven acá. Tu y yo podemos hablar.
Ven acá, ven acá. Esto se puede arreglar.

Hay dos niños peleando
y el otro dice,
"Tengo coraje, tengo coraje."
Pero el pequeño quiere hablar.
"Ya yo no quiero pelear."
Hablemos, hablemos.
Dímelo, dímelo. Esto se puede arreglar.
Dímelo, dímelo. Esto se puede arreglar.

True Story: How Anna Talked It Out

Actual stories of the process of talking out conflicts really carry weight with children. They like to know what other people their age can do. Tell this story or use puppets to act it out.

If you had been standing on the playground of St. Philip's School in Bemidji, Minnesota, here's what you would have heard. In their school, the phrase "I to I" means talking things out. Sue Liedl trains students, teachers, and parents on how to do an "I to I." She's also the mother of two boys at the school. One day at recess, two second-grade girls named Anna and Carol ran up to her. They looked very upset.

> *Anna*: I'm so mad at Jake.

> *Sue Liedl*: It sounds like you need to have an "I to I" with Jake.

> *Anna*: I don't really want to.

> *Sue Liedl*: I know you can do it.

Anna straightens her shoulder and goes to find Jake.

> *Anna*: Remember that game we had just now, Jake. I felt it got too rough. You see this scab on my knee? Well, it's bleeding now.

> *Jake*: I thought we all had fun.

> *Anna*: I wasn't having fun. Do you think you can be more gentle? If you think you can be more gentle, Carol and I still want to play with you.

> *Jake*: Yes.

> *Anna*: Okay, let's go.

Discuss with your students how this dialogue follows the plan of "Talk it Out" or whatever method of face-to-face problem solving you are teaching.

Anna gave Jake an "I"-message telling him how she felt.

She suggested a solution—that he could play if he was more gentle.

He agreed to the plan.

They went off to try it.

Story Repeat Role Play

Ask the children to retell the same story by acting it out. One plays the part of a child who gets hurt during recess play. The other listens and responds.

A Reminder Song

Lois Bascom, director of Mohawk Nursery School, approaches children ages 3, 4, or 5 who are in conflict and starts to sing this song. This gives them a moment to calm down and refocus. She sings just the beginning to remind them of the option of talking together, and then she helps facilitate their conversation.

Practice Finding Words

When you feel like hitting or pushing, what are some words you can use instead? Make a list with children of helpful phrases.

Please stop.

I don't like that.

Watch out.

Wait.

Will you talk to me?

The short version of "When I Say Stop, I Mean Stop" (Song 29) is a good companion to "Two in the Fight" because it supplies that simple word—stop.

Conflict Resolution in the Media

Ask: When people get into an argument or have a problem on television, what are some of the ways that they solve it? How do these ways help or hurt the people in the argument?

Finger Play: Talk It Out Practice

Follow up this finger play by using fingers to act out a common classroom problem. Pick a situation, such as pushing in line, and ask children to pretend their fingers are children. Ask them to pretend their fingers are talking it out. Then discuss what words they came up with. Ask: What could they say to each other when pushing happens?

Tip!

Keep a file of your own examples of real-life moments where children talk out problems themselves.

27 Heart To Heart/ Corazón A Corazón

Pairs stand palm to palm and sing affirmatively to each other.

• •

OBJECTIVES

- to choose a healthy expression of feelings
- to use your heart to stay connected
- to agree to talk things out

PROCEDURE

1 Gather the children together and teach them the song.

2 Help the children form pairs. Start by asking pairs to create a bridge together. They face each other and use their hands to connect in a way they both enjoy. Every time they hear the chorus, their hands come up in a bridge again.

> *Heart to heart we can listen.*
> *Heart to heart we can talk it out.*

Make sure that all partners are able to do this successfully before moving ahead. Sometimes a child will pound her partner's palms or will squeeze hands too tightly. Talk about keeping the motion friendly.

3 Now work on dramatizing each verse. Pause to talk about how our faces look when we are angry or scared. Clarify that everyone gets angry. Anger sends an important message that something is bothering us. We can talk about what that message is.

4 During each verse, have the children move away from each other and pretend to be angry by making angry faces in verse one and pretend to be scared in verse two. During each chorus, have the pairs come back together to make a bridge. To ease the transition between moving away and reconnecting you can say, "Remember here's your friend who wants to know what you're feeling. Come on back and look at her."

Note: *The chorus to this song is by my friend Robin M. Smith, from her song "Heart to Heart" © 1992. The words to the chorus were adapted with permission. You can hear her song on the recording,* Love Makes A Family, *recorded by Two of a Kind.*

Heart to Heart / Corazón a Corazón

©1997 Words and Music by Sarah Pirtle
Discovery Center Music, BMI

Chorus

Heart to heart we can listen,
heart to heart we can talk it out.

Verse 1

Sometimes I feel angry.
I don't want to hit or shout.
When I know I'm angry,
I can talk it out.

Verse 2

Sometimes I feel scared.
I don't want to hide away.
When I know I'm scared,
I'll tell what I have to say.

Chant

Hand in hand, mano a mano
Heart to heart, corazón a corazón

Round Part 1

Mano a mano, hand in hand.
Mano a mano, hand in hand.

Round Part 2

Corazón a corazón, heart...to heart.
Corazón a corazón, heart...to heart.

Closing (same melody as chorus)

Hand in hand we can understand.
Hand in hand we can talk it out.

SNAPSHOT

How it Looks

· ·

Kindergartners at Craneville School in Dalton, Massachusetts are enjoying looking at their partners. They giggle as they touch palms. Some swing their arms, others rock back and forth together. When the song is over, they ask to sing it again. They act out the first verse by moving apart and pretending to look angry. Then on the chorus, they rush back to their partners and sing eye to eye, *"Heart to heart we can talk it out."*

Role Plays

With children in first grade and older, this activity is a helpful preparation for role playing. Sing the song in two facing lines. Next, provide a situation that needs to be talked out. For example, "You are working at the same desk. Everyone in line A is trying to draw a line carefully. Everyone in line B is tapping the desk with a pencil because it helps them think. How can you talk about this?"

Round Singing

Half the group sings Round Part 1 while the other half sings Part 2. Add gestures to contrast "mano a mano" (hand in hand) with "corazón a corazón" (heart to heart).

Movement

Divide into four groups. Each group works on one part of the song: the chorus, the chant, or the two parts of the round. Each group memorizes the words and invents gestures or dance movements to fit them.

RELATED SONG

"The Anger Chant" (Song 28)

Discussion

Ask the children, "How can you use your heart when you are upset to help you reconnect with someone you care about?"

Tip!

You can use the phrase "Do a Heart to Heart" as a way of signaling that it's time to talk things out.

Recommended Lesson Plan

Here's an effective sequence of activities for K–Grade 3:

1. "Cloud Hands" mirroring activity (p. 243)

2. "Heart to Heart" with same partners (p. 184)

3. "Under the Bridge" (p. 247)

Ages	3 to 8
When to Use	Discussion and drawing about anger, or conflict resolution skills development
Language	English
Location	Side 2, Song 28
Source	Sarah Pirtle

28 The Anger Chant

Children sing about listening to their anger.

OBJECTIVES

- to recognize feelings
- to identify what you need when you are angry.

PROCEDURE

1 Read over the words to the song youself and study what they say.

Verse One—We all feel strong anger at times.

Verse Two—People respond in different ways when they are angry.

Verse Three—We can pay attention to ourselves and learn how to figure out what is upsetting for us.

2 Guide your students through an open-ended drawing activity. Assemble crayons or markers and enough paper for all children to have two sheets each. Pass out the supplies first so that they are ready before the class hears the song. As you introduce the song, explain, "Everyone gets angry. Anger is a message inside us that says—pay attention! Something is really bothering me." After children listen to or sing the song, ask them to draw whatever they want.

Next, focus on the last line: "you know I'm gonna listen to me!" Ask, "What helps you when you are angry? You can add to your first drawing or make a new one." Here are some drawing suggestions:

You could draw a person listening to someone who is angry.

You could show a person or an animal understanding the angry child and helping them.

You could draw what a child likes to do when they feel angry.

When the drawings are complete, ask if anyone wants to show what they drew or talk about it. Keep the sharing optional. If appropriate, help children gather in pairs and share their drawings.

3 Choose an activity such as "Anger Messages" or "Make a Classroom Plan About Anger" to help children work constructively with anger.

Anger Chant

Verse 1

Fee Fi Fee Fi Fee Fo Fum
I'm getting angry. Here it comes.
My anger's here like popcorn popping.
My anger's here like rabbits hopping.
What am I gonna do? Hmmm?

Verse 2

Sometimes I feel like growling.
And sometimes I hide away.
And sometimes I want you to hold me,

And hear what I have to say.
Till my anger's slowing down.
I got my feet back on the ground—
Ummm!

Verse 3

When my anger's here, knocking on the door.
I say, come on in and tell me more!
Come on in, I've got the key.
You know I'm gonna LISTEN TO ME.

Note: *This chant is designed so that with three- to five-year-olds you can use just the first two sections. The last part, which is more advanced and abstract, is optional.*

. . . .

E X T E N S I O N S

. . . .

Anger Messages

Here's an important phrase I learned from Betsy Evans, director of the Giving Tree School in Gill, Massachusetts, and High Scope trainer and author:

"Will hitting tell him or her what you want?"

You can use this phrase to assist children in the heat of the moment to communicate their needs, or you can convey the concept with a puppet play using two puppets.

For example, the bear puppet says it wants to hit the monkey puppet for taking the yellow ball. The teacher talks to the bear puppet: "I see you're angry. Hitting is one thing people do when they feel angry. But will hitting tell monkey what you want? What words could you say to the monkey?"

The children then suggest words to the bear puppet.

Anger Face Masks

Explore how you look when you are angry. Ask people to cover their faces. On the count of three, everyone (including you) uncovers their face showing what they look like when they feel angry.

Discuss: How do you know when you're angry? What happens to your body? How do you know when other people are angry?

Affirm the children by explaining that once we know we're angry, we can get help to find out what feels upsetting.

Calming Corner

. . . .

Create a place that children can go to at any time that has a soothing effect. Make it clear that anybody can use it anytime—to read in or sit. If you are angry you can also choose to be there. Engage the children in helping to decide what they want to have in the calming corner: stuffed toys, soft scarves, soft blankets, a comfortable chair.

Overview On Anger

Anger is a normal part of human experience. How do we make room to live with the anger that will inevitably be expressed by children in our classroom and will inevitably arise within us as well? If we look at anger as an integral part of our makeup, without its negative connotations, what does anger do for us?

Anger gives us an opportunity to learn about ourselves and what we want, and sometimes connects us with needs and concerns that have been buried. When we are angry, we're often affected at a level where we don't have words. We may feel flooded with hurt, disappointment, surprise, or confusion that may be hard to immediately comprehend. Often things feel out of our control. It's challenging for people of any age to find words to say in the flood of anger. In that sense, feeling anger creates great vulnerability. This may seem like a contradiction because an angry child may be hitting or scratching or feel like a threat to others, but the cause of this aggression is a sense of being vulnerable and a feeling of powerlessness.

Anger sends us an important message that we want something to change—this is portrayed in the chant as a knock on the door. Conflict resolution trainer Marchall Rosenburg says, "Anger is a thwarted desire for closeness. Anger is a poorly disguised request for nurturing."

The cause of the anger may seem irrational or trivial—"I want the red cup!"—but the underlying cause is a need for caring. If we keep an eye on how to communicate care and connection, rather than how to give the child the specific thing he is asking for, we will stay closer to the mark.

When I see the toughness of a clenched fist, what I hear unspoken are the words: "No one is going to hurt me!" That child needs to feel safe. From that defiant stance he is keeping away hurt and keeping away contact. A certain firm but gentle quality is needed to help the angry child listen to his underlying needs.

In general, our goal is to keep connected to the child who is angry. Each child and each situation is different. How we respond will depend on the circumstances. Here are many ways we can connect to an angry child:

> Tell him the truth. For instance, "We're all having blue cups today because those are the ones that are clean." Stand by what is real, while at the same time conveying care and warmth. Give reasons. Speak affirmatively not mockingly, firmly and gently.

> Come close to the angry child and stay next to him using open body language and words that mirror his reality. "I see you're very upset and I'm right here with you. I want to listen to you." This helps the child "bail" out the imbalance of feelings he is awash in, to use an image I learned from trainer Betsy Evans. This approach may result in the anger getting momentarily more intense before the wave of feeling diminishes.

> Assist children in identifying their anger and what is upsetting. Even if they don't know why they are feeling the way they do, we can offer a guess. For instance, "I wonder if it was upsetting for you when _____."

> Don't pressure a child to find words if he isn't ready.

> If a child is hitting, biting, or scratching, set boundaries to indicate you will make sure that no one gets hurt. You can say, "I see how angry you are, but hitting is not okay. I'm going to help you." Or, use a firm hug that holds the child with you as he calms down. By doing this we indicate that these ways of communicating are both unacceptable and not useful. At these times it's particularly important not to turn away from the child, unless you both agree he needs time to cool off by himself. Children need us there giving guidance.

If a child wants to be alone, we can help him take time in a comfortable place and come back when he feels calmer. Let isolation be the child's choice, rather than sending him away as punishment and, as he returns, show he is welcome and accepted after the outburst of anger. We are looking for what will help a child return to a centered feeling again.

Anger is not a trump card that gives the angry child or adult the right to win in a social situation. It's our job to create a fair atmosphere. When a child displays strong emotions, people are tempted to give the child what he wants—anything to have the yelling or tantrum stop. Yet our common sense and our group agreements need to be stronger and more prevailing. Anger is meant to be a messenger but not a governor.

Two goals to keep in mind as you stay connected with angry children are both encapsulated in the song:

1) Help them "get their feet back on the ground." Help them return to a calmer place where they can think about what they want.

2) Help them "listen to themselves." Help them identify what they are asking for and help them learn how to ask for it in a way that others can hear and respond to. In other words, "We don't know how to help when you're hitting."

Make a Classroom Plan about Anger

Say, "In our classroom, do you think that all of us here will probably get angry about something at one time or another? Yes! So let's make a plan about anger."

"'I'm gonna listen to me!' says the chant. Let's agree that we want to help people here understand themselves when they are angry and help them be heard."

a. Begin by providing information about anger. Say, "Your anger gives you a message. When you figure out what is upsetting you, then you can tell someone. In our classroom, we want to know about the things that bother you."

b. Think together. Ask, "In our classroom, what are things we do when we are angry to try to get other people to hear our message?" Make a list and discuss it.

Extend the exploration: "If we hit when we are angry in our classroom, is it easy or hard for other children or teachers to listen to us?" Go over other examples such as shouting, screaming, threatening, accusing,

biting, or scratching. Ask, "What are ways we can tell each other something is wrong that make it easier to be heard?"

c. Suggest a plan and ask for modifications until there is group agreement. Here is an example: "What if we say this year that when you are angry that you'll try to do something that helps. You could:

- find a teacher or friend who can listen to you and help you find a way to say what you're upset about;
- make an angry drawing that shows what you are angry about;
- go to a calming corner that we will create together with stuffed toys and a comfortable chair—a place where children can be at any time;
- go to a peace table or get the peace spoons to hold (refer to whatever concrete materials you have chosen for conflict resolution) and talk about it."

"We'll try not to hit or do the things that make it hard to understand us. Do you have any other ideas of what would help?"

What Does Anger Feel Like To You?

Start by referring to the words in the first verse. Ask, "Does popcorn popping or rabbits hopping describe how anger feels to you?" Affirm the group by asking them to describe what their anger feels like. Use the same chant rhythm to repeat their words while everyone keeps the beat, tapping knees. Example:

> *I feel like boiling water.*
> *I feel like I'm going to boil over.*

Volcano Pictures

Ages: 6 and up

Many times children say that their anger feels like a volcano to them. You can use this image to help them get in touch with things that are bothering them. First ask, "How is anger like a volcano?" For example, like a volcano, anger is unexpected, and causes movement. "Sometimes we're afraid that anger will destroy things, just like the hot lava and the shaking of a volcano could hurt people nearby."

Add this scientific fact: volcanoes bring up rich minerals from deep inside the earth and these minerals help enrich the soil.

Say, "We're going to do drawings called 'The Messages of the Volcano.' First draw an animal or person in one corner of your drawing who is going to stay safe while the volcano explodes. They will listen to the volcano and find out what it's trying to say. Draw the volcano exploding, but this volcano doesn't destroy anything. It brings up gems you didn't know were there. Draw a volcano with words coming out of it. Write messages to yourself of things that bother you."

Zip in Children's Words

I explained to third graders at Westminster West School in Vermont that they could add words to the song: "Who'd like to tell us what it feels like to be angry?" A girl in the back row was eager to speak. We chanted her words:

> *I feel like a volcano.*
> *I feel ready to pop.*

After class she asked if I would help her write down the words because she wanted to bring them home to show her mother.

Hand Motions

Add hand motions as you sing the song.

Verse 1

Keep a rhythm, tapping legs then clapping, while singing

> *Fee Fi Fee Fi Fee Fo Fum.*
> *I'm getting angry. Here it comes.*

Rub your hands together on the final lines about popcorn popping and rabbits hopping. As you ask the question, "What am I going to do?" Stop all movements and pause to think, "Hmmm?"

Verse 2

On *"growling,"* form hands in a claw shape and circle them like a bear clawing.

On *"hide away,"* hands run behind back.

On *"hold me,"* hug yourself.

For *"back on the ground,"* make a definite motion like stomping legs.

Verse 3

Return to the starting rhythm of tap and clap.

On *"listen to me,"* touch your heart.

Convey the Message of Anger

a. Help the children identify a current problem. Ask them to write or draw about a time recently when they felt angry: "Write or draw as much of it as you can—show what happened, or what you felt, or what you looked like." This expression anchors the experience and helps them reflect.

b. Introduce phrases that get to the heart of the feeling: What is bothering you? What do you want another person to know? What do you want them to remember?

c. Take examples from their drawing or writing and help children explore what they want to express and how they could express it.

> *Lee*: I wish I could hit my brother.
> *Teacher*: What do you want your brother to remember?
> *Lee*: I don't want him going in my room.
> *Teacher*: How can you tell him that?
> *Lee*: I don't know. He'll just beat me up.
> *Teacher*: Would you be okay if other people in the class helped brainstorm ideas of how you could send him the message?

d. In pairs, have children share drawing or writing. Have them help their partners figure out a way to express their anger that doesn't make the situation worse. They can practice finding words that aren't attack words that address the heart of the matter. For example, "You covered up my poster on my door and I'm furious."

SNAPSHOT

Tantrums and Boundaries

Once I was leading a song and a third-grade boy accustomed to tantrums began to interrupt the group. It was a song that built in layers and his interruption was unusual. I was pretty sure no one else wanted to stop the fun we were having. I liked this boy and I knew his contribution would be interesting, but I felt he was banking on the threat of his tantrums to push through what he wanted. I knew I couldn't join him.

I decided to treat him as an equal member of the classroom community. I nodded to him, acknowledged that he had something important to say, told him I would like to hear it at the end of the song, and kept on singing while he displayed the warning signs that he was going to let loose with a full explosion. I kept nodding and calmly singing while his sounds and body language heightened. He didn't leave the room. At the end of the song, I turned to him and matter-of-factly asked him what he wanted to say.

It was a brief moment, but in many ways it was a turnaround in the life of that group. During the next week teachers and other children came up to me and thanked me privately. Here's what I was trying to do: I was indicating that anger wasn't going to rule the group, just as his anger didn't need to rule him. I kept maintaining a sincere, friendly attitude toward him. I was trying to signal to him at a nonverbal level a way out of his dilemma—he could release the anger's hold and still respect and affirm himself. He could send his message and be heard without a tantrum.

Home Culture Interfacing with School Culture

Culturally we have different ways of expressing anger; some cultures favor suppression, some favor strong expression. Individual families have different messages about hitting; some parents coach children to hit back. Be sensitive to helping children make sense of differences between home and school. Spell out that families make the home rules and schools make school rules.

Providing Appropriate Emotional Support

There will be children in your group who see parents and caregivers out of control with anger, and children who have anger about emotional, physical, or sexual mistreatment they are receiving in their lives. They will likely feel they have no avenue to stop mistreatment by adults. Use the guidelines of your school community to give them the protection, help, and encouragement that you can.

Using Full Body Movement

Ask children to stand in their own personal space and practice methods of refocusing like stretching and deep breathing while they sing affirming words relating to the expression of anger.

Use the tune of "My Space/Mi Espacio" (Song 8) or "My Roots Go Down" (Song 33) and sing any of these new verses:

> *I can listen to what I want. (3x)*
> *I can find the words I need.*
>
> *I'll tell you what I'm feeling today. (3x)*
> *Cuz I've got a lot to say.*
>
> *I know you're going to listen to me. (3x)*
> *I want you to hear what I have to say.*

Teaching About Anger

Just bringing up the topic of anger can be enough to create agitation among some members of a class. I've seen children begin to play-fight and point their fists at each other during the first verse of the chant. Name what is happening and expand upon it to focus the issue — what is anger all about?

Here's an example of how to work with what is presented with children ages six and older. Let's say two children hold their fists up to each other's faces as you say the name of the chant. You can respond by saying: "I see your fists. How many other people also think of clenched fists when you hear the word anger? When you are really angry, how do you know it? What happens to your body?"

Young children ages three to five can get stuck in this posture of anger. Convert the shape of a fist to an open hand. Hold up your own hand in a fist, then one at a time touch one of your fingers and peel it open, while you chant: 1, 2, 3, 4 until you have an open hand, palm up.

At this point open your hand in peace:
> *I'm going to tell you more.*

Ages	3 to 10
When to Use	Social Skills Development
Language	Bilingual
Location	Side 2, Song 29
Source	"When I Say Stop" by Sarah Pirtle; "Cuando Digo ¡Ya!" words and music © 1997 by Roberto Díaz and Sarah Pirtle

(29) When I Say Stop/ Cuando Digo ¡Ya!

Children affirm their boundaries.

● ●

OBJECTIVES

- to make a clear, affirmative declaration of needs
- to respect boundaries
- to use words to send a social message

PROCEDURE

1 In preparation, think about the basic information presented in the song. Plan to lead an extension activity or a discussion to explain the meaning:

- We can tell people what we need.
- We can set limits.
- People don't want to be hurt, and no one deserves to be hurt.
- Part of being a friend is responding to the messages that our friends send us.

2 Gather the children together and listen to the recording of the two songs. Discuss what you have heard and talk about what the song means to them. Ask:

- What did you think about as you heard the music?
- Has there been a time when you wanted to say "stop" to someone you know? Was it when someone was hitting you? Was it when someone was teasing you? Other times?
- What words can you say in those situations?
- If you can't think of words, what motion can you do with your body to say you don't like what's happening?

Distinguish between words and motions that help and words and motions that make it worse. See the related song, "How Can We Be Friends Again?/ Amigos De Nuevo" (Song 25).

3 Teach one or both songs. When you are leading the longer song, teach the basic three lines first.

> *When I say stop, I mean stop.*
> *When I say no, I mean no.*
> *When I say enough, I mean enough.*

Cuando digo ¡Ya! Quiero decir ¡Ya!
Cuando digo ¡No! Quiero decir ¡No!
Cuando digo ¡Para! Quiero decir ¡Para!

4 Use motions to emphasize the meaning of the words. Ask the children to help choose the movements. For example, hold your palm out in front of you on "stop" and "ya." Shake your head on "no" while folding your arms. Cross your arms to form an X on "enough" and "para."

"Tell Jack to Stop"

At Circle Time at Mohawk Nursery School four-year-old Jack pushes and hits five-year-old Eddie, but as usual he doesn't respond. I describe what I see happening, "Jack just hit you, Eddie, didn't he? We can use words to ask someone to stop. Can you turn toward Jack and put up your hand to say stop?" Eddie did this while Jack watched with interest, equally absorbed in this new direction. "Let me teach you a song as a reminder that we can tell someone with our hands or with our words to stop." The whole class was interested in learning the song. Their teacher Lois Bascom told me that the children adopted "When I Say Stop" for the rest of the year. In fact, sometimes during free play, if Jack was pushing Eddie and he wasn't responding, other children encouraged him, "Tell Jack to stop."

When I Say Stop

©1997 Words and music by Sarah Pirtle
Discovery Center Music, BMI

When I Say Stop

When I say stop, I mean stop.
When I say no, I mean no.
I want you to hear me.
Listen to my words.

Cuando Digo: ¡Ya!

Words and Music
©1997 Sarah Pirtle and Roberto Díaz
Discovery Center Music, BMI

Verse 1

Cuando digo ¡Ya! Quiero decir ¡Ya!
Cuando digo ¡No! Quiero decir ¡No!
Cuando digo ¡Para! Quiero decir ¡Para!

Bridge

Quiero que tú escuches, lo que estoy diciendo.
Quiero que me entiendas, porque te estoy queriendo.

Verse 2

When I say stop, I mean stop.
When I say no, I mean no.
When I say enough, I mean enough.

Bridge

I want you to listen to what I'm saying.
Understand my words, I am not just playing—and I care about you.

Cuando digo ¡Ya! Quiero decir ¡Ya!
Cuando digo ¡No! Quiero decir ¡No!
Cuando digo ¡Para! Quiero decir ¡Para!

When I say stop, I mean stop.
When I say no, I mean no.
When I say enough, I mean enough!

Note: *We wanted to sing this message both in Spanish and English so we made up a new tune and a longer song.*

Translation Note: *Alternate words--another way to express "enough" is "basta."*

Send Your Message

Materials: 2 Puppets

Use two puppets to help children practice expressing their needs. Ask, "What can you say when someone teases you, and you don't want to be teased?" Suggest: "I don't like that," or "I don't think that's fun."

Illustrate that same situation with puppets. Give children practice at setting limits. Use a puppet—such as a monkey—who takes the part of the teaser. The monkey teases a child or another puppet, and children help supply the words needed to set limits. Ask children what other situations they'd like the puppets to act out.

Puppet Play to Teach Negotiation

Materials: 2 Puppets

Use two puppets and the "How to Talk It Out Together" negotiation chart (see page 153) to teach children about negotiation. Tell the following story: "The monkey and the bear (or whatever puppets you are using) both want to use the same ball at recess. Yesterday the monkey called out, 'I get it first tomorrow.' But today, the bear ran out and took it first."

Now move through the following questions and responses: "How do you think the monkey feels?"

1. Show the puppets choosing to get together. The monkey is following the first step of negotiation by agreeing to talk out the problem instead of making it worse.

2. Ask, "What happens next?" Show the stage of negotiation of taking turns to talk and listen. Ask children to hold one of the puppets and say what the puppet is feeling and what that puppet thinks the problem is.

3. Summarize what the problem is. Then ask, "What are some ideas for how they could solve this?" Show the monkey and the bear suggesting ideas. Examine the ideas the children suggest by asking, "How would that work?"

4. Ask, "Which ideas do you think they'll try?" Show the monkey and the bear agreeing on a plan.

5. "Can you repeat what their plan is? What will they do first to carry out their plan?" Show the monkey and the bear beginning the first step of their plan.

Show That You Get the Message

Materials: 2 Puppets

I like to tell the following real-life story to children to illustrate the concept that part of being a friend is responding to the messages that our friends send us.

A boy is teasing another boy in a school cafeteria. The boy who is being targeted is cringing and cowering.

A teacher asks the teaser, "What message is your friend sending you? Can you show that you get the message?"

Talk about this story: "What did you think the boy noticed? What do you think each boy did next?" Tell the children, "Sometimes our friends talk to us in words, and sometimes they talk to us without words. Being a friend means responding to these messages."

Act out this scene with puppets and take it stage by stage. Ask the group, "What do you think the puppet who is getting teased is feeling? What tells you this? What words could the puppet use?"

Pick another situation that is of interest to the class such as pushing in line and act it out with puppets or as a role play. Focus not only on giving the message as in the activity above, but also explore how the person who is asked to stop receives the message.

Tip!

Use the short version of "When I Say Stop" to intervene directly when children need guidance and help saying "stop."

Ages	4 to 12
When to Use	Teachable moments, class meeting, or brainstorm training
Language	English
Location	Side 2, Song 30
Source	Sarah Pirtle

30 There Is Always Something You Can Do

Children recognize they have positive options.

• •

OBJECTIVES

- to explore different ways of solving problems
- to expand options by brainstorming

PROCEDURE

1 Ask children to listen to the song and think of a time that they faced a problem. Provide an opportunity for children to share their thoughts.

2 When appropriate, give children the song lyrics and have them sing along. As a variation, provide rhythm instruments to emphasize the marching beat.

3 Practice thinking of "something else you could do." Use a puppet to introduce a common problem such as pushing, wanting the same object, or feeling teased. Ask the group to think of all the different things the puppet could do.

4 Introduce the word "brainstorming" to describe this process of finding alternatives.

Songwriter's Note: *In preparation for writing this song, I asked Charles Walker, cofounder of Peace Brigades International, what was the main idea he conveyed in conflict resolution training? He answered, "That there's always something you can do."*

Since this song was first released in 1984 on my cassette "Two Hands Hold the Earth," it has been used widely for conflict resolution training. ESR's Resolving Conflict Creatively Program (RCCP) brought it into New York City schools as a theme song in their training. It appears in the Kids' Conscious Acts of Peace teaching guide from Ben and Jerry's, written by RCCP. The Children's Creative Response to Conflict Program includes it in their book, Songs for a Small Planet. It has also been used as a theme song for conflict resolution videos.

Our Agreements When We Brainstorm

1. We're going to give everyone who wants to a chance to speak.

2. Please raise your hand so I can call on one person at a time. I'll put your words into a short phrase and write it down so that we can remember your idea.

3. When we're brainstorming, we're not deciding what we want to do. Deciding on our choice comes second. Right now we're thinking.

4. If you hear an idea you really like or you really don't like, please don't call out and tell us your opinion. Don't say "no" or "hurrah." Right now we're listening to all the ideas. We'll make the list as long as we can.

5. If you don't understand someone's idea, we'll stop and let the person explain how it would work.

SNAPSHOT

Young Children and Brainstorming

Children ages three to five at the Giving Tree School had a problem. When they got ready for outdoor play, some children would rush off the designated waiting spot—a porch area—and run onto the driveway while others were still putting on their coats. Director Betsy Evans engaged the children in solving the problem. She asked them to brainstorm solutions. After they had a list, she helped the children evaluate solutions by taking an idea and asking, "Now how would that work?" Children were able to see that some ideas were unrealistic. After much discussion and many suggestions, they came up with a solution— they created a stop sign to post on the porch which could be flipped to "go" when it was time to depart.

The children liked "brainstorming." When two children were in an argument, others enjoyed coming over and helping them brainstorm ways they could solve it. Betsy Evans believes that we underestimate the ability of young children to engage in problem solving and brainstorming.

There Is Always Something You Can Do

©1984 Words and music by Sarah Pirtle
Discovery Center Music, BMI

There is always something you can do,
do, do
when you're getting in a stew, stew, stew.
You can go out for a walk.
You can try to sit and talk.
There's always something you can do.

Whether in a school or fam'ly argument,
when you feel you'd really like to throw a fit.
Don't be trapped by fights and fists and
angry threats,
reach for this ordinary plan.

There is always something you can do,
do, do
yes, it's difficult but true, true, true.
See it from each other's eyes.

Find a way to compromise.
There's always something you can do.

You can use your smarts and not your fist,
fist, fist,
you can give that problem a new twist,
twist, twist.
You can see it 'round about and upside
down,
give yourself the time to find a way.

There is always something you can do, do, do
when you're getting in a stew, stew, stew.
When you want to shout and scream, find
the words for what you mean.
There's always something you can do.
There's always something you can do..

Tip!

The message of this song can be useful to help children "hear each other out" when anger and hurt feelings prevail. Remind children who are in conflict that "there's always something you can do," i.e. we can be creative and solve problems in many different ways.

Brainstorming Practice

Children often chuckle when they hear the word "brainstorm." Explain that it means to "stir up your brain to come up with as many different ways to solve a problem as you can."

Practice brainstorming with a common problem that is general and not currently "charged" or of pressing concern for the class. For example, you could address the problem of losing a pencil, wanting the same ball, or needing help from older children to learn a new game at recess. Write down all the solutions children can devise and see how long a list of options you can create.

For children ages three to five, act out the problem with puppets and ask children to suggest all the different ways the puppets could solve the problem.

For children ages six and older, have pairs think together and then share their ideas with the class.

Brainstorming a Real Problem

After you've practiced, you're ready to address a problem that is a "hot topic" or a topic that really affects the group. For example, you could brainstorm solutions for how to share blocks in the block corner, how to handle a problem on the school bus, or what activities they want to do at a class party. Before you make your brainstorm list, present "Our Agreements When We Brainstorm."

Moving from Brainstorming to Decision Making

Step One Read all the ideas on the brainstorm list and ask if anyone would like to hear any item explained. If someone does, test for understanding by asking a child who did not give the idea to put it in his or her own words.

Step Two Help the group evaluate options. Ask, "How would that work?" to help explore whether ideas would be effective.

Step Three Narrow the options either by crossing out ideas that couldn't be carried out and giving reasons for their elimination, or by asking which idea is the most interesting and testing for consensus.

Step Four If more than one idea is favored, see if it is possible to combine several ideas or ask children to explain their reasons for liking a particular option. Now test again to see if there is common agreement.

Ages	4 to 10
When to Use	Teaching communication skills or before recess
Language	Bilingual
Location	Side 2, Song 31
Source	Roberto Díaz, Sarah Pirtle, and Luz Rodríguez

31 ¡Dilo!/Talk To Me

Children urge each other to talk out their problem.

OBJECTIVES

- to develop conflict resolution skills
- to develop bilingual language ability
- to become aware of the choice of talking out problems

PROCEDURE

1 Begin with the first verse. Decide whether you will use Spanish, English, or both languages. Teach the repeating phrases, "Dilo," and/or "Talk To Me," which have a similar meaning. Play the recording or sing the song. Ask students to join in on these repeating phases. For children ages seven and up, post the words so that students hear and see them at the same time.

2 Illustrate how to dramatize the first verse. Either work with one volunteer in front of the class or ask two students to act it out. At the start of the song, the two people are back to back, turned away from each other with their arms folded. They are in the midst of a conflict, and they aren't communicating. Gradually as the song is sung, first one and then the other turns around, until they are face to face. End the song with a handshake.

Now ask for other volunteers and form two lines of partners. Each pair starts back to back. Again, use just the first verse. As the song progresses, pairs turn around, dramatizing the decision to talk together. At the end, they conclude with a handshake.

Lead a discussion for children ages five and older. Play the tape or sing the whole song and ask students to tell you what thoughts they have about it. Ask: "How does the speaker in the song feel? Does the song remind you of something that has happened to you?"

Review the method used in your class for resolving conflicts.

¡Dilo! / Talk To Me

©1997 Words and Music by
Sarah Pirtle, Roberto Díaz, and Luz Rodríguez
Discovery Center Music, BMI

¡Dilo! Yo sé que es difícil.
¡Dilo! No debes rendirte.
¡Dilo! Es muy importante
que conservemos nuestra amistad.

Talk to me! I know it's not easy.
Talk to me! Don't give up now.
Talk to me! It's really important.
I want to be friends.

¡Dilo! ¿Qué es lo que piensas?
Dime. En qué puedo ayudarte.
¡Dilo! Es muy importante
que conservemos nuestra amistad.

Talk to me! What are you thinking?
Talk to me! How can I help you?
Talk to me! It's really important.
I want to be friends.

Translation Note: *Singing in Spanish, you may want to use "dime" instead of "dilo." "Dime" means "tell me," and "dilo" means "say it."*

Pronunciation Note: *"Conservemos" is pronounced "cone-ser-VAY-mos."*

· ·

E X T E N S I O N S

· ·

Find Your Words

· ·

As teachers we urge children to use their words, but they also need practice in knowing what words to say.

Chant Activity

Use your words. (Clap, clap)
What kind of words? (Clap, clap)
What kind of words will help? (Clap, clap)

Guess the Feeling

Ages: 6 and up

One person who is "it" pantomimes a feeling in response to a certain situation and the class will attempt to name the feeling being pantomimed. Present a situation to the person who is "it." Students or the teacher can prepare cards with suggested situations, or whisper their idea to the person who is "it."

1. The person who is "it" non-verbally communicates what he is thinking and feeling in that situation.

2. The person who is "it" picks one person to guess his feeling.

3. The person guesses the feeling.

4. The class calls: "¡Dilo!"

5. The person "it" says exactly what his or her feeling was.

Waiting For A Swing

Tell the class, "She is at recess waiting for a swing."

Tell the person "it," "You are at recess waiting for a swing. You are feeling upset because recess is almost over and you want a turn, but you are afraid to ask the person on the swing because he or she is a lot older then you."

Ripped Paper

Tell the class, "She has just finished writing a story she really likes."

Tell the person "it," "You feel angry when someone accidentally rips your paper without knowing it."

Lost Pet

Tell the class, "He has just walked around the neighborhood."

Tell the person "it," "You feel sad because your pet is lost."

Talk It Out Together Practice

Ages: 6 and older

Review the basic steps of negotiation and post them in words or pictures.

Using a role play, lead two volunteers through the Talk It Out Together Process. Provide one situation for a pair of students. Here are two examples:

Friends Want To Play Different Games
Setting Up The Role Play

Say, "Have you ever wanted to play a different game than your friend wanted to play? Let's think of two kinds of games, and each of you will pretend you want to play a different one. I'll be the person who is helping you talk out the problem. Why don't you start off by pretending to look upset?"

Leading the Negotiation

"I see there's a problem here. Can each of you tell me what you are feeling?" Give each child a turn to talk. "So the problem is that you both want to play different things. Can you think what you could do next? How can you work this out?"

Help them name solutions and check with both people until they find a solution that is agreeable to both.

A Special Book Gets Accidentally Hurt
Setting Up the Role Play

Say to the children, "Let's pretend that one of you has a book that you like a lot and you gave it to the other person to read. Pretend he took it home and on the way the book accidentally fell into a puddle. Which person do each of you want to be? Talk with each other and decide how damaged the book is. Can you still read it? Both of you begin by looking upset and I'll come over and ask if I can help you."

Leading the Negotiation

Ask, "Do you need help talking out a problem? Let's give each of you a turn explaining what the problem is." They explain the situation from their points of view. When they have finished, restate the problem and help the children move toward solutions. "I see. So the problem is when you borrowed the book, it accidentally got dirty from the puddle. Let's get some information. What does the book look like now? Can you still read it? What will help us?"

Start with the child who owns the book and ask what he or she would need to make the situation better. Then check which ideas are agreeable to the child who accidentally dropped it. Keep working until they have a plan both like.

Simultaneous Role Plays

Divide the whole class into pairs standing in two facing lines.

Before the drama starts, ask the students to clarify the situation, invent more details, and clarify who has which part. Following the role play, process it by asking for pairs to volunteer to show what they said to each other.

Examine each stage of the negotiation. Find out what partners said and identify how well they are using their skills. For example, one pair might be able to do step two and describe why they are upset, but might get stuck on thinking of ways to solve it.

Talk It Out Role Play: Audience Help

Grades 2 and older

Two friends are deciding what to do together after school.

Tell two volunteers the situation out of earshot of the rest of the class.

Tell person A, "You hurt your leg during recess and want to do less active things."

Tell person B, "You insist on playing soccer and don't give time for the other to explain that he or she can't play because of a hurt leg."

Give Person B these words to begin the drama: "Come on. You never want to play soccer."

Begin the drama. End the action by saying "cut" once both persons A and B have had a few chances to speak. Ask the class how Person A could respond. Then ask each actor to describe his or her thoughts and feelings about the problem.

With the whole class, brainstorm solutions to the situation.

Let the actors choose the ending.

Ask the actors to dramatize the implementation of their plan.

Afterwards ask a volunteer to go to the problem-solving chart and point out how the actors followed each step of the process.

RELATED SONGS

"Two in the Fight" (Song 25) is a complementary song. It introduces similar concepts through a humorous finger play.

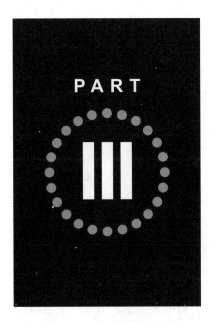

PART

III

Songs for Movement Games

●●

Let's get together with our hands.
— from "Let's Get Together" (Song 40)

Since time immemorial children have loved movement games. Whether engaged in "Ring-around-the-Rosy" from the British Isles or singing "Little Johnny Brown, lay your blanket down," from the Georgia Sea Islands, children feel nourished by the vitality and the camaraderie of group games. While they are having fun during movement games, they are also developing their ability to cooperate and collaborate with others.

The fifteen songs in the next three chapters ask children to move together in a range of different ways. Movement song games can be used throughout the day:

- For a movement break to help children re-focus.
- When the class can't play outside because of inclement weather.
- During transitions, such as when there are five more minutes before lunch or at the end of the day.
- To both the group together and build a close feeling of community.
- To help children feel anchored and centered.
- To enhance your curriculum (specific songs in this section compliment a science unit on animals, a social studies unit on boars, or a cultural study of Native American music.)

The songs in Part III are arranged in five different thematic Song Sequences on the recording:

1. Joining with Nature (Chapter 5)
2. Moving Together (Chapter 6)
3. Creating Mirrors, Bridges, and Shapes (Chapter 6)
4. Exploring Peace (Chapter 7)
5. Celebrating Community (Chapter 7)

HOW DO MOVEMENT EXPERIENCES AFFECT A CHILD?

Movement anchors us. It provides a sense of —I am!

I first heard that phrase from a dance teacher. I remember when she told our class, "Now we're going to get into our I am's." I knew what that meant. I'd bounce from leg to leg and really experience my feet in contact with the ground. I'd shift my shoulders and sway from side to side. I'd stomp the ground. Here I am. This is me. I can feel myself being me. When a child dances to "My Space/ Mi Espacio" (Song 6) she connects to the ground and to her own basic affirmation of "Here I am."

Anchoring is essential for everything a child does during the day. Whether learning addition, or reading, or talking out a conflict, growth depends upon a child feeling centered in his or her physical self and coming home to his or her own body.

Reggie moved like a spider, with his arms and legs extended. He often hit other children while laughing with a disconnected expression. Jeremy talked in a whisper. His body seemed retracted. His head pulled in and his arms extended only cautiously into the world.

A song that helped Jeremy was "Jump, Jump, Jump" (Song 7). Vigorously he jumped and experimented with moving farther away from his chair. I liked to see him jump with his mouth open in excitement and a light in his eyes.

When Reggie danced "My Space/ Mi Espacio" (Song 6) he didn't want to stand alone in his own space; he wanted to stand in another child's space. Alone he couldn't concentrate on which motions he wanted to do. His eyes darted around the room. Gradually he learned how to find his own personal space sufficient. He also benefitted from collaborative songs, like "Let's Get Together" (Song 40). As the year progressed, he learned how to look directly at the other children in his small group.

PROVIDING STRUCTURE DURING MOVEMENT GAMES

You'll need to provide clear guidelines for children to ensure everyone's safety during movement games.

Summary: How to Work with the Story Framework

Think about movement games like a story. Children completely enter the world of the characters. What is true for the characters–hunger, danger, curiosity–becomes true for them. Modify any story framework to add elements that insure group safety.

Example: Running Horses
Situation: Kindergarteners choose something they want the whole group to be, such as a cat, a horse, a monkey or a tiger as they move to the song, "My Roots Go Down" (Song 33).

Teacher: What do you want to put into the song, Kisha?

Kisha: A horse.

Teacher: What do you want the horse to do?

Kisha: Run around.

Teacher encourages child to add details.

Teacher: Okay. The horses are going to run. When horses run, they watch all around them and turn away before they bump into anything. Horses, get ready to look in every direction while you're running and galloping so no one will get bumped. Are you ready?

Teacher adds reminders to insure group safety.

Teacher leads new verse using child's words:

> *I am a horse. I'm running all around. (3x)*
> *I'm a running horse.*

WHEN A CHILD BRINGS IN POWER RANGERS

Summary: Extending the Story Framework

When a character from a TV show or other scripted toy is introduced, expand on the usually narrow story line. Offer alternatives to negative behaviors.

Example: Power Rangers

Situation: A child wants to be a Power Ranger for a verse of "My Roots Go Down" (Song 33). You have two responsibilities at that moment:

1. affirm the individual child
2. make sure that any story framework is congruent with group safety and mutual respect

Not recommended: "Well, we're certainly not going to be Power Rangers today." Instead, reframe the script. Children are attracted to the "power" of the Power Rangers. Provide a positive direction to express that power such as offering a job or responsibility that the character will carry out.

Look for other parts of a day in the life of a Power Ranger you can explore: What about Power Rangers having food together?

- Ask questions to involve children in elaborating upon the story framework: Is it a picnic? Where do they carry their food? Is it in their backpack? Where are they going to go to eat? How about if they have their picnic by a river?

- Develop opportunities for pantomime: They arrive and take out their favorite sandwich and favorite drink.

- Suggest a storyline which encourages positive human qualities: Maybe there are people nearby who have fallen out of a boat near a waterfall and need help.

Lee: I want to sing–I am a Power Ranger.

Teacher: And where are the Power Rangers going to travel?

Traveling is a different frame than fighting.

Lee: To the mountain.

Teacher: Okay. Let's imagine there are baby animals on that mountain and they are lost. They need help from the Power Rangers.

Suggests a powerful activity. Looks at Lee to see if this feels like acceptable framing. Lee nods and teacher feels it is okay to go ahead. Asks a question to return storyline to Lee.

Teacher: Lee, where in our room do you want the mountain to be?

Lee: The blocks.

Teacher recognizes the block area can create a bottleneck. Keeps suggestion but reframes.

Teacher: We'll need not to get too crowded on the top of that mountain. Whenever we need more space, we either stay in partners or stay in a line. How do you want to do this, Lee? Partners or a line?

Refers to previous space plan.

Lee: A line. I lead.

Teacher: Okay. You're the line leader to the mountain. Everyone think about what kind of baby animal you want to rescue. When we get to the mountain, we'll pick up that animal and bring it back. Let's practice picking up a baby animal. How can we help them feel safe?

The whole class is engaged.

Teacher sings:

> *I see that baby animal. I pick it up. (3x)*
> *Now you're safe.*

This gives children a chance to select their animal concretely by pantomime.

Lee: Power Rangers do it.
Teacher: You're the line leader to the mountain.
Teacher sings while the group dances.

> *I am a Power Ranger. I fly to the mountain.*
> *There's a baby animal that needs my help.*
> *I'll find that animal and bring it back.*
> *I can use my power.*

WHEN YOUNG CHILDREN DON'T GO ALONG WITH THE MOVEMENT

Summary: How to Follow Children's Lead

Follow children's lead and treat the unexpected behavior as a suggestion rather than a threat to your authority. React to the behavior as impulsive exploration or self-expression instead of as misbehavior. The children are giving us information about what they need to do. Modify the motions and bring them into the group as part of the song. "Let's try that together." By following their lead, we are modeling an essential skill—social responsiveness.

Consider:
- The developmental level of the child and the group members.
- Whether the behavior goes against a specific group agreement.

Example: An Outbreak of Stomping

Situation: The group is singing, "Wheels on the Bus."

Teacher: *The horn on the bus*
           goes honk, honk, honk.

(Four-year-old Gladys starts stomping her feet.
Half the group joins her.)

(Teacher stops leading the verse and watches the stomping feet).	**Teacher stops focus on horn honking and observes.**
Teacher: *The people on the bus* *go stomp, stomp, stomp.*	**Invents words to match with stomping.**

(Teacher observes wilder stomping and is concerned that children might lose self-control.) She changes the verse:
    People with their lunch
    say, chomp, chomp, chomp.
	Maintains safety.
	Keeps the vitality, but redirects the stomping to a new motion.

(Teacher pantomimes holding a sandwich while moving upper body with the same side-to-side motion as stomping.)	**Focuses the energy of the group.**

Children sing new verse:
    People with their lunch
    say, chomp, chomp, chomp.

(Some stomp and chomp at the same time.
All are more focused.)

Points to note:
- At every moment the teacher is firmly guiding the group.
- Song verses provide a boundary. A verse has a specific length—short and predictable. Children can stomp safely for the length of the verse and then stop.
- A large potentially aggressive motion (stomping) is changed to a focused, nonaggressive motion (chomping).

HOW TO FOLLOW CHILDREN'S LEAD

1. Let go of your plan and reshape it.

2. Observe what children are doing. Address needs they are expressing.

3. Acknowledge children with open body language and look for a way to connect with a child in words or movement.

4. If possible, take the movements children are showing you and bring them into the song or game. Frame their actions into an activity everyone can do.

5. Evaluate whether the action would be unsafe or disruptive and make modifications to insure group safety. If actions are inappropriate, offer limited choices.

6. Provide a clear framework. Make up new words or a game that correspond to the actions they are suggesting.

CHAPTER 6 Nature Exploration Songs

My roots go down,
down to the earth.
— from "My Roots Go Down" (Song 33)

The three songs in this chapter help children know they are part of the earth. In Native American culture, songs are used to allow children to enter the natural world, and with it, a whole value system. The "Night Critters Game" (Song 34) includes two traditional Native American songs I learned from Ernest Siva. He says, "I think it is important to keep other worlds alive in our imagination. We actually go to these different worlds through song and story."

Songs can take children to a sacred timeless space. When children become engrossed in being eagles leaving their nest in the "My Roots Go Down" game, it is as if they have entered into another dimension. They are the eagle and they feel their feathers and the wind. These are moments that allow for transformation, where a child previously stuck in a behavior or thought can become unstuck. And by asking children to create movements, their actions bring them more fully into the sphere of the song. When we touch the earth, we link to one another.

Old-Fashioned Teachings in a Song by Ernest Siva

In this so-called modern world of ours, we see all sorts of social problems around us. We cannot read a newspaper without noticing senseless acts of violence, especially involving our youth. Poverty of spirit and lack of time-tested values appears to be key.

Without a belief in something greater than one's own being, you have a false sense of pride. My grandfather called this, 'tirvatc ahurki.' This means people with shallow roots, like the grass, which quickly withers and dies. There is no depth to their life and being. When they look at a tree, they may see it as a nuisance, or maybe as a nice shade tree. They do not see the great beauty and mystery of spirit.

For me growing up, instruction for living was a daily affair. Respect for older people was especially important, because they were the keepers and purveyors of great knowledge. They knew the plants, the animals, the stars and planets, kinships, the history of the people, stories, and songs.

We were told that everything was alive and special. That is, all of creation was put here for a purpose, and that we, too, were special and had life as a gift. There was power all around us. We had to do good by our neighbor, to respect him. In fact, we were to respect all of creation. Most of this knowledge was encapsulated in special songs. The songs were the key to enter the next world. Is it any wonder then, why songs are held in such high regard?

Ages 3 to 9

When to Use Science integra-
tion, movement
exploration, or
developing lan-
guage in Spanish
and English

Language Bilingual

Location Side 2, Song 32

Source Traditional Latin
American

32 El Caracol/ The Snail's Dance

Children pretend to be snails moving in and out of their shells.

● ●

OBJECTIVES

- to cooperate in pairs or small groups
- to imitate a snail's undulation

PROCEDURE

1 Read the words of this song as a poem in Spanish or English, using whichever language is more familiar for your students. If possible, show a snail shell or a picture of a snail.

2 Using one hand as the shell of the snail and the other hand as the body, dramatize the story by moving your hands as you say the words again. Ask the children, "Why does the snail come out?" Let children give their own imaginative explanations.

3 Tell the children, "Snails don't have bones. Their muscles move in waves." Select a movement activity from the extensions that best fits your group.

Some Facts About the Common Air-Breathing, White-lipped Snail

● ●

Size
the shell is one inch when full grown

Habitat
the forest

Speed
crawls across a two-inch leaf in a minute

Food
soil, fungus, plants such as the leaves of the nettle

Eaten by
mice, birds, shrews, moles, glow worms, immature fireflies, some other snails.

Habits
hibernates in the winter under a stone until the spring rains.

Reproduction
Lays 30 to 40 eggs when mature.

NOTE

Snails need to be cool and damp, which puts the traditional words a bit at odds with the scientific facts. The words imply that the snail is attracted to the sun, yet many snails live underwater, and those on land avoid the hot noonday sun, preferring cool and cloudy days.

Here's an alternate text in English that you can use as a substitute. It doesn't emphasize the sun, but focuses on the time of day and the action of coming out of the shell:

> *Little snail come out. Now the morning's here.*
> *Come out of your house for your food is near.*

Snails absorb rainwater through their skin and store water inside their shell. This allows them to excrete the mucus they need to create a sticky path. If they are out of water, they seal up until rain comes. Here's an additional verse that recognizes snails' need for water:

> *Little snail come out. Can you feel the rain?*
> *You can fill your shell, then you'll glide again.*

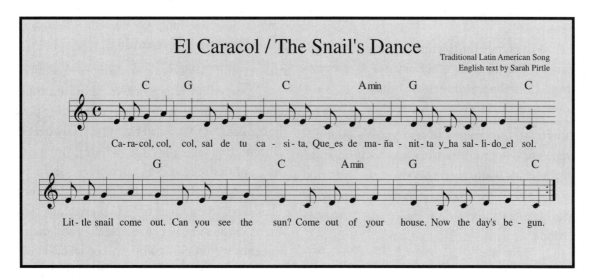

El Caracol / The Snail's Dance

Traditional Latin American Song
English text by Sarah Pirtle

Ca-ra-col, col, col, sal de tu ca-si-ta, Que_es de ma-ña-nit-ta y_ha sal-li-do_el sol.

Lit-tle snail come out. Can you see the sun? Come out of your house. Now the day's be-gun.

Caracol, col, col, sal de tu casita,
Que es de mañanita y ha salido el sol.

Little snail come out.
Can you see the sun?
Come out of your house.
Now the day's begun.
La, la, la, la, la (4x)

Caracol, col, col, vuelva a tu casita
Que es de nochecita y se ha puesto el sol.

Little snail go home.
Now the sun is gone.
Go back to your house

for the day is done.
La, la, la, la, la (4x)

Pronunciation Guide
Kara COL COL COL sal de TU ka-see-ta
Keh-es deh MAN-nyah-NEE-ta ya-sa LEE
doel sol

Kara COL COL COL vuel-va TU ka-see-ta
Keh-es deh NO-chay SEE-ta ee-seh-ah
PUES tuel sol

Note: *I learned this song from Cherie Greene Moraga. She urges teachers to let children find their own ways of moving to the words.*

Movement Activities

Be a Snail

Ages: 3 to 5

Have children start by pretending to be snails curled up in their shells. Play the songs. As they hear the words, ask them to move out of their shells and then return. They can also move in pairs. Cherie Greene Moraga suggests that children take turns as the sun and the snail and then switch places.

The Snail Dance

Ages: 5 to 8

Learn the lyrics line by line in one or both languages. Form small groups of three to five children. Help the children discuss how they want to act out the story.

Illustrate the process of group decision making. Ask one group to work with you in front of the class while the others watch. Your role is to be a coach. Ask questions and provide guidance as the children make their own decisions.

Ask, "What part do each of you want to take?" Go around the circle and let each child choose his or her part. Agree that every child can be exactly what he or she wants to be, even if it means having five snails. Children can also choose to be a part of nature not directly mentioned in the song.

Say, "Knowing who you each want to be, how will you work together? Where will you each be when the song starts?" Encourage them to try their movements together.

Sing or play the song. Give them a chance to act out leaving and returning.

After seeing the decision-making process modeled, have all groups work on planning their dance using these same steps. After they pick their roles, let them practice at their own pace without the tape playing. When groups are ready, play the music as they move. Children like to repeat the song and act out different roles. Give them more time to plan again. Ask them to select one way of doing the snail dance that they would like to show to the whole class. Share the dances. Watch one or two groups at a time.

Tip!

- Expect noise as children plan together and experiment with how they want to move. Use a bell or drum as a come-back signal.

- Use the game "Let's Get Together" (Song 40) as a warm-up to develop cooperation skills in small groups before creating the snail dance with the same group of children.

- Support the children's way of telling the story. Instead of saying, "A snail doesn't move like that. Snails are supposed to be slow," or "Why did you put a tree in the song? It's not in the words," give them freedom to create it their own way. As they select their parts, ask: "Do you want to be a snail, the snail's house, or the sun? You can make the story your own way. It's fine to add extra parts like a tree, the rain, or a flower."

- The actions of retreating into and then coming out of a hiding place are deeply satisfying for many children. Some like to create elaborate snail shell houses. Some like to stay inside their shells.

ADDITIONAL RESOURCES

The Sunshine Reading Series published by the Wright Group features three big books about snails by Chris Brough: *How Snails Live, How Snails Protect Themselves,* and *The Life Cycle of a Snail.* For orders and information call 1-800-523-2371.

Ryder, Joan. *Snail in the Woods.* (San Francisco: Harper and Row, 1979.) This is a Nature I CAN READ book for ages 4 to 8.

Latin American song games: *Ritmos, Cantos Y Juegos / Rhythms, Songs and Games* by Francisco Aquino y Cherie Greene Moraga is a bilingual guide of 32 Latin American game songs including "El Caracol." Book and tape are available from: Rayito de Sol Publications, 1311 Lodgewood Way, Oxnard, CA 93030-3313.

Ages	2 to adult
When to Use	Cooperative movement game, whole language, or science studies
Language	English
Location	Side 2, Song 33
Source	Sarah Pirtle

33 My Roots Go Down

Children act out movements that connect them to nature.

OBJECTIVES

- to create new words and movements
- to collaborate with others
- to bond with nature

PROCEDURE

1 Preview the song "My Roots Go Down" to familiarize yourself with the music, the lyrics, and the pattern of the song.

2 Have the children stand with enough room to move in place without bumping into others. During this song children keep their feet anchored in place and swing their arms, as if their arms were the branches of a tree. During the chorus of the song, encourage children to feel the earth under their feet. Notice whether children's movements indicate that they are feeling rooted and anchored. Ask the children, "Can you feel your feet planted firmly on the ground?"

3 Have the children create different movements as they sing the chorus. For example, suggest stomping.

4 Sing verses that connect children to animals, trees, and places in nature. Some examples:

I am a willow swaying in a storm. (3x)
My roots go down.

I am a wildflower pushing through stones. (3x)
My roots go down.

I am a waterfall skipping home. (3x)
My roots go down.

My Roots Go Down

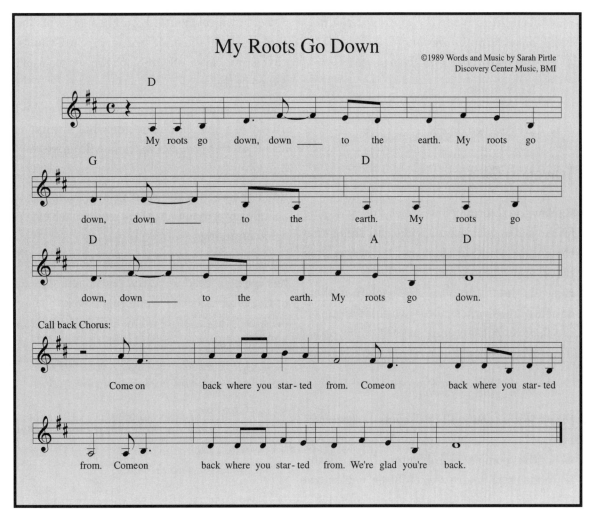

©1989 Words and Music by Sarah Pirtle
Discovery Center Music, BMI

Chorus

My roots go down, down to the earth.
My roots go down, down to the earth.
My roots go down, down to the earth.
My roots go down.

Verse

I am a pine tree on a mountainside.
I am a pine tree on a mountainside.
I am a pine tree on a mountainside.
My roots go down.

. . . .

E X T E N S I O N S

. . . .

Children Invent New Words

Ask the children for a suggestion of an animal or something else in nature that they like a lot. Ask, "What shall we put in the song to-day?" Example: A child could answer, "Jumping beans." Then the teacher can extend the thought to create a whole verse. The group jumps as everyone sings:

I am a jumping bean, jumping to the sun. (3x)
My roots go down.

Whenever possible, ask the children to expand upon their ideas and use their words to extend the verse. Example:

> **Teacher***: What do you want to be?*
> **Isabelle***: Dolphins.*

Teacher: *What do you want the dolphins to do in the song?*
Isabelle: *Dive into the waves.*

New verse

I am a dolphin diving in the waves (3x).
My roots go down.

Traveling Game

Review the recording and notice the variations in the lyrics that are provided. In this game the children act out their own verses as they travel around the room. Then the revised chorus calls the children to come back from their dancing and sit once more with their group on the floor or on their chairs:

> *Come on back where you started from. (3x)*
> *We're glad you're back.*

Plan the area that will be used for large movement. Use a scarf or rope to close off any areas of the room as "out of bounds." Clarify the boundaries of where the children can move.

Set clear agreements. Examples: stay on the rug, or stay in the middle of our circle of chairs, or the rope closes off our block area so we won't dance in there.

Using the songwriting method described above, ask one child to decide what animal or other part of nature everyone will be as they dance.

Set agreements for safe group movement. Examples: remember to look out for each other, or no bumping.

Children dance and dramatize the story that has been created until the "call back" chorus of the song calls the group to go back to their original places.

Verse

I am a deer running in the wind. (3x)
and come on back.

Chorus

And come on back where you started from. (3x)
We're glad you're back.

Expanding on Children's Ideas

Here's how the Eggs in a Nest game first got started. When I invited first graders in Port Reyes, California, to make the shape of a nest, to my surprise, one boy unexpectedly got inside the center of the nest and curled up very small. "I'm a rotten egg," he said. The class had been reading a chapter of *Charlotte's Web* that morning, where a rotten egg makes a big stink in the farmyard. Knowing that he often made disparaging comments about himself, I wanted to explore what would happen if I worked with the image and offered more possibilities.

"Rotten?" I said. "It looks like there's a bird growing inside here." I led the group in singing new words: "This is the day the new bird is born." We watched as he gradually uncurled himself and came out of the shell as a newborn eagle. Then others took turns being eggs in the center and emerging.

Check on the agreements. Discuss if anyone bumped into anyone else. Make sure that all feel safe as they travel. On the recording this process is modeled:

> **Ryan**: *Let's do—I am a bear catching fish.*
>
> **Peter**: *But last time we did that somebody caught me.*
>
> **Teacher**: *What agreements could we make?*
>
> **Ryan**: *How about if we say that the people aren't the fish. We're all the bears and we have to pretend we see fish.*

Give other children a chance to create new verses. Add any reminders or additions to the "story framework" that are necessary to ensure that all will feel safe.

Variation

Instead of all children dancing at once, pick four at a time to dance while the others sing. Singers clap, tap their legs, or drum on the floor to retain their interest.

Birds in Flight

Review the lyrics on the recording.

> *I am a bird flying through the sky. (3x)*
> *And come back to your nest.*

Make a nest by joining hands with your whole group or in small groups of three to eight people. Children ages five to eight enjoy inventing their own ways to link with each other, either standing or sitting (i.e., all hands in the center like spokes of a wheel or hands up high meeting in the middle like a roof).

To help children be aware of each member of their group, ask them to wave good-bye before they leave the nest. Children fly away from the nest as they dance, then return and form the nest shape again.

Tip!

Use the eggs in the nest game to bring a feeling of calm to your class. This game has a particular poignancy. As children have the chance to transition from being in an egg to pecking their way out and being greeted by friendly faces, a hush and expectancy comes over the game. Take time in the narration to help the children emerge slowly from their eggs.

Science Extension

Be an Eagle

Eagles are social birds and enjoy gathering together when they aren't raising their young ones. Explore what it would feel like to fly with the strength of the eagle. Imagine watching an eagle soaring above the plains. The bald eagle's broad wings stretch as far as seven feet. Think about the way an eagle can look from high above and spot tiny objects. Ask children to fly with the feeling of an eagle.

Eggs in the Nest

Ask for volunteers to pretend to be eggs curled up in the center of the nest. Those standing around them are the parents waiting for the babies to be born.

Tell the children, "This is the day the eggs are waking up. The baby birds inside the eggs feel warmth and they start to peck their way out of the shells. Their parents are waiting. They are so glad to see them come out of their eggs. When they are ready the parents teach them to fly."

Encourage those children playing the parent birds to help the babies fly around the space. Sing words that relate to the process.

Examples:

Show us your strong wings as you fly.
We're happy to see you flying with us.
The babies are learning to fly so far.
Now come back to your nest.

Cooperation in Small Groups

Divide the class into small groups of three to five children who will move together, sitting or standing, on each verse. Ask them to sit or stand together in a circle. Provide verses that lend themselves to collaboration:

- *We are whales swimming with our friends. (3x)*
  And come on back.

- *We are a stream with swirling ripples. (3x)*
  And come on back.

- *We are flowers opening to the light. (3x)*
  And come on back.

- *We are monkeys jumping through the vines. (3x)*
  And come on back.

After the children have collaborated on acting out verses you suggest, have them work in their small groups to develop their own dance using a verse that they make up. Invite each group to show their dance to the whole class.

Cooperative Songwriting

A classroom of second graders in Conway, Massachusetts, assembled in groups of three. For their science studies each individual had studied an animal she particularly liked. First, they each discussed the animal's habits, and then chose a phrase to form the verse of the song. Next, they created motions to go with their animals. Here is a verse from one of the small groups:

I'm a sidewinder snake sliding over the desert.
I am a prairie dog popping from my hole.
I am a lion prowling the savanna.
My roots go down.

All three children acted out all three animals together, changing from snakes, to prairie dogs, to lions.

When experience with collaboration is limited, participation within the groups may be uneven. One child may dominate and not listen to the ideas others offer. Some may look away or distract others. If needed, guide your class step by step through the process of collaboration:

Step One: Provide a clear image in the verse, like: "We are beavers building a new lodge."

Step Two: Ask each person on his own to create a movement that fits the story framework the group selected.

Step Three: Number off (each child gets a number from 1 to 3, 4, or 5). One at a time have each child show her movements to the group. For example, to the words, "We are beavers building a new house," one person might decide to concentrate on tapping the mud, while another thinks of carrying branches. Let the children know that is okay to pass.

Step Four: Say, "Put all the ideas together. Make sure to use at least one idea from each person."

Ages	4 to 10 years
When to Use	Circle Time or Native American studies
Language	Cahuilla and Serrano
Location	Side 2, Song 34
Source	Ernest H. Siva teaches these two songs from his Cahuilla and Serrano traditions

34 Night Critters Game

Children become nocturnal animals who explore the world when the sun is down and hide when the morning star comes up.

● ●

OBJECTIVES

- to be aware of other dancers
- to enter the animal world
- to sing in the Cahuilla and Serrano Native American languages

PROCEDURE

1 Explain that two Native American songs will alternate in this game. One song is Cahuilla and one Serrano. The Serrano and the Cahuilla are two Native American nations of southern California. Play the "Night Critters Game" on the recording.

2 Help children picture the contrast of night and day in the song. Explain that nocturnal animals hide when the first star comes up. They don't want the light to illuminate them so that other critters can find them.

3 Help children learn the songs by walking together in a circle. Tell them that first they will be the night critters and then the morning star. Start with "Kaich Akuum/The Mountain Sleeps." All children stalk slowly as night critters. Ask the children to stay in line, leaving space for each person to have enough room. Younger children may enjoy crawling.

Next, as the slow music changes to the rapid tune of "Soweta Nena/Song of the Morning Star," stand in place. Tell the children, "Now we are the morning star. Let's face each other and flick our fingers like we are sending rays of light. You can also stomp your feet." Explain to the children, "We're not doing a traditional Native American dance, but we're making up our own way of moving to the music. That is part of the tradition—we make up movements to help us go into the story of the song."

4 Explain the meaning of both songs (see the following "Accurate translation" and "Modified translation").

Kaich Akuum, The Mountain Goes to Sleep

Accurate translation

The mountain sleeps, the mountain sleeps!
Let's go sneak, let's go wander.
The mountain sleeps, the mountain sleeps!

Modified translation

Wander around, sneak around,
the mountains are sleeping.
Wander around, sneak around,
the mountains are sleeping.

Note: *Ernest Siva explains that this song instructs children about the mountain. When the mountain goes to sleep, all of the night critters come out. They are the ones who wander around for food. They call to each other: "Let's go sneak around. Let's go wander."*

Soweta Nena, The Morning Star
A traditional Cahuilla dance song

Chorus/Pronunciation Guide

Soweta nena (3x)
´So - we-eh -eta néy-na

Modified Translation

The morning star appears. The owl and the other creatures talk to each other and say, "Hide." The morning star tells us soon the sun will be here.

"Soweta" means star. "Nena" means aunt or revered one.

Note: *This section of "Soweta Nena" is a small refrain in one of the bird song cycles. These are migration songs. They reflect the life of the people moving around like birds in the seasons, following what the earth offered for food, moving from winter to summer houses. In the bird song cycles, five or six related songs are grouped together. The next sections of "Soweta Nena," not included here, sing of the California Thrasher and other birds calling to each other.*
When a song becomes your own, you change it. So even though I worked with Ernest Siva to be as accurate as possible, these traditional songs are now a step removed from their source. Ernest Siva invites non-Native Americans into this music, and encourages us to acknowledge, "This is the way that I sing this song."

Facilitating "Song of the Morning Star"

Second graders in Andover, Massachusetts, stand in a circle. "Who will be the mountains for the dance?" I ask. Three children come into the center and stand tall with their legs apart. Those who remain in the outside ring choose to be animals who stalk for food at night. During "The Song of the Morning Star," the fingers of the children in the outer ring flick like the rays of the star. When the sun goes down and the mountains are asleep, they become the animals leaving their sleeping spots. They stalk around, in and out of the mountains. The mountains keep their eyes closed until suddenly the sun returns. As the mountains awaken, the animals hurry back to their original spots.

After several groups have taken turns being mountains, the children are asked to explain what animals they were. They take turns going into the center and pantomiming their animal while we guess. Then, I take out the book, *The Cahuilla*, and talk about the origins of the songs.

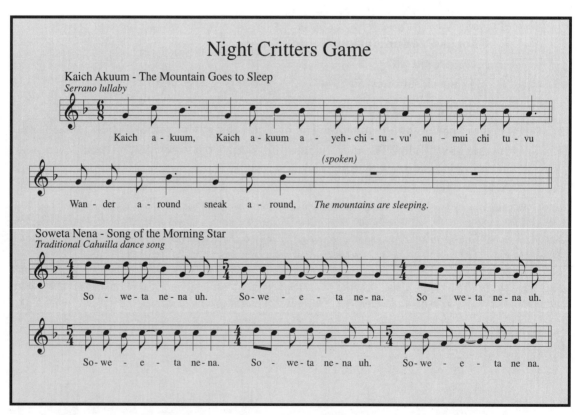

Kaich Akuum, The Mountain Sleeps
Traditional Serrano lullaby

The mountain goes to sleep—kaich akuum—and all of the night critters come out and look for food. We sneak around and we sing:

*Kaich akuum, kaich akuum
ayehchituvu' numuichituvu'
kaich akuum, kaich akuum.*

[Pronunciation: Ki-cha-kum, Ki-cha-kum
Uhya chit a-voo neh-moy chit a-voo
Ki-cha-kum, Ki-cha-kum.]

Enter the Animal World

Explain that everyone will be animals throughout the whole song. Help the children to find a place on the floor that will be their home. They begin there and return after they wander. Invite the children to become involved in creating their movements.

Set the stage: "Animals, the sun is up and that's not the time when you like to explore the world. Curl in your home and wait for the sun to go down."

Then begin "Kaich Akuum/The Mountain Sleeps." Say, "Now the mountains are sleeping. The sun is down. It's safe to come out and look around. As you wander around, the animals you see are not your food. They are your friends. You can say hello to them as you sneak by. What are the places you are exploring?"

Then say, "Remember, the morning star will be returning. Get ready to go back to your home. Animals, here comes the light. Be careful of each other as you find your own space." Begin "Soweta Nena/Song of the Morning Star." Tell them, "Time to rest while the light is shining. Wait for the night to return when the mountains go to sleep again."

Mountains in the Center

Everyone begins in a circle. Ask, "Who wants to be a mountain?" Select two to four children and ask them to stand very still in the center. Leave space between the children in the center and the outer ring. Children in the outside ring are the animals or the night critters.

If you like, as a transition to the song, invent a story about the mountain: "The mountain had a busy day. Bears walked on his shoul-

ders. Birds perched on his head. And then the sun went down and he went to sleep."

Instruct the mountains to stay standing but to droop their heads and close their eyes.

Have everyone chant "Kaich Akuum/The Mountain Sleeps" and play the song recording. Children from the outside circle tiptoe and walk lightly around each other and the sleeping mountains. They listen for the sudden switch in the music.

"Soweta Nena/Song of the Morning Star" begins. Everyone—mountains included—imitates the rays of the star's light by extending their hands and waving their fingers with emphasis on the beat.

Keep contrasting the two songs, singing first one and then the other. End with "Soweta Nena/Song of the Morning Star."

Nocturnal Animals

Discuss specific animals who are primarily nocturnal. Examples of nocturnal animals who hunt or forage at night include raccoons, skunks, and opossums. Animals who travel either in the daytime or in the night include coyotes, bears, fox, and mice. The owl is a nocturnal bird. The most valuable animals to the Cahuilla are the mule deer, mountain sheep, and antelope (pronghorn deer). Ask each child to select what animal they will be during the dance. If you like, children can keep their choices secret and reveal them at the end of the game.

Social Studies

The Serrano and the Cahuilla are Native American nations of southern California. They are the first people of the inland Los Angeles region. Some lived in the desert and some in mountainous areas. Ernest H. Siva, from Banning, California, is preserving the songs and the language of his culture. He is an ethnomusicologist and has now retired as a professor at UCLA.

Serrano Language

When you see the mark ('), it indicates a glottal stop. A glottal stop is an interruption of the breath stream during speech.

Serrano numbers:

1. Hoopk
2. Worh'
3. Paahi'
4. Wachah
5. Mahatc
6. Pavorhi'
7. Wachowik
8. Wawch
9. Mukovik
10. Wahmahatc

Some Serrano words and phrases:

Hakop a'aih! "It is very good!"

Haminut omih' nupuyam. "How are you my friends."

Tumurntc "antelope"

ADDITIONAL RESOURCES

The Cahuilla by Lowell John Bean and Lisa Bourgeault, (New York: Chelsea House Publishers, 1989).

You can receive booklets on either the Cahuilla or the Serrano ($2 each) or receive an extensive lists of books on language, healing with plants, and other customs from: Malki Museum Press, Morongo Indian Reservation, Banning, CA 92220.

CHAPTER 7

Collaboration Songs

Wave your hands like clouds in the sky.
Look each other in the eye.
— from "Cloud Hands" (Song 38)

Songs in this chapter develop children's awareness and skills around collaboration through movement. When a child is standing with a partner to move hands like clouds or working with others to create the shape of a boat, he or she has an important invitation—to contribute cooperatively toward the shared experience. Learning happens concretely. A child calls out "I'm squished," instead of pushing in frustration. Others listen to the message, react responsively, and accommodate the shape of the circle to make room. Moments like these develop collaboration skills.

The lyrics to the six songs in this chapter provide clear instructions for the movement actitivies as well as guidelines to help the game progress smoothly. For instance, the words of "Cloud Hands" (Song 38) urge participants to focus on their partners—"Look each other in the eye." "Under the Bridge" (Song 39) encourages children making the bridge to watch out for the children going underneath. And "Shake, Shake, Freeze" (Song 36) contrasts free movement with sudden stops helping children practice self-control.

In preparation for using these song games, it will be important to ask yourself:
- How much space does this song require? What part of the room will we use?
- Are there sections of the song that we will need to practice in advance before we play the game? For example, to play "Under the Bridge" (Song 39), can children form bridges with their hands and leave enough room underneath for children to pass?
- If the game uses partners or small groups, how will the groups be assigned? Which children do you want to work together?
- Has the class had enough practice with self-control and with respecting the personal space of others to be able to do the more challenging game "Let's Get Together" (Song 40)?

Additionally the songs in this chapter can be used without leading singing, if you like, by playing them on the recording.

Ages 4 to 9

When to Use Circle Time,
work projects

Language English

Location Side 2, Song 35

Source Sarah Pirtle

35 Build A Boat

Children pretend to row across a river together.

● ●

OBJECTIVES

- to synchronize movements
- to collaborate
- to build community

PROCEDURE

1 Teach the song in a circle. Describe what it means to row a boat. Join hands around the circle and pretend to row together as you play the recording or sing the song.

2 Create movement patterns to accompany the song that are simple or complex. Here's a simple one: children group together in pairs or trios. They hold each others' waists and move together in a conga line with the leader of the line making the rowing motion. After a few minutes, reverse direction so that the person in the back is now the leader. Another idea is to stay together as a whole group all pretending to row. Move in one direction together around the circle or around the classroom. As a variation, hold scarves to keep connected.

3 If you are playing an instrument to accompany the song, you may prefer to use easier chords than the ones listed in the transcription. The song is recorded and transcribed in the key of B flat. You can sing it instead in the key of C. Play these chords:

Part A

C
Build a boat now to cross the sea.

G   C
There's room for you and there's room for me.

C   G   C
There's room for the whole family to cross the water now.

Part B

C
Don't give up, keep on going.

F
Don't give up, keep on going.

C
Don't give up, keep on going.

G   C
Cross the water now.

1. This song can be used to heighten focus during work projects because of the rhythm and the repeating line, "Don't give up."

   Example:
   A kindergarten class is moving the block corner to a new location. They assemble in a line and use the song to add focus and fun to their work. First, they change the words:

   Pass the blocks now across the sea.
   There's help from you and there's help from me.
   There's help from our class family.
   We're going to move them all.
   Don't give up, keep on going ...
   We're going to move them all.

2. Lead a classroom unit on boats. Each day during the week repeat the song, adding something more to the movement pattern.

Monday	Circle the classroom.
Tuesday	Small groups make a conga line.
Wednesday	Give each small group a long scarf or cloth to share.
Thursday	Groups start on different sides of the river.
Friday	Carry stuffed toys across the river.

Build a Boat

©1997 Words and Music by Sarah Pirtle
Discovery Center Music, BMI

Part A

Build a boat now to cross the sea.
There's room for you and
there's room for me.
There's room for the whole family
to cross the water now.

Part B

Don't give up, keep on going.
Don't give up, keep on going.
Don't give up, keep on going.
Cross the water now.

Optional words

Don't give up, keep on rowing.

A Look At Boats

Create a bulletin board of pictures of boats. Include boats propelled by a group paddling together. Talk about the group effort needed to sail the boat. Look for pictures of indigenous peoples of the past and of today. Represent a variety of cultures such as the Mayans, Egyptians, Vikings, the Pacific Islanders, and the people of the Caribbean.

Cross a River

Ages: 4 to 6
Materials: Ribbons, scarves, or chairs to use as boundaries

Define where the river is by using ribbons, scarves, or chairs. Choose a method to travel across the river. Here are some examples:

- Children row their own way as they stay in line and cross over the river with a teacher leading the group.

- Keep together. Using synchronized rowing, the group crosses together, stepping to the beat as they walk across.

- A line leader pantomimes rowing. The others hold the waist of the person ahead of them like a conga line.

- Form two lines that pass by each other, each from different banks of the river.

Small Boats

Ages: 5 to 9
Optional Materials: Scarves, streamers, or cardboard.

A small group of three or four children creates the shape of a boat by the way they hold their arms and link up. Children connect to each other and move together across the river. Try these methods of crossing:

- One person stands in the middle of a circle of hands. He or she pretends to look out of a spyglass or acts the part of the sail.

- One foot: the members of the small group each stand on one foot, stay connected, and hop across.

- Carrying (for ages 7 to 9): One person in a small group is carried by the other members, making sure all feel safe.

Optional Props:
Give each group scarves to use as sails for their boat. Create the waves of the ocean by shaking scarves or streamers. Half the class makes the waves while the other half dances, then they switch roles. Or, use cardboard to create the sides of the boat.

Symbol of Change

For older groups, talk about the symbol of crossing a great body of water. This symbol appears in many cultures to represent a big change for an individual or for a community. The song can be used to celebrate a big change or turning point in the life of a classmate or to mark a transition made by the whole class. Add new words to the song to reflect the change. Form two facing lines. The child being honored walks down the aisle while the others sing and clap to the beat.

Ages	4 to 9
When to Use	Circle Time or for an energizing break
Language	Bilingual
Location	Side 2, Song 36
Source	Sarah Pirtle

36 Shake, Shake, Freeze

Children explore movement in a stop-and-go rhythm.

● ●

OBJECTIVES

- to alternate movement and self-control
- to respect social boundaries

PROCEDURE

1 You can play this game from any seating arrangement—in a circle, in rows, or chairs by desks. Plan ahead which area will be used when the children start to move.

2 Begin with the children seated. Clarify that when children hear the word, "freeze," they become completely still. Ask the children to make a movement with their hands and arms when they hear the word, "shake." Check that the children stop their movements on "freeze."

3 This song develops incrementally. Use motions that work when children are sitting down:

- roll your hands
- bounce
- flick (flicking your fingers open and shut)
- tap feet
- move your fingers
- rock
- wave elbows (sing, "elbows")
- lift shoulders

4 As you explore different movements you can modify the lyrics of the song. For example, while exploring finger movements sing, "Fingers, fingers, fingers, fingers, fingers, and FREEZE." When moving the elbows sing, "Elbows, elbows, elbows, elbows, elbows, and FREEZE."

5   For the next round, ask the children to stand. Suggest movements that are easy to do standing in place:

- twist (while keeping feet in place)
- twirl
- stretch
- make waves
- shake
- jump
- bend
- sway
- stamp
- hop

Again, have children stop their movements when they hear the word, "Freeze."

6   For the next round, suggest motions for moving through space:

Note: *Before you begin this section, tell the children it is very important to watch for each other and not to bump into anyone.*

- walk
- wave (to the people you pass by)
- shake hands
- curl (clasping hands in front, stay standing but curl and curve around the other people)
- swim (press hands together like a fin, stay standing)
- skip
- leap
- gallop
- skip

Again, have children stop their movements when they hear the word, "Freeze." Check back to see if anyone got bumped. Encourage children to interact as they move through space by waving and shaking hands.

At the end of the song, the music slows down.

The lyrics are:

> *Moving slow like you're going through*
> *peanut butter.*
> *Moving slow like you're going through*
> *peanut butter.*
> *Moving slow, moving slow, and end up in*
> *your place.*

Teacher Facilitation Guidelines

Overview: Your goal as leader is to meet the children where they are. Select movements children can do successfully. Build the movements incrementally:

- seated, e.g., rolling your hands
- standing, e.g., stretching
- moving through space slowly, e.g., walking
- moving in and out of the other movers, e.g., flying

Use these guidelines for choosing motions:

1. Work within the movement abilities of the group. Example: If you notice that children lose self-control while seated, wait until another day to progress to standing.

2. Build up at a pace that suits the group. Example: If they are eager and able to go directly to full body movement, use only one seated motion.

3. Provide contrast. Examples: Follow fast hopping with slow wave movements; use eye blinking to give a moment to rest.

4. If they need a framework while moving in space, try slow sustained motions like "swimming" through the space with hands pressed together, but not fast motions like "flying."

5. Acknowledge the movement abilities of individuals. If there are children who cannot walk or have other physical limitations, give directions with inclusive language that provide choices: "On this next section you can walk or you can shake your fingers." Sing, *"Walk or shake your fingers and FREEZE."* Select a movement that a child with physical disabilities can do and begin the game there: "Nod your head and nod and FREEZE," or "Twist your shoulders and twist and FREEZE."

6. Consider the types of movements that might benefit your group that day. As you watch for nonverbal signals, what actions do children seem to need? Do they want more vigorous activity? Do they want more connection with each other? Examples: If the group needs forceful expression, have the children stomp. If the group needs to look at each other and make connections, have them shake hands as they walk.

7. Ask the children what movements they would like to do. Say, "What shall we do next? You decide." Include nonverbal children by recognizing their preferences. For example, "Let's join Jamie. I notice that you like to blink your eyes, Jamie. How about if we do, 'Blink your eyes, and blink and freeze.'"

Help the children respect social agreements. Notice whether children are holding the freeze and whether boundaries are being respected. The attitude I use is firm but playful. I don't want to imply that I expect certain children to have trouble, so I scan the whole group equally. I take the attitude of a firm boundary holder.

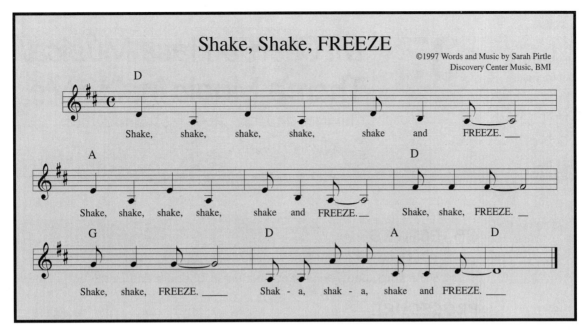

Shake, Shake, FREEZE

©1997 Words and Music by Sarah Pirtle
Discovery Center Music, BMI

English

Shake, shake, shake, shake, shake and FREEZE.

Shake, shake, shake, shake, shake and FREEZE.

Shake, shake, FREEZE.

Shake, shake, FREEZE.

Shaka, shaka, shake and FREEZE.

Spanish

Muevete, muevete, muevete y PARA.

Muevete, muevete, muevete y PARA

Muevete, PARA.

Muevete, PARA.

Muevete y PARA.

These are the six motions heard on the recording.

1. *shake / muevete*
2. *stretch / estirate*
3. *hop / salta*
4. *walk / camina*
5. *swim / nada*
6. *moving slow like you're going through peanut butter / muevete como si estuviera caminando a través de mantequilla de maní*

ADDITIONAL RESOURCES

Ella Jenkins has inspired generations of educators. Her work sustained me as a classroom teacher. When I heard her song, "You Walk and You Stop" twenty years ago, it taught me to make use of pauses in songs. Ella Jenkins' recordings are available through Smithsonian/ Folkways Recordings, 414 Hungerford Dr., Suite 444, Rockville MD 20850.

Ages 3 to 12

When to Use Active movement at Circle Time or for an energizing break

Language Bilingual

Location Side 2, Song 37

Source Puerto Rican traditional

37 Mi Cuerpo Hace Música/ There's Music Inside Me

Children clap, tap their feet, and dance to a lively rhythm.

●●●●●●●●●●●●●●●●●●●●●●●●●●●●

OBJECTIVES

- to move slow and fast with self-control
- to sing about parts of our bodies in Spanish and English

PROCEDURE

1 The song was recorded in the key of A flat, but you may find it easier to play the song a half step lower in the key of G. Here are the chords:

Chorus

```
      G                  C         G
Mi cuerpo, mi cuerpo hace música.
      G                  D         G
Mi cuerpo, mi cuerpo hace música.
```

Verse

```
      G     C
Mi boca hace la, la, la
        D              G
Mis manos hacen cla, cla, cla. (clap)
      G       C
Mis pies hacen ta, ta, ta. (tap)
          D                      G
Mi cintura hace...(¿Están listos?) cha, cha, cha,
C                      D        G
cha, cha, cha. Mi cintura hace cha, cha, cha.
C                      D        G
cha, cha, cha. Mi cintura hace cha, cha, cha.
```

2 Begin seated. Lead the children in following along by clapping their hands and tapping their feet. On "cha, cha, cha" stand up and dance to the beat. As the song starts again, once more sit down, follow along with the hand and foot motions, and get ready to dance, "cha, cha, cha." For children who only speak English, review the body parts in Spanish:

> *boca* = mouth
>
> *manos* = hands
>
> *pies* = feet
>
> *cintura* = waist and hips

Tip!*

If your children don't like music, try this song. When I see that the children are bored, and I want to get their attention, I say, "Okay, let's sing 'Mi Cuerpo,'" and they love it. They move and express themselves. Or one child will say to me, "Can we do Cha, Cha, Cha?" That's what they call it. After they've sung it twice, I pick one child to stand on the table and show their "cha, cha, cha." The others can't wait to see what each person will do.

* from Roberto Diaz

3 Next, dance the whole song standing, but vary the speed. Begin slowly moving back and forth from foot to foot. On the ending, "cha, cha, cha," pick up speed.

4 Line up the children. Say, "Now we'll dance the whole song in a conga line. Hold onto the person in front of you. Tell the person behind you whether you want them to hold onto your waist or shoulders."

SNAPSHOT

Adding Favorite Dance Steps

In a fourth-grade class at Conway Elementary School, Conway, Massachusetts, half the class plays rhythm instruments while the other half dances to the song. The dancers stand in two lines and face each other. They embellish the chorus with their favorite dance steps. On the verse, they take turns going forward and back in alternating lines.

Mi Cuerpo Hace Música

Puerto Rican Traditional

Chorus

Mi cuerpo, mi cuerpo hace música.

Mi cuerpo, mi cuerpo hace música.

Verse

Mi boca hace la, la, la.

Mis manos hacen (clap, clap, clap)

Mis pies hacen ta, ta, ta. (tap feet)

Mi cintura hace ... (Spoken: ¿Están listos?)

Cha, cha, cha. Cha, cha, cha,

Mi cintura hace cha, cha, cha.

Cha, cha, cha.

Mi cintura hace cha, cha, cha.

English

Chorus

*There's music, there's music, there's music
inside me. (2x)*

(literal translation: my body has music)

Verse

My mouth says la, la, la.

My hands say (clap, clap, clap)

My feet say ta, ta, ta. (tap feet)

*My waist and hips say... (Spoken: Are you
ready?)*

Cha, cha, cha. Cha, cha, cha.

My waist and hips say cha, cha, cha.

Cha, cha, cha.

My waist and hips say cha, cha, cha.

Alternative translation

Chorus

My body, My body, I make music.

Verse

... My body does the cha, cha, cha.

38 Cloud Hands/Manos Como Las Nubes

Partners take turns mirroring each other while they move as slowly as clouds.

Ages	3 to 12
When to Use	Partner work, developing conflict resolution skills, Chinese studies
Language	Bilingual
Location	Side 2, Song 38
Source	Sarah Pirtle

OBJECTIVES

- to affirm another child's movements
- to respond to others
- to adapt motions so that they are easy to copy
- to experience safe movements close at hand

PROCEDURE

1 You may begin by standing or sitting. Observe clouds together on the playground or outside your classroom window or show photographs of clouds. Ask the children to move their arms as slowly as clouds. While they are learning the song, each person moves her own way.

2 Next, introduce mirroring. Ask the whole group to mirror you while you lead. Emphasize that the game is about connecting and moving together. As you model the game, say what the leader is thinking: "Am I moving slowly enough for my partner to follow me? Are we sticking together? Are my movements clear?" Choose the descriptive verb that will work best for your group: matching, following, sticking together, copying, or mirroring.

3 Help students form pairs. Tell children, "To start off, stand and face your partner. Leave enough space between you so that you can move your hands. Think about the ways you've seen clouds move in the sky. One of you will start as the cloud leader. Decide who will be the first cloud leader and who will lead second." Check to see if they've

Play-fighting: Facilitate Teachable Moments

The goal of this song activity is to give children a chance to stand in front of another child and experience gentle, safe movements. The image of slow clouds guides children away from play-fighting movements, but if a child begins punching or making any other kind of threatening gesture, you have an opportunity to intervene. Help children experience the difference between safe and unsafe movements. Explain, "I don't like the way it feels when somebody makes punching movements near me. I want to feel safe in my space."

Note: *Since partners need to respond to each other for the game of "Cloud Hands" to feel satisfying, this activity helps teach a fundamental concept: it is important to be able to respond to other people. Hearing what others say to us, verbally or nonverbally, and responding to them is an important skill.*

made a clear decision: ask all children who are leading first to raise their hands. Now tell the cloud leaders, "Move slowly enough that your partner can stay with you." On the recording, "Cloud Hands" is sung twice to provide one time for each partner to lead. To repeat the game, rewind the tape or ask children to sing the song to each other as they move or ask cloud leaders to begin by showing their partner their starting shape.

Tip!

Make A Starting Shape

Here's a method that helps you notice whether students have the basic skills of mirroring before you begin the song. Tell the cloud leader, "Show your partner where you want your hands to be when you start the song. Partners, place your hands exactly like that and get ready to begin."

Can they all stand and face a partner? Can they all mirror their partners with their hands when they are still? Look around the whole group and assist any child who isn't facing her partner or isn't matching this first hand shape. Once they get familiar with this concept, you can refer to it as "make your starting shape." This method gives you a quick idea of who needs assistance.

4 As the children take turns leading and following, remind them to think about working together. They should pick movements that are easy to follow. In other words, they are not trying to trick or challenge each other with fast or difficult movements. Their goal is moving as one.

SNAPSHOT

Facilitating Different Learning Styles

A first grader in Bemidji, Minnesota begins the "Cloud Hands" game. Instead of facing his partner, he positions himself shoulder to shoulder. As I ask partners to match hands in a starting shape before the song begins, he turns away from the boy who is the cloud leader. I go over to find out what will help. I stand next to him and coach him. I discover that it is hard for him to copy movements opposite him. It's easier to copy movements next to him. I help place his hands in a matching shape. As the song begins, I stay alongside him. When his partner leads, I also follow his partner. After staying with him twice through the song, he is ready to continue independently. He feels proud that he has done something that he thought he wasn't able to do. When I ask, "Which partners would like to show the class the way they move together?" he puts his hand up quickly.

VARIATIONS

- Model the song first with a partner while the group watches, or pick two children to illustrate the game.
- Stand in two lines with partners facing each other. All the children in one line start as cloud leaders. As the song says, "Now the other one leads," all the children in the facing line become cloud leaders. Working in lines makes the switch easier.
- After the children have tried mirroring, ask them to try the song without a designated leader. Both watch and follow so that the movement unfolds together.
- For young children, have children face each other, but instead of one following the other, both move their own way. During the transition, sing, "And let's try it again," instead of, "Now the other one leads."

Cloud Hands
©1997 Words and Music by Sarah Pirtle
Discovery Center Music, BMI

Wave your hands ___ like clouds ___ in the sky. Wave your hands ___ like clouds ___ in the sky. Wave your hands ___ like clouds ___ in the sky. Look each o-ther in the eye. ___ Now the o-ther ___ one leads.

English

Wave your hands like clouds in the sky.
Wave your hands like clouds in the sky.
Wave your hands like clouds in the sky.
Look each other in the eye.

Transition: Now the other one leads.

Spanish

Como las nubes mueve las manos.
Como las nubes muévelas.
Como las nubes mueve las manos.
Mirémonos a los ojos.

Note: *On the recording, the song is sung only in English.*

Transition: Y ahora el otro dirigirá.

Cloud Drawings

Have children draw clouds while they listen to slow music.

Chinese Studies

"Wave hands like clouds" is one of the classic movements found in forms of Tai Chi, an ancient system of movement. The movements in Tai Chi developed from watching animals like the snake, the crane, and the tiger. I began studying Tai Chi in 1973, and have tried to apply Taoist insights to the teaching of conflict resolution. The clouds teach us how to live flexibly, how to respond to people just as clouds respond to wind currents, and how to balance the roles of leader and follower.

 **Yin/Yang Symbol**

Draw the yin/yang symbol for your students and explain that we all have rhythms in our life. We have day and night, waking and sleeping, noisy and quiet, activity and rest, talking and listening just as the symbol shows dark and light, empty and full. The Taoist approach is to include and balance opposites rather than treating one element as the dominant one. The application to conflict of this concept is to treat the needs of both people as important, and in-stead of seeing which will dominate, to seek a balance of needs.

Practice Responsiveness

Ask children, "Have you seen a cat move its head when you are scratching it? Have you felt the way it tells you where it wants to be scratched?" One child in a pair is the cat, and the other scratches its head or neck or back according to nonverbal signals. Now switch roles.

Scarves

Materials: one scarf per child

Master teacher and dance therapy pioneer, Anne Lief Barlin, identifies what is at the core of mirroring: "The most important thing is not how creative or how beautifully you can move but how connected you can become. Trust will inevitably follow." She uses scarves for mirroring with a partner. She asks each child to hold a scarf at its corner in one hand while mirroring: "Our scarves are magic. If we are very quiet, your scarf can hear my scarf saying 'Move with me. I like you. I want to be your friend.'" (From *Goodnight Toes! Bedtime Stories, Lullabies and Movement Games* by Anne Lief Barlin and Nurit Kalev, a Dance Horizons Book, Princeton Book Company, 1993, P.O. Box 57, Pennington, NJ 08534. Tel.1-800-220-7149.)

RELATED SONGS

"My Space/ Mi Espacio" (Song 6) and "When I Say Stop, I Mean Stop" (Song 29).

ADDITIONAL RESOURCES

You can learn more about the movement games Anne Lief Barlin has developed over the past fifty years by contacting Learning Through Movement, 2728 N. County Road 25E, Bellvue CO 80512. (970) 482-6098. The books *Goodnight Toes!* and *Hello Toes!*, coauthored with Nurit Kalev, are available separately or with accompanying cassette tapes.

39 Under The Bridge

Children build a bridge with their hands and take turns going underneath.

●●●●●●●●●●●●●●●●●●●●●●●●●●●●

Ages	4 to 10
When to Use	Circle Time or to give affirmations
Language	English
Location	Side 2, Song 39
Source	Sarah Pirtle

OBJECTIVES

- to cooperate in forming bridges
- to be aware of others
- to affirm the child passing under the bridge

PROCEDURE

1 Decide in advance how you will form the bridge shape: You can use one long bridge built by the whole group. To form this kind of bridge, children stand in two facing lines shoulder to shoulder, then raise their arm, and touch palms with the person across from them.

Or, separate bridges can be built by partners. These may be scattered randomly throughout the space. This format is often easiest for younger children.

Help children stand in the pattern you have chosen.

2 Decide in advance how children will travel underneath. Here are some options:

- One person at a time.
- A short line of children led by one child.
- Three pairs following each other.
- Partners go all the way under, then hold hands and form an extension of the bridge. (This is the most difficult.)

3 Use the term "fish" to designate the children who go under the bridge. Choose the "fish." Ask, "Is the bridge ready? Are the fish ready? Let's start our song." Everyone forming the bridge sings to those passing under. Make sure that all children who want to be fish get a turn.

Tip!

Before you play, "Under the Bridge," play a different activity which uses pairs, and then ask the same partners to form the bridge or bridges. "Cloud Hands" (song 38) appears directly before this song on the recording. "Across the Wide Ocean" (song 11) and "Heart to Heart" (song 27) also provide partner activities.

How To Create Bridges That Work

1. Check for safety. Practice holding hands up before anyone passes underneath. Help the group think about how high they'll need to hold their arms. Agree to keep hands up and not capture people as they pass underneath.

2. Provide choice. Ask, "Do you want to go under the bridge?" Not all children do at first. If pairs are traveling together, ask partners to talk and decide if they are ready to take a turn. Have them raise their hands if they are interested.

3. You may want to discuss "capturing." Find out whether the class wants to agree not to capture or wants to find a safe way to use capturing (holding the bridge briefly down over the child who is passing through). If there is a strong interest in capturing, and the children have the ability to maintain safe boundaries, ask the group to help make rules and set up the game so that this is fun for everyone. Make an agreement to release captured children immediately. Create a signal that any child can say or show with his or her hands, "I don't want to be captured."

SNAPSHOT

Sending And Receiving Social Messages

I start a conflict resolution training for first graders in Putnam Valley, New York by telling the children that part of being friends is responding to the signals that your friend gives you. As I'm speaking, I see a boy push a girl in the back row. I can't tell what led to that conflict, but they appear to be friends. I ask them if they would both help demonstrate the game of "Cloud Hands," and they agree. First, I add a role play. I provide the children with a situation where they each need to tell the other, "Stop, I don't like that." They practice using the words to set limits, just as they might have needed those same words earlier in the class.

Next, they demonstrate the "Cloud Hands" game. Now it's time for the whole class to work on the concepts. As I set up two facing lines for the game, I ask partners to shake hands. Will some children purposefully squeeze hands too hard? I suggest that they can say, "Stop," if a handshake hurts. This is a litmus test: in that one moment of the handshake, I can learn a great deal about the participants even before we start the game. Now they play "Under the Bridge" using the most challenging formation—re-forming the bridge. We focus upon giving verbal instructions to help each other.

Three Variations

A Short Line Goes Under Separate Bridges

· ·

Five-year-olds have finished playing "Cloud Hands." I ask them to sit down with their partners. I invite them to clap while they listen to "Under the Bridge." I divide the room into four sections. I tell them that each section will get a turn being "fish." Partners stand and form bridges while one section takes a turn passing in and out of the bridges scattered throughout the room. I ask one child who is a fish to lead the others as they go under each so that they don't collide with each other. We sing the song four times through, once for each of the four sections. Children have the option not to take a turn as fish.

Three Pairs At A Time Go Under One Long Bridge

· ·

First graders have been working in pairs on the song "Across the Wide Ocean." They have mirrored each other's movements and have established a trusting connection. Now I ask them to find a way to make a bridge with their hands high enough that other children could go underneath. I say, "We'll use these bridges for a new game." I tell them, "First, we need to put all of our bridges together." I place two nearby pairs shoulder to shoulder, and then add a third to create two facing lines. "Do you see the pattern?" I ask the group. All other partners join the bridge, each facing their partners. I ask pairs to talk together and decide if they'd like a turn traveling underneath as the "fish." They raise their hands, and I pick three pairs at a time to be fish. We continue until everyone who would like to be a fish has a turn.

Partners Re-form the Bridge After Passing Through

· ·

Since the size of the bridge will extend further, I take time at the beginning to make sure that there is enough space at the end of the bridge so that children passing through will have some place to go as they continue to rejoin the bridge. The children at the entrance to the tunnel go through first. We pause to watch them re-form the bridge on the other side. Each new partner at the entrance takes a turn until the original pair is back at the start.

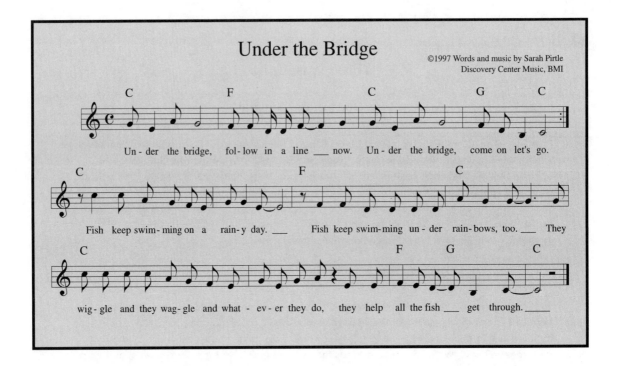

Under the Bridge

©1997 Words and music by Sarah Pirtle
Discovery Center Music, BMI

Un - der the bridge, fol - low in a line ___ now. Un - der the bridge, come on let's go.

Fish keep swim-ming on a rain-y day. ___ Fish keep swim-ming un - der rain-bows, too. ___ They

wig - gle and they wag - gle and what - ev - er they do, they help all the fish ___ get through. _____

Chorus

Under the bridge, follow in a line now.
Under the bridge, come on let's go.
Under the bridge, follow in a line now.
Under the bridge, come on let's go.

Verse

Fish keep swimming on a rainy day.
Fish keep swimming under rainbows too.
They wiggle and they waggle and what-
ever they do,
they help all the fish get through.

- -

E X T E N S I O N S

- -

Affirmation Bridge

As one person passes through, classmates shower her with positive comments. Practice the statements to use: "I like the way you throw the ball to me." "I like the way you laugh." Encourage the child passing under the bridge to walk slowly enough to hear the comments. Or instead of thinking of comments, sing affirming words to the same tune as the refrain.

For example:

I'm glad you're here.
I'm glad you're in this class.
I'm glad you're here.
It's fun to play with you.

Affirming one to four children a day is about right for keeping the activity fresh. Keep a list and give everyone a turn over a period of a week or two. Or use the Affirmation Bridge as one of the choices children have on their birthdays.

40 Let's Get Together/Juntémonos

Children create connecting shapes.

● ●

Ages 4 to 10

When to Use Song Circle, indoor recess game, or as an energizer

Language Bilingual

Location Side 2, Song 40

Source Sarah Pirtle

Note: *This is the game depicted on the cover of this book.*

OBJECTIVES
- to interact in small groups
- to build community
- to increase awareness of others

PROCEDURE

1 Help the children stand in small circles of four to six participants. Tell them, "Connect to the other people with your hands until everyone is linked. Everyone doesn't have to connect in the same way." Sing, "Let's get together with our hands," or "Juntémonos con nuestros manos."

2 Play the recording and allow the children time to discover different ways of connecting. Translate into Spanish if you wish.

3 Stop the recording and discuss the different methods of connecting that the children have invented. For example, crossing hands, touching palms, fingers meeting in the middle. Clarify that it's fine to try ideas that you see other groups using. This isn't "copying," but part of the game. Each group creates movements they find fun. It's also okay for individuals within a group to select different motions than the rest of the group.

4 This is a zipper song. Zip new movement directions into the pattern.

Let's get together _____.
Let's get together _____.
Let's get together, let's get together,
Let's get together _____.

Spanish
Juntémonos _____.
Juntémonos _____.
Juntémonos, juntémonos,
Juntémonos _____.

The recording presents these suggestions. Also, here are translations into Spanish of the English words you hear.

Tip!

> Let's get together with our hands.
> *Juntémonos con nuestros manos.*
>
> Let's get together like a wheel.
> *Juntémonos como una rueda* or
> *Formemos juntos una rueda.*
>
> Let's get together round and round.
> *Juntémonos y demos vueltas.*
>
> Let's get together like a roof.
> *Formemos juntos un gran techo.*
>
> Let's get together like a flower—whoo!
> *Juntémonos como una flor.*
>
> Let's get together our own way.
> *Juntémonos como querramos.*
>
> Let's get together with our elbows.
> *Juntémonos codo a codo.*
>
> Let's get together with our fingers.
> *Juntémonos con nuestros dedos.*
>
> Let's get together like a train.
> *Juntémonos con un tren.*
>
> Let's get together like a bridge.
> *Juntémonos como un puente.*

Have half the class link onto one another to form a train. The other half should form a tunnel by holding hands in pairs across from each other.

Sing: Let's bring our train through the tunnel.

Other possible verses:

> *Let's get together like a star.*
> *Formemos juntos una estrella.*
>
> *Let's get together on one leg.*
>
> *Let's get together like a T (or the letter A, M, S, or C).*
>
> *Let's get together like a web.*
>
> *Let's get together like a pretzel.*

5   Make a group agreement to keep the game fun for everyone. Notice whether children are looking out for each other. Is one child in a circle crowded out? Are children squeezing hands too hard? You can sing a reminder. Here's a new verse to encourage awareness of others:

> Let's make more room in the circle.
> Let's make more room in the circle.
> Think about each other, think about each other.
> Keep it fun for everyone.

6 Watch the group and see what movement directions would be beneficial. For example: Do they need more time to explore how to connect with their hands because they are coming up with interesting shapes? Then repeat that verse again.

Do they need a very specific suggestion to help them focus because they are having trouble responding to open-ended directions? Suggest they use their fingers or form the letter T.

7 Choose a final activity to bring closure. Provide a definite motion that feels like an ending such as:

"Let's end the song touching palms."

"Let's end together like a roof."

"Let's end the song with our hands crossed."

Or, ask the children to invent a motion that feels like an ending.

Tip!

1. Give each small group a chance to teach one shape they invented to the rest of the class.

2. Stop the recording if you need to have more time for a group to complete a motion, or if you need to assist a group in identifying how to work together more successfully.

3. Invite students to invent the next verse. Follow their lead and encourage them to create new possibilities.

4. Give groups a choice between two possibilities. Examples: "Make a tree or a flower." "Make a boat or your own shape."

Facilitating Collaboration

. . . .

This song provides an opportunity for children who have difficulty collaborating with others to get assistance. One second grader in Ashfield, Massachusetts kept impeding the work of his group by falling on the floor. I stopped the song to meet with them. I asked the child, "Can you figure out something you're doing that's making it hard for your group?" He didn't answer. I asked the others, "Can you describe for him what's making it hard?" A member of the group said to him, "We can't do this when you're falling down." Hearing their specific request helped him refocus and become integrated into the process. For the rest of the song he was engaged.

In one second-grade class at Brightwood Magnet School, one particular boy who had a lot of leadership qualities had sometimes been intimidating others. The first time he participated in this song game he became entranced with the possibilities of the verse—let's make a flower—and announced that he would make up the next verse, and he would be a butterfly. A large group of twelve children gathered around him. We sang to him, "We'll watch you change to a butterfly," as he metamorphosed from a caterpillar into a butterfly.

Facilitating Discovery Time

Every day for the whole year my first-grade class met with me for thirty minutes before lunch in an open room in our school basement for a cooperative movement session we called Discovery Time. After experimenting with different ways to lead the session, I came upon a format that worked day after day. Here's the method I repeated.

1. Family groups are made at the start of each week.

Children stayed in the same small group, called a "family," for one week to give them practice working together. I used an inclusive way to make groups which also gave individual choice. I marked five spots on the floor. The class lined up on Monday and one by one chose one of the spots. When a spot had four children, the family was full. This worked for a class of twenty. Readjust the number of spots to divide your class into small groups of three or four people.

2. Make a shape.

This movement game explores going away from a group to move alone and then returning and re-forming as a group again. Just like the song, "Let's Get Together" (Song 40) all children in the same "family" connect with elbows, hands, or heads, in any combination of their choosing. Then they temporarily part from each other to walk, skip, or travel around the room. Use a call-back signal to bring individuals back. Once more, all "family" members make a shape together. To mark the two sections—traveling and shape making—you can use taped music for the traveling section and then stop the music when it's time to make a shape. Or use one sound such as a drum beat to mean go apart and another sound to mean return to your group.

To help teach shape-making, say, "Freeze in a shape touching…"
- with elbows
- with noses
- with knees
- with heads
- very low
- with one foot off the ground

To help teach traveling, provide suggestions such as:
- skipping
- walking backward
- touching your hand to at least one person
- jumping
- being a monkey
- being a fish
- zooming like a star

3. Hold a Family Dance or Play

The whole class regroups and sits together. Set up an array of costumes and props including rhythm instruments.

For kindergarten and grade 1: Each group takes a turn. One by one give "families" a chance to choose costumes or props and invent a scene or dance on the spot. Each member of the group can select one or two costumes or props. Spontaneously they have a chance to make up a dance or quick dramatic play improvising from what they chose. If the dance or scene is too long and the attention of the watchers is fading, give a signal: "Now it's time to make an ending."

For grades 2 and 3: Divide up the props and costumes. Each group creates a quick scene, skit, dance, or situation.

Each group shows what it has invented. At the end of their dance or scene, the "family" stands facing the other members of the class. Each dancer/actor selects one observer to say a specific thing he or she noticed or liked about what that person did. In this way everybody receives immediate positive feedback, and the observers have a reason to watch the dancers closely.

4. Close with a Goodbye Dance

The class lines up at a distance from the door. While taped music plays or the teacher drums, one by one children invent a dance of their own movement sequence as they travel across the floor to line up at the door.

Let's Get Together

©1997 Words and Music by Sarah Pirtle
Discovery Center Music, BMI

Let's get together with our hands.
Let's get together with our hands.
Let's get together, let's get together,
Let's get together with our hands.

. . . .

E X T E N S I O N S

. . . .

Flower Pattern

Second-grade children at Brightwood Magnet School in Springfield, Massachusetts invented a particular way to make a flower that children ages five to ten have really enjoyed. One person ducks down in the center. Others bring their arms out over them like flower petals but they don't press down and touch her head. When the song says "Whoo!" the arms go back and the person in the center jumps up. Repeat the verse, "Let's get together like a flower—whoo!" over and over until more children have had a turn in the center. This is described on the recording.

CHAPTER 8: Linking Up Songs

Peace is me being me.
Peace is you being you.
And we're jumping, and we're dancing.
Peace is us being true
to the happiness inside
that sings out like a lark.
Peace is already here in my heart.
           — from "Peace is Me Being Me" (Song 43)

What's the opposite of violence? Connection.

I want to tell you about an unusual meeting that redirected my thinking about peace. In fact, it was through this meeting that the word "link" took on a whole new meaning for me. By chance, I met Riane Eisler. We were on the same television program in Boston to address the increase in violence and to speak about alternatives. Her ground-breaking book, *The Chalice and the Blade*, had just been published, and so had my young adult novel, *An Outbreak of Peace*. To my surprise and excitement, she said that a great source of inspiration for her is the evidence from history that violence hasn't always been part of people's lives. She spoke about acclaimed archaeologist Marija Gimbutas, whose work reveals 4,000 years in which humans worked in partnership with one another during the period before the historical record.

Riane Eisler describes two basic ways that groups of people can organize themselves: in partnership or in domination. She uses "linking" to describe collaboration in partnership. She uses "ranking" to represent stratification in a system where some people are dominated by others. To her, violence is the outgrowth of the model of domination. She states that in the partnership model "diversity is not equated with either inferiority or superiority." (*The Chalice and the Blade*, San Francisco: Harper and Row 1988, p. xvii). Eisler writes that it's important today now "that the present system is breaking down, that we must find ways to break through to a different kind of future." (p. xxiii). We have a choice to rank each other or to link with each other.

PEACE IS OUR HOMEBASE

I first became aware of the different ways people think of the word "peace" in 1983. I was searching for elementary classrooms where I could pilot peace education activities I had created. A school principal invited me into the school, but added the stipulation, "Just don't say the word 'peace.' It's too controversial. I wouldn't want the board of education to hear about it." Ironically, the word did slip out when I was sharing a biography of Jane Addams. I mentioned that she had won the Noble Peace Prize, and, to my surprise, a fourth-grade girl lit upon the word and suddenly exclaimed, "Peace! I love peace!"

What does peace mean to us? Is peace a concept that is political, controversial, not for discussion in schools? Is it a touchstone of hope, but hope for something far away in the future? Is peace something we have to wait for? Is it out of reach, a pipe dream, an unattainable goal?

I invite us to understand peace in a whole new way: as something personal and immediately attainable through a shift in attitude.

Here are the connotations of peace that I grew up with: quiet, in agreement, all the same, no wars, obediently cooperative.

But that kind of peace doesn't feel empowering—rather it feels passive and static.

If we expand our understanding of peace to be dynamic and active, peace could be noisy or quiet, it could happen alone or with others, it could be a time we feel engaged, a time we are reaching for what we value, or an experience of sticking together through thick and thin.

Then peace becomes a choice we can make.

Here's a snapshot of peace in a second-grade classroom. Here peace is not the absence of conflict. Instead, peace refers to the quality of the dynamic relationship. Three girls named Angela, Bette, and Carla are working together to make a snail dance with the song "Caracol" (Song 32).

> *Angela*: I want to be the snail. (She points to Bette.) You be my shell.
>
> *Bette*: No, I don't want to be a shell. I want to be a snail, too.
>
> *Angela*: Then we can both be snails.
>
> *Bette*: Carla, you be the shell.
>
> *Carla*: Not me. Pretend you have shells.
>
> *Bette*: Who you gonna be?
>
> *Carla*: Hm... I'll be the sun.
>
> *Angela*: Yeah. You're the sun and we're the snails.
>
> *Bette*: The snails stand over here.
>
> *Carla*: No, that's a good place for the sun.
>
> *Angela*: Why?
>
> *Carla*: The sun can hide there and then it comes out.
>
> *Bette*: Okay, the snails will be nearby watching the sun.

The three girls created a snail dance with each other, not against each other. They said what they wanted and found ways to relate to each other. What comes through in this dialogue is a positive intention and a desire to work things out.

They could have made things worse. When Angela said to Bette, "You be my shell," Bette could have responded, "I don't like you. You're no fun. You never let me do what I want," and Angela could have asserted, "You have to do what I say or I won't be your friend." But this would have destroyed the fun for all participants. In one sense, battles between friends, family and community members cannot be won. We may win an argument or dominate a situation but leave the encounter with lingering hurt or even a lost friendship.

I like to look at peace as a framework or an attitude. We declare: I care what you think and feel. I will speak up for what I think and feel. We might not agree, but I want to talk about it. I'm important and you're important. That includes standing up to bullies and speaking up if there is unfairness or injustice. At any moment in our lives, we can declare our own outbreak of peace in the attitude we carry.

Here are activities that you can use to help the concept of dynamic peace become more vivid for your students.

ACTIVITIES FOR UNDERSTANDING PEACE

Help children construct an active understanding of the word "peace."

1. Peace is Here Today

During Peace Week at Giving Tree Nursery School in Gill, Massachusetts, children drew pictures of their own peaceful places, heard songs about peace, made a multicultural collage of people in the world, invented peace symbols, and listed things that made them feel peaceful. Here are some of their answers:

- Peace is being silly.
- Peace is not pulling hair.
- Peace is sharing toys and something real tasty.

At recall time, children reflected upon these questions:

- What is something friendly that you did today?
- What is something you did that took two people to do?

You can help children reflect back at the end of the day or immediately after a play period. Ask children to identify times that they felt peace that day. Raise questions to expand their thinking.

- Can we have peace that is noisy?
- Can we feel peace alone?
- Can we feel peace when we're with other people?
- What is it about the way we feel when we're playing together that makes it feel like peace?
- If we're angry and we talk about it together, can this be peace?

Look for times when they felt engaged, excited, and connected. Look for times when they worked through a problem. As you start to collect examples and discuss different interpretations of peace, an awareness of peace as part of life develops. Be sure to give children an opportunity to ask questions, to discuss, and to disagree. Leave the conversation open-ended; don't force the children to come up with immediate conclusions.

2. Noisy Peace

Ask children to draw themselves doing activities that they enjoy. Look at the drawings together and ask: When you were doing these things, did it feel like peace? Can we call these pictures of peace?

3. Peaceful Places

Ask children to draw a place they like to be. Introduce the activity with a book that includes pictures of a special place that a child enjoys, such as by a tree, in a playground, or under Grandma's dining room table. Help children consciously experience peace.

4. Cooperative Drawing about Peace

Materials: Large paper, pencils, markers, or crayons.

   a. Supply groups of four with one piece of large paper and drawing supplies.

   b. Ask the children to make one big picture together with as many people as they can fit on the paper. Ask them to draw people who are doing peaceful activities. Add the words that they have come up with about what peace means to them. For example, "Draw peaceful people —like the things we've said before about people having fun and feeling safe."

   c. Depending on the developmental stage of the group, you can ask them to plan the scenario for their drawing first. In other words, they can discuss and agree upon what they want to have in the landscape—buildings, streets, rivers, mountains, houses—so they have a congruent background on which they add their figures.

   d. If they like, at the end they can sign their names on the group picture and give it a name.

This cooperative activity gives children a peaceful group experience and helps them solidify their understanding that peace can include exciting, challenging experiences, such as jumping on their front steps, running, or dancing. If there is disagreement about what activities are peaceful, promote discussion and let the children themselves make a decision.

> *Caleb*: What do you mean I can't draw kids playing army? It's fun.

> *Teacher*: Mayer, do you want to tell what you were thinking when you asked Caleb to take it out of the drawing?

> *Mayer*: I don't know. It seemed surprising.

> *Caleb*: They aren't hurting anybody.

> *Mayer*: If they aren't pushing each other down, maybe it's okay.

> *Caleb*: What if they're just chasing?

> *Mayer*: Okay. But don't put guns in.

Note*: The teacher has the option to promote a discussion of what each of the children mean when they say, "no hurting."*

As a variation, have children draw people first on separate sheets of paper, show them to the others in their group, and then cut them out and paste them on the common drawing.

5. Echo Game: Building Bridges with Sounds
Materials: Rhythm instruments

Here are three ways to play this game.

a. A pair of children sit in the center of a circle. Each selects an instrument. One child begins by making a simple pattern of three to six beats using their instrument. The other child tries to copy it exactly. Then they switch, so the second child initiates a pattern and the other echoes back what they heard. Give other pairs a turn in the center.

b. Everyone remains in the circle. Each class member holds a rhythm instrument. Take turns giving each child a chance to send a signal of beats. The whole class, in unison, copies what they heard.

c. Take turns sending a message with sound. Pass a drum. Each person takes a short turn playing it their own way.

Discuss:
- Did this game feel like peace?
- Does peace have to be quiet?

6. Musical Conversation: Walls and Bridges
Materials: Eight or more rhythm instruments.

a. Create a hand signal that means start and another hand signal that means silence. Assemble rhythm instruments in the center of the circle or on a desk and choose five students to come forward and choose instruments.

b. Tell the group that first they will play their instruments as if they are all alone and they aren't thinking about the other people around them. Say, "Imagine that there's an invisible box with walls around you." Set ground rules. "Take care not to touch each other as you play and be careful not to harm the instruments." Give the signal to begin, and when they've had a full noisy exploration, give the signal for silence. Discuss what that felt like.

c. Say, "Now feel your invisible box come off of you. Look around at the other musicians. Get ready to listen to each other. The next time you'll play together like you are building bridges to each other using your sounds." If needed, give them repeated tries until they feel that they've portrayed making bridges with sounds.

d. Give other groups a chance to try this exercise or do the activity with the whole class.

Discuss:
- What have you found out about building bridges?
- Can you think about yourself and another person at the same time?
- Can you think about the sounds you want to make and the sounds the other people are making at the same time?

Help children maintain their inner sense of worth.

7. Teachable Moments: Returning to Peace After Name-Calling

When a child is targeted by name-calling or put-downs, one way we can assist is to help him return to his own center. Here's a conversation with a second grader.

Teacher: Hello, Jared. You look upset.

Jared: Lee called me stupid.

Teacher: I see you didn't like that. Do you know that you aren't stupid?

Jared: Well, yes. But he called me stupid.

Teacher: He could be trying to get you mad.

Jared: Yeah.

Teacher: I want to let you know that you're in charge of how you feel about yourself. If he calls you something, that doesn't make it true.

Jared: Hm.

Teacher: If he calls you stupid, does that mean it's true?

Jared: No way.

Teacher: That's it. No way. You know who you are.

Jared: Right. I'm not stupid. (He returns to playing).

8. The Friendly Voice Inside Us

All of us, both children and adults, can develop a friendly voice inside of us. We can all speak to ourselves in encouraging ways. Every day we teachers have opportunities to model this friendly voice in the way we speak to children.

41 Two Hands Hold the Earth/Mis Dos Manos

Children sing about their physical connection to the earth.

●●●●●●●●●●●●●●●●●●●●●●●●●●●●●●●

Ages	All
When to Use	Ecology unit, peace unit, or for an energizing stretch break
Language	Bilingual
Location	Side 2, Song 41
Source	Sarah Pirtle

OBJECTIVES

- to revitalize through full-body movements
- to experience the self as part of nature
- to care for the earth

PROCEDURE

1 Gather the children together and have them stand. Say, "Let's begin by stretching." Sing, "*My head is in the sky, sky, sky.*" Lead the children through movements to accompany each part of the song. Keep the directions general such as, "Move like waves," so that children have the opportunity to move in their own way.

Lyrics	Movement
Sky, sky, sky	Stretch upward
Ground, ground, ground	Stamp
Blood / from the sea	Wave movements
Bones / mountains	Make fists; gesture like making a muscle, raising arms to the beat
Hands / hold this land	Eight claps
Two hands hold the earth	Make a sphere

2 Focus on the last line. Pantomime that you are holding the sphere of the earth. Illustrate how to curve your hands to indicate that you are holding a round ball. Leave six to twelve inches of space between your hands. To rotate this earth you are holding, suggest to children that they put one foot in front of the other, sink onto the back foot, and then rock forward while turning their waist—this moves the earth.

Note: *The phrase and posture "two hands hold the earth" come from the ancient Chinese system of movements called Tai Chi.*

3 To foster ecological awareness, discuss how the poetry of the song corresponds to scientific reality. Tell children that our blood has the same proportion of salt as ocean water has, and that our bodies are 75 percent water.

4 Try these variations:

Small groups of two or three children face each other. They find ways to do each motion together and, at the end, hold the same sphere. Or the whole class pantomimes that together they hold one earth.

5 After repeating the song, bring it to closure. It ends with a poignant thought–"My two hands hold the earth." At the end, as a joke, sometimes students smash their hands together and laugh about smashing the earth. I redirect the group, "Bring the earth back again, and let's end more slowly. Make the earth smaller and smaller until it becomes the size of a stone on the beach. Just like you would save a favorite stone, put it in your pocket."

SNAPSHOT

Into the Woods

• •

At summer camp at Giving Tree School I lead the children into the pine forest to sing this song. "When we stretch our hands up, we see the blue sky and the clouds. When we sing our feet are on the ground; we stomp our feet on the forest floor covered with pine needles." The meaning of the words comes across with greater clarity and several children continue to hum the song throughout the day.

MELODY VARIATION

In some measures the tune is slightly different when singing in Spanish. Here are the notes to sing:

C D F D   C A A A F
¿Y mi sangre? Es como el mar.

C D F D   F G F A A F
¿Y mis huesos? Como montañas son.

A C A G F D F F D C
Mis dos manos sostienen la tierra.

Two Hands Hold the Earth

My head is in the sky, sky sky. ___ My feet are on the ground, ground, ground. ___ And what a-bout my blood? It's from the sea. And what a-bout my bones? Like the moun-tains be. And my hands, ___ oh ___ my hands. I be-lieve with my hands I could hold this land. My two hands hold the earth. _____ My two hands hold the earth. _____

Spanish

Mi cabeza está en el cielo, cielo, cielo.

Mis pies están sobre el terreno.

¿Y mi sangre? Es como el mar.

¿Y mis huesos? Como montañas son.

Y mis manos, ay, mis manos

Mis dos manos sostienen la tierra.

¡Sostienen la tierra!

¡Sostienen la tierra!

. . . .

E X T E N S I O N S

. . . .

Holding the Earth

As you hold the earth at the end, ask, "What would you like to say to the earth?" One classroom came up with this idea: bring your hands closer, making the ball smaller. Lean into your cupped hands and imagine you are talking to the earth and making a promise to it.

Here's what third grader Dawn Fleming of Duxbury, Massachusetts, said when she talked to the earth: "I hold the earth and it's new everyday." I like to share Dawn's words with other students and ask them to explain what they think she means.

Ages	5 to adult
When to Use	Peacemaking unit, Circle Time
Language	Bilingual
Location	Side 2, Song 42
Source	Words and music by Roberto Díaz, English translation by Sarah Pirtle

42 Canto Por La Paz/ I Sing For Peace

Children alternate Spanish and English in a song of peace.

● ●

OBJECTIVES

- to think about peace
- to develop bilingual awareness

PROCEDURE

1   As a first step in learning to sing the song, repeat back the words as illustrated on the tape. Here are places to echo:

- *canto por la paz*
- *de la humanidad*
- *en el corazón*

Notice how the sounds of the Spanish words blend together when the song is sung.

The last syllable of one word often blends into the first syllable of the next.

2   Photocopy or post the English and Spanish words to the song. Whichever language is "homebase," point to a word in that language and ask students to find its translation.

paz	peace
amor	love
corazón	heart
humanidad	humanity
verdadera paz	true peace
canto	I sing
canto por la paz	I sing for peace

3   Select and lead an activity from "Activities for Understanding Peace" (see p. 259) such as "Peaceful Places" or "Cooperation Drawing about Peace." See the essay on peace in chapter 8 (p. 257).

Canto Por La Paz

©1997 Words and Music by Roberto Díaz

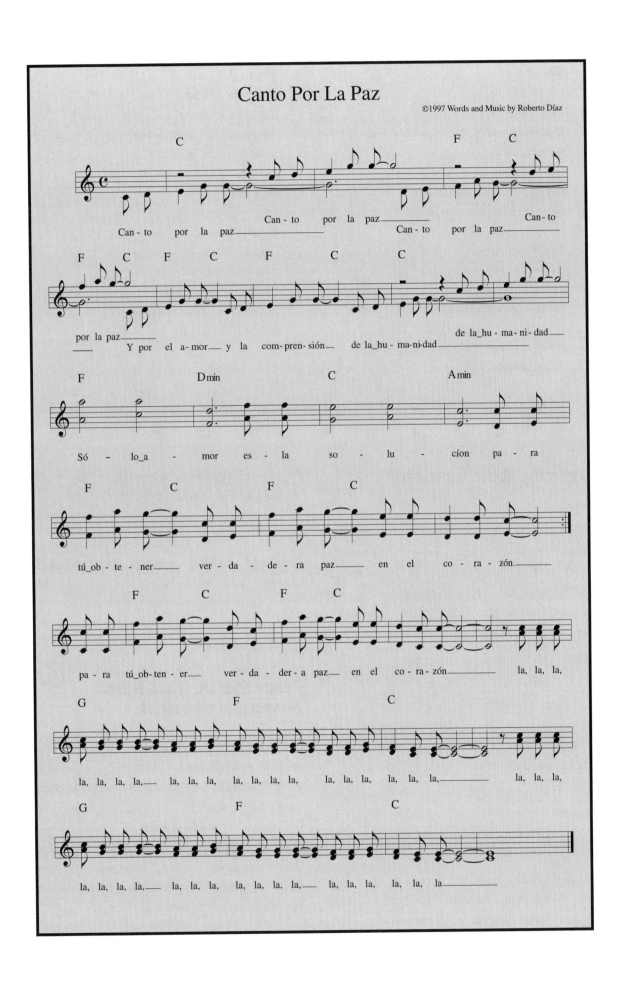

Verse 1

Canto por la paz,
Canto por la paz.
Y por el amor y la comprensión de la
humanidad.
Sólo amor es la solución
para tú obtener verdadera paz
en el corazón.

Verse 2

I sing for peace,
I sing for peace.
I sing to love and understand humanity.
Only love is the way peace starts.
We find peace, I mean true peace
in our hearts.

Verse 3

Canto por la paz
Corazón a corazón.
Sólo amor es la solución
then love can start
para tú obtener verdadera paz
en el corazón.

English

I sing for peace.
May our hearts meet,
Then love can start.
Love brings true peace
inside our hearts.

. . . .

E X T E N S I O N S

. . . .

Learning about Translation

Grades 2 and older

Explain to the children that a translator some-times changes the exact meaning of a phrase to a near meaning in order to fit the rhythm of the song or in order to create a rhyme. Examine the translation for "Canto Por La Paz" in two sections.

Here's the opening of the song:

Canto por la paz. Y por el amor y la
comprensión de la humanidad.

The literal meaning of this passage is: "I sing for peace and for the love and understanding of humanity."

The translation tells that same thought, but condenses it:

I sing for peace. I sing to love and un-
derstand humanity.

Now, look at the second part:

Sólo amor es la solución para tú obtener
verdadera paz en el corazón.

Try saying the literal meaning in time to the music and rhythm of the song:

"Only love is the solution to have true
peace in your heart."

Compare to the translation that includes a rhyme:

Only love is the way peace starts.
We find peace, I mean true peace in
our hearts.

Peace Search: Good News Newspaper Headlines

. . . .

Songwriter Roberto Díaz wrote this song for a concert at his church in 1988. "Since then I've sung 'Canto Por La Paz' every year in my class-room. Even students who don't speak Span-ish learn it quickly. I want children to think about things happening in this world. When they talk about the song, they say that they don't see peace very often, and they are wor-ried that we need to do something."

Ask students to search their school, neighborhoods, churches, synagogues, temples, and mosques for examples of peaceful activities. Newspapers most often focus on problems; they show what's not working and focus on outbreaks of violence.

Make a list of the events you notice. List them as if they were headlines for a "Good News Newspaper" that focuses on what is working well in the community. Where are people cooperating? What are people doing together? For example, "Girl Scout Troop Cleans Litter in Park."

Ages	5 to 12
When to Use	To promote discussion, or for a group folk dance
Language	English
Location	Side 2, Song 43
Source	Sarah Pirtle

43 Peace Is Me Being Me

Children personalize their conceptions of peace and happiness.

OBJECTIVES

- to build an understanding of peace
- to explore happiness
- to build community with group movement

PROCEDURE

1 Play the recording of "Peace is Me Being Me" for your class and discuss the meaning of the words. Explain that a lark is a song bird. Ask children:

- When have you felt happiness inside that sings out like a lark?
- Does peace already live in your heart?
- Does it feel like peace when you are you being you?

2 Add movement and dance to the beat of the song. Stand and move around in a circle as you sing the words.

3 Select and lead an activity from "Activities for Understanding Peace" (see p. 259) such as the "Echo Game: Building Bridges with Sounds."

Peace is Me Being Me

©1997 Words and Music by Sarah Pirtle
Discovery Center Music, BMI

Verse 1

Peace is the boat that we ride,
and the song that we sing,
and the gathering tide.
Follow it in to the happiness inside that
sings out like a lark.
Peace is already here in my heart.

Chorus

Sing it from the mountains,
down to the sea.
Sing it from the valleys
in your family.

There's a happiness inside that sings out
like a lark.
Peace is already here in my heart.

Verse 2

Peace is me being me.
Peace is you being you
and we're jumpin' and we're dancin'.
Peace is us being true
to the happiness inside
that sings out like a lark.
Peace is already here in my heart.
Peace is already here in my heart.

E X T E N S I O N S

Happiness Exploration

Draw or write about a time that you felt happiness welling up inside you, "happiness inside that sings out like a lark." Through writing or drawing explore these phrases:

> I can choose peace.
> I can be happy right now.

Group Collaboration: A Folk Dance

Stand together in a circle and use the words of the second verse to create a folk dance.

Lyrics	Group movements
Peace is me being me.	Each person walks forward proudly into the center of the circle without holding hands.
Peace is you being you.	Now walk backward to your place. Open your arms to acknowledge others.
We're jumpin' and we're dancin'.	Jump and dance.
Peace is us being true.	All point to the ground.
To the happiness inside that sings out like a lark. Peace is already here in my heart.	Invent the motions you want to use.

44 Carry the Candle

Children sing about the light in their hearts.

●●●●●●●●●●●●●●●●●●●●●●●●●●●●

Ages 3 to adult

When to Use For friendship ceremonies and times of closure or celebration

Language English

Location Side 2, Song 44

Source Sarah Pirtle

OBJECTIVES

- to honor friends
- to celebrate community

PROCEDURE

1 Teach the song by call and response. Sing the first line or play the first line on the recording and then ask children to echo it back. Teach subsequent lines in the same manner.

2 Incorporate a candle into the song in any of the following ways:

- Watch a candle flame as you sing.
- Ask children to dance while pantomiming that they are holding a candle.
- Pass an unlit candle or a dripless lit candle around the group.

Tip!

Make up new verses to match the purpose of your gathering.

3 Learn the melody using the short version of the song on the recording. Then look at the suggestions below of new words you can add to the song.

Three Snapshots

Times of Celebration and Loss

· ·

This multipurpose song helps children develop a feeling of closeness. It can be used at times of celebration or at times of honoring transitions or loss:

- Three- to five-year-olds and their parents sang "Carry the Candle" for a graduation ceremony at their nursery school. Children who were going into kindergarten or who were moving away took turns passing the lit candle. They felt proud that the adults trusted them to be careful with a candle flame. They added the following verse:

  Now it's time to leave our school.
  Now it's time to leave our school.
  We'll remember our teachers and friends
  And the light will keep on going.

- Second and third graders pantomimed that they all held candles as they danced around their room at a birthday celebration. They added this verse:

  Bring the light to our friend Roberto.
  Bring the light to our friend Roberto.
  Happy Birthday and many more.
  And the light will keep on going.

- Children of various ages gathered at a hospital bereavement program. All had lost family members due to illness, accidents, or family violence. We passed a candle around the circle as we sang these new verses:

  Here is a place to show what we feel.
  Here is a place for hearts to heal.
  The strongest force is the love in our hearts
  and the love will keep on going.

  When you blow a candle out
  I don't believe the light just dies.
  When you blow a candle out,
  then the light flies inside.

  Hold in your heart a candle flame.
  Hold in your heart a candle flame.
  All of your love never is lost
  and your love keeps on going.

Carry the Candle

©1997 Words and Music by Sarah Pirtle
Discovery Center Music, BMI

Carry the candle around the room. (2x)
Hold in your heart the light of love.
And the light keeps on going.
And the light keeps on going.

Bring the light wherever you go. (2x)
Hold in your heart the light of love.
And the light keeps on going.
And the light keeps on going.

Songwriter's note: *Most of my ancestors are from the British Isles. I gave the melody a Celtic mood in keeping with this tradition. With this song I honor the life and death of my sister Lucy Ann Pirtle, whose light lives on.*

Friendship Circle

End the week in a circle. Light a candle and place it in the center. Prepare a bowl with special objects like shells, rocks, acorns, or chestnuts. Each child takes one to hold during the circle, and then places it back at the end. Ask if anyone wants to mention something that happened that week. If you like, sing their words using a zipper pattern:

We remember _____.
We remember _____.
We remember _____.
And the light keeps on going.

OR:

We liked the time that _____.
We liked the time that _____.
Hold in your heart the light of friends.
And the light keeps on going.

End by singing these words:

We grow and learn more every day. (2x)
Hold in your heart the light of this class.
And the light keeps on going.

Adiós/Goodbye

Children sing an ending song.

● ●

Ages	3 to 8
When to Use	Transitions, closing, Circle Time, or ending the school day
Language	Bilingual
Location	Side 2, Song 45
Source	Music by Sarah Pirtle; words by Sarah Pirtle and Roberto Díaz

OBJECTIVES

- to help with closure
- to teach appropriate responses to social endings

PROCEDURE

1 Announce an ending with this song. Make the transition clear. What will happen next? Snack, recess, lunch, lining up to go home? Children need assistance during transitions. In fact, conflicts are reduced when there is clarity about transitions.

2 Wave goodbye as you sing together. Look at each child as you wave. For younger children it makes a clear parenthesis around the experience of a song circle to start off by waving hello and end the circle by waving goodbye.

3 As needed, change the wording of the song to fit your situation. For example, on Friday, you can end the verse by singing:

> *Pero cuando llega el lunes,*
> *nos volveremos a reunir.*

> *But when it's Monday,*
> *we'll be back I know.*

At the end of the day:

> *Pero mañana temprano*
> *nos volveremos a reunir.*

> *But tomorrow morning*
> *we will meet again.*

SNAPSHOT

Easing Transitions

● ● ● ● ● ● ● ● ● ● ● ● ● ● ● ● ● ● ● ●

The Giving Tree School in Gill, Massachusetts posts a picture to represent each event in the daily schedule. This helps children anticipate changes and look for predictable daily rhythms.

Adios / Goodbye

©1997 Words by Sarah Pirtle and Roberto Díaz
Music by Sarah Pirtle
Discovery Center Music, BMI

Spanish

Verso

Ha llegado el momento
que tenemos que partir.
Pero despúes de almorzar
nos volveremos a reunir.

Coro

Adiós amigos, (clap, clap) (3x).
Nos volveremos a reunir.

English

Verse

Our time is almost over.
Now it's time to go.
But right after lunchtime,
we'll be back, I know.

Chorus

Goodbye my friends (clap, clap) (3x).
I'll see you again.

46 Linking Up

Children join in a song of connection.

●●●●●●●●●●●●●●●●●●●●●●●●●●●

Ages 5 to adult

When to Use Ceremonies, celebrations, or as a closing song

Language English

Location Side 2, Song 46

Source Words by Sarah Pirtle; music by Roberto Díaz

OBJECTIVES

- to appreciate the intangible quality of togetherness
- to build self-esteem
- to create connecting motions in a group

PROCEDURE

1 Play or sing "Linking Up" so that the children can become familiar with the words. Talk about the tangible parts of the song:

- Can you see grass grow?
- Can you see the roots of a tree below ground?

Then talk about feelings:

- Can you see love?
- Can you tell when you're with people who care about you?
- Have you stood near a mountain and heard the wind whistle like music?

2 Use motions to connect the group. Try these movements or modify them.

Lyrics	Movements
Verse One	
Grass growing	Fingers of one hand push upward through the thumb and index finger of the other hand.
Important	Thumbs up.
Roots grow	Fingers push downward through the thumb and index finger of the other hand.
Chorus	
Linking	Make up ways to link with hands and elbows.
River	Keep your arms linked and make circular waves together.
Verse Two	
Wild voice of the sea	Carefully lean back and kick your feet with out touching anyone.
Mountain	Feet touch and make a mountain
Important	Thumbs up.
Chorus	Sit up and link arms.

Note: *These movements were invented by Nancy Edwards, Dan Post, and their children Allie and Julian, along with my family.*

Linking Up

Who can see the grass grow? Day by day it grows so slow.

You are im - por - tant in this world.

Who can see the roots grow? Un - der - ground the roots don't show.

You are im - por - tant in this world.

Link - ing up like the grass - es, link - ing up like the trees. Link - ing

up like the ri - ver as it goes in - to the sea.

Who can see the love shin - ing ve - ry near? I

see it. I feel it. It's here.

© 1997 Words by Sarah Pirtle and Music by Roberto Díaz

Verse 1

Who can see the grass grow?
Day by day it grows so slow.
You are important in this world.
Who can see the roots grow?
Underground the roots don't show.
They know you are important in this
world.

Chorus

Linking up like the grasses,
linking up like the trees.
Linking up like the river as it goes into
the sea.

Who can see the love shining very near?
I see it. I feel it. It's here.

Verse 2

Who can hear the river with the wild
voice of the sea?
You are important in this world.
Who can hear the mountains sing to you
and me?
You are important in this world.

Last chorus:... Who can see the love shin-
ing very clear?

Songwriter's Note: *I began this song on an airplane. I flew to Macon, Georgia, to work with teachers and students I'd never met before. During our time together I experienced circle after circle of caring people, from four-year-olds who invented a new way to play "Build a Boat" by hugging each other, to staff practicing conflict resolution skills. Coming back, I searched for words to express the warmth I was taking home with me. Later Roberto Díaz shared a beautiful melody he had created, and I wove words and tune together.*

. . . .
E X T E N S I O N S
. . . .

Linking Up Drawing

Draw animals and people and other parts of nature, saying to each other, "You are important in this world." Keep the drawings where you can see them and be reminded frequently of the message.

The Spiral Handshake

Stand or sit in a circle. Each child identifies her right hand and reaches it forward. She curls her fingers inward to make a backwards C, and reaches into the center to hook on to

and nest with all the other hands. The group's shape looks like curved petals coming out of the middle of a flower. If you have too many people to fit in one circle, then make two tiers, with one spiral under the other.

Note: *I learned this from Jenni Allard and Beth Hick's class in Leyden, Massachusetts. This handshake originally was developed in the Cooperative Learning Network.*

Appendix

· ·

Song Sequences

Building Character Through Music

How Songs Can Teach Reading

How Songs Develop the Social Health of a Class

Teacher Training for Linking Up

OVERVIEW OF SONG SEQUENCES

Part I: Songs for Circle Time
Chapter Two: Starting Songs
1. The Colors of Earth
2. Good Morning to the Sky/ Buenos Días al Cielo
3. This Little Light of Mine

Song Sequence One: Connecting with Self and Others
4. Come Join in the Circle

Chapter Three: Friendship Songs
5. Chocolate
6. My Space/Mi Espacio
7. Sitting in the Soup and Jump, Jump, Jump

Song Sequence Two: Awareness of Self and Others
8. Our Own Song and the Spoony Song
9. Creeping Mouse Game
10. Across the Wide Ocean/A Través Del Inmenso Mar

Song Sequence Three: Spanish Bilingual Songs
11. ¡Hola!/Hello
12. Pajarito/Little Bird - traditional
13. Step by Step/Paso a Paso
14. En La Feria /At the Fair
15. Llegó la Hora /Now's the Time

Song Sequence Four: Affirming Differences
Part II: Songs for the Social Curriculum
Chapter Four: Diversity Songs
16. In the Very Middle
17. Speak Up
18. I Want to Know Your Name

Song Sequence Five: Unity and Inclusion
19. Grandmother Spider
20. We Won't Leave Anyone Out
21. Sing About Us/ Cantemos De Nosotros

Song Sequence Six: Empathy and Community
22. Canción de la Nube/ Song of the Cloud
23. Sleeping Birds / Los Pajaritos Duermen (Back Patting Game)
24. Full Circle (The Village)

Connecting with Self and Others

1. Unify

Come Join in the Circle   (Song 4 – Ages 3 to 9)
Children wave and sing each name.

Extension
Children sing about the activities they did right before Song Circle.

2. Anchor in the Present

Chocolate   (Song 5 – Ages 3 to 9)
Hand motions anchor children physically.

3. Build a Skill

My Space/Mi Espacio   (Song 6 – Ages 4 to 9)
The children practice staying in their own personal space. They progress from twisting and stomping to painting the sphere of their space.

Extension
As children spontaneously do new movements, we incorporate them and sing a phrase such as "I wiggle in my space."

4. Expand Their Involvement

Sitting in the Soup   (Song 7 – Ages 3 to 8)
Jump, Jump, Jump variation
Children are reminded to be careful of each other as they share the space. This is the climax—the main activity.

5. End Together

Our Own Song revision   (Song 8)
"Time to end the circle" is sung to the tune of "Come Join the Circle." Or, summarize what the children did in Song Circle using the tune of "Our Own Song." This closes the experience.

Awareness of Self and Others

1. Unify

Our Own Song   (Song 8 – Ages 2 to 5, with variations for Ages 5 to 9)
The group sings about the activities each child did before Song Circle.

2. Anchor in the Present

Creeping Mouse   (Song 9 – Ages 3 to 7)
Bond the group in a circle using gentle touch.

3. Build a Skill

Across the Wide Ocean   (Song 10 – Ages 3 to 10)
Children move with self-awareness. They recognize their own movement preferences as they invent wave motions.

4. Expand Their Involvement

Across the Wide Ocean   (Song 10 – Ages 3 to 10)
The song is expanded as the whole group mirrors movements of individuals (ages 3 and up), or partners mirror each other's waves (ages 5 and up).

5. End Together

Children return to sit in a circle. Using the tune to "Our Own Song," (Song 8) make a clear transition with an affirmative statement, such as "I like dancing with all of you, (3x), and now it is time for snack."

Song Sequence 3

Bilingual Songs

UNIFY

1. Unify

"¡Hola!/Hello" (Song 11 – Ages 4 to 8)
Greet every child by name.

ANCHOR

2. Anchor In The Present

"Pajarito/Little Bird" (Song 12 – Ages 3 to 8)
Children act out the song as a fingerplay while seated.

BUILD

3. Build A Skill

"Pajarito/Little Bird" (Song 12)
Children stand in a circle and act out "Pajarito/Little Bird."

"Step by Step/Paso a Paso" (Song 13 – Ages 3 to 10)
Children sing "Step by Step/Paso a Paso" moving with self-control in a circle, walking slowly then stopping to jump.

EXPAND

4. Expand Their Involvement

"En La Feria/At the Fair" (Song 14 – Ages 3 to 10)
Children pantomime playing musical instruments.

END

5. End Together

"Llegó La Hora/Now's the Time" (Song 15 – Ages 3 to 8)
Make a clear transition to the next activity.

Affirming Differences

UNIFY

1. Unify

In the Very Middle (Song 16)

Help children find pairs so that no one is left out. Play the "Partner Game."

ANCHOR

2. Anchor In The Present

In the Very Middle (Song 16)

After pairs share ways they are alike and ways they are different, they sing the song, "In the Very Middle" to each other standing face to face and palm to palm.

BUILD

3. Build A Skill

Speak Up (Song 17)

Use the song "Speak Up" to explore ways to intervene in a friendly but firm way if you hear someone make fun of differences. Learn the song and then do the activity, "Standing Up for Fairness." Practice finding words that will help using one or two of the "Four Situations of Bias."

EXPAND

4. Expand Their Involvement

I Want to Know Your Name (Song 18)

Recognize a few specific people known to the class from the school or your community who stand up for fairness. Use the pattern of the song, "I Want to Know Your Name," to sing a short statement about each person. Variation: Assemble books or posters of famous people who promoted fairness and respected diversity, such as Cesar Chavez, Jane Addams, and Mary McLeod Bethune. Create brief phrases to summarize what they did. See the activity, "Singing About Peacemakers."

END

5. End Together

In the Very Middle (Song 16)

Repeat "In the Very Middle" in pairs, asking children to send a feeling of respect to their partner.

Song 5 Sequence

Unity and Inclusion

UNIFY

1. Unify

Grandmother Spider (Song 19)

Sing "Grandmother Spider" in a circle. Use the image of a web to describe the feeling of connection between classmates. Learn the movements which accompany the song.

ANCHOR

2. Anchor In The Present

We Won't Leave Anyone Out (Song 20)

Stand in a circle and pass out interesting objects for each person to hold while you play "Name Echo." Next teach "We Won't Leave Anyone Out" and play a passing game, "Everyone At Once," using special objects. Collect the objects and discuss what it means to say "we won't leave anyone out."

BUILD

3. Build a Skill

Sing About Us (Song 21)

Teach "Sing About Us." Discuss the words in the chorus, "You don't have to be just like me to be my friend."

EXPAND

4. Expand Their Involvement

Sing About Us (Song 21)

Lead the class in songwriting to make new verses for "Sing About Us." First set group agreements to respect each person's ideas. Selct a topic from the heading which will be most useful for your group:

> affirming our preferences,
> affirming our physical identities,
> affirming our cultural and family identities.

END

5. End

Grandmother Spider (Song 19)

Repeat the Grandmother Spider Song. Tell your class that you'd like to hear from children whenever they are feeling left out of the web.

Song 6 Sequence

Empathy and Community

LESSON PLAN FOR GRADES K-1

1. Unify

Full Circle (Song 24)

Play the song "Full Circle" and ask children to cycle their hands on the chorus. Ask them to reach to each other on the words, "between you and I."

2. Anchor In The Present

Canción de la Nube/Song of the Cloud (Song 22)

Today we're practicing thinking about each other. Introduce "Canción de la Nube/Song of the Cloud." This song talks about a cloud thinking about a thirsty flower. Use one hand to be the cloud and the other hand to be the flower to act out the song.

3. Build A Skill

Repeat the story of the cloud and the flower. Use the activity "Two Lines." The children in one line are the clouds and they face their partners in the other line who are the flowers. Then have them switch roles.

4. Expand Their Involment

Sleeping Birds/Los Pajaritos Duermen

Now we're going to give each other some care. We'll play a game where some children will be sleeping birds while others help me pat their backs. At the end of the game, sit up together in a circle. Say, "Let's keep thinking about each other for the rest of the day. As you look at other children you can notice if they need help or you can ask each other for help." See the extension activity, "Solidarity and Empathy."

5. End

Full Circle (Song 24)

Repeat just the chorus of "Full Circle." Children look at each other and repeat the motion on the words, "between you and I," extending their hand from their heart.

Finding Words That Help

UNIFY

1. Unify

Two in the Fight   (Song 26)

Repeat from previous lesson. Say, "Have you heard people say use your words when you are angry? Today we're going to work on finding words that help."

ANCHOR

2. Anchor In The Present

The Anger Chant (Song 28)

Sing or listen to "The Anger Chant" and tap the beat. Next, engage the children in creating hand movements to accompany the words, and repeat the song. If children get stuck in making fists or showing their fists threateningly, use the short reframing activity, "Converting Fists to an Open Hand."

BUILD

3. Build A Skill

When I Say Stop/Cuando Digo ¡Ya!   (Song 29)

Reinforce that we can send a message with our words or our body language that says, "Stop, I don't like that," and "Let's do something different."

EXPAND

4. Expand Their Involvement

Use puppets to help children find words that help. Lead one or two of these activities from the song games:

> How Anna Talked Out A Problem (Two in the Fight)
> Anger Messages (The Anger Chant)
> Send Your Message (When I Say Stop)
> Show That You Get the Message (When I Say Stop)

END

5. End Together

Heart to Heart/Corazón a Corazón (Song 27)
When I Say Stop/Cuando Digo ¡Ya! (Song 29)

Choose the ending song that fits your group best.

Song 8 Sequence

Choosing to Talk it Out Together

1. Unify

How Can We Be Friends Again?/Amigos de Nuevo   (Song 25)

Teach just the chorus in English, Spanish, or both.

2. Anchor In The Present

Two in the Fight   (Song 26)

Illustrate the choice of talking out a problem together. Teach the fingerplay Two in the Fight. Ask children for their ideas on how people talk things out.

3. Build A Skill

How Can We Be Friends Again?/Amigos de Nuevo   (Song 25)

Teach the whole song: "How Can We Be Friends Again? / Amigos de Nuevo"

Make a list of what makes a problem worse (using the symbol of the growing tornado) and what makes a problem better, (using the symbol of the sprouting seed.) Use the words from your list to create new verses to the song.

4. Expand Their Involvement

Heart to Heart/Corazón a Corazón (Song 27)

Children act out the song, turning away from one another on the verses and then returning to face each other on the chorus. Either stop the song before the chant or suggest that children invent movements on that section of the song.

5. End Together

Heart to Heart/Corazón a Corazón (Song 27)

Sit down together and hold hands. Sing the Heart to Heart chorus once more.

Solving Problems

1. Unify

When I Say Stop/ Cuando Digo ¡Ya!   (Song 29)

Repeat the three lines of "When I Say Stop/ Cuando Digo ¡Ya!" from the previous lesson. Then share the whole song, tying in the overall theme of the lessons—having options, saying things different ways, looking at things from another person's view point.

2. Anchor In the Present

There is Always Something You Can Do   (Song 30)

Ask children to explain in their own words what that phrase "there's always something you can do" means.

3. Build A Skill

Present a conflict situation that would be familiar for your class. Ask children to come up with as many possible solutions as they can. Teach how to brainstorm.

4. Expand Their Involvement

¡Dilo!/Talk to Me   (Song 31)

Teach the first verse of "¡Dilo!/ Talk To Me" in both Spanish and English. Use the method described in the procedure of acting out the song with partners.

Then connect this song with the process of brainstorming.

5. End

¡Dilo!/Talk to Me   (Song 31)

Sit together and sing the song one more time.

Joining With Nature

UNIFY

1. Unify

El Caracol/The Snail's Dance (Song 32)

Sing as a finger play.

ANCHOR

2. Anchor In the Present

My Roots Go Down (Song 33)

Ask each child to stand in his or her own space. Invite the children to make up their own way to move to the chorus.

BUILD

3. Build A Skill

My Roots Go Down (Song 33)

Ask them to select an animal they would like to be. Use the verses to sing their animals as they dance. On the chorus, have the children return to the same spot on the floor where they began.

EXPAND

4. Expand Their Involvement

Night Critters Game (Song 34)

Explain that the next songs are Native American. Talk about nocturnal animals who hunt at night for food. Play the recording of the which has both a Serrano lullabye and a Cahuilla song. Dance to it in a circle. As a variation, extend the game by asking a few children to go into the center of the circle and act as mountains while the rest of the children in the circle role play animals.

END

5. End

Serrano Lullaby

Sit in a circle using hands to act out the Serrano lullabye one last time: "Kaich akuum, kaich akuum." With your fingers show the animal going to sleep.

Option: begin or end with

Grandmother Spider (Song 19)

Song Sequence 11

Moving Together

1. Unify

Build A Boat (Song 35)

Sing the song in a seated circle. Clap along. Repeat the song and pretend everyone is rowing in a boat together.

2. Anchor In the Present

Shake, Shake, Freeze (Song 36)

Play while sitting down. Shake fingers, roll hands, shake shoulders. Make sure everyone is able to stop and freeze.

3. Build A Skill

Shake, Shake, Freeze (Song 36)

Stand up but stay in place. Play with standing motions: shake your whole body, stretch, hop, twist.

4. Expand Their Involvement

Mi Cuerpo Hace Música/There's Music Inside Me
(Song 37)

Say, "We've been moving all different parts of our bodies. Now we're going to sing about our hands, feet, mouth, and hips in Spanish and English." Lead song. Next, move in a line around the room, repeating the song. Option: Repeat "Build A Boat" (Song 35), this time hooking on to each other in a line and moving around the room.

5. End

Build A Boat (Song 35)

Return to sitting in a circle. Once more, repeat song. For the last line sing, "And now it's time to stop."

Song 12 Sequence

Creating Mirrors, Bridges, and Shapes

UNIFY

1. Unify

Cloud Hands (Song 38)

Ask children to mirror you as you move. Select children to lead the movement.

ANCHOR

2. Anchor In the Present

Cloud Hands (Song 38)

Help children find partners. Face your partner sitting down. Take turns leading song.

BUILD

3. Build A Skill

Cloud Hands (Song 38)
Under the Bridge (Song 39)

Play Cloud Hands standing up. Next, partners form bridges for Under the Bridge. Decide whether one long bridge or separate bridges will be more effective for your class. Take turns going under the bridges.

EXPAND

4. Expand Their Involvement

Let's Get Together (Song 40)

Put partners together to create groups of four or six. Begin by connecting with hands, and then create shapes together like wheels, a roof, or a flower.

END

5. End

Let's Get Together (Song 40)

Ask everyone to return to sit in a circle. Use the tune to "Let's Get Together" and sing, *"Let's wave now to each other. (2x) Let's wave now, let's wave now and it's time to stop."*

Song 13 Sequence **Peace Songs**

1. Unify

Two Hands Hold the Earth/Mis Dos Manos (Song 41)

Stand together and follow the motions to the song.

2. Anchor In the Present

Two Hands Hold the Earth/Mis Dos Manos (Song 41)

Partners face each other and do the motions. Form one earth together with all four hands.

3. Build A Skill

Canto Por La Paz/I Sing for Peace (Song 42)

Learn the song and talk about its meaning.

4. Expand Their Involvement

Peace is Me Being Me (Song 43)

Create a dance to the song. Option: Use a peace activity with drawing or rhythm instruments as described in this chapter.

5. End Together

Two Hands Hold the Earth/Mis Dos Manos (Song 41)

Repeat song. At the end, the whole class pantomimes that it is holding together one earth.

Option: Begin or end the sequence with "This Little Light of Mine" (Song 3).

Build Community

1. Unify

Carry the Candle (Song 44)

If possible, light a candle in the room, have a candle for display, or pass a candle.

2. Anchor In the Present

Carry the Candle (Song 44)

Use as a zipper song: ask children for new words they want to sing.

3. Build A Skill

Linking Up (Song 46)

Play the recording for children to listen to this song.. If possible, deepen their listening in one of these ways:

- ask them to close their eyes and sense pictures in their imagination

- supply one large sheet of paper or individual sheets and ask them to draw what they are thinking about

- provide a basket of objects from nature such as a shell, a rock, or a nut and give every child one object to hold.

4. Expand Their Involvement

Linking Up (Song 46)

Share thoughts, feelings, or pictures from listening together. Talk about the words, "You are important in this world." Make a spiral handshake and sing along to "Linking Up." At the end of handshake, let go while saying affirming words as a group. For example, everyone says, "Here we go," "Carry the light," or "You are important."

5. End Together

Adiós/Goodbye (Song 45)

Option: Include related songs such as "This Little Light of Mine" (Song 3), "Full Circle" (Song 24) or "Grandmother Spider" (Song 19).

BUILDING CHARACTER THROUGH MUSIC

Respect, responsibility, caring, fairness—how do we teach these qualities?

Words alone aren't enough. When we tell children how to behave, our words fall flat. However, if we tie the concepts to a social activity, children can learn by doing. You can use the songs in this book to provide a context for developing these important traits.

Responsibility

1. Shake, Shake, Freeze (Song 36)

   I can control how I move.

2. My Space/Mi Espacio (Song 6)

   I can contain large movements in my own space.

3. Let's Get Together/Juntémonos (Song 40)

   I can move with others and take responsibility for my movements.

4. Under the Bridge (Song 39)

   I am careful of others as we make bridges together.

Respect

1. Cloud Hands (Song 38)

   I show respect for others as I follow and lead a mirror game.
2. Across the Wide Ocean/A Través del Inmenso Mar (Song 10)

   I work with you respectfully as we invent wave motions together.
3. My Roots Go Down (Song 33)

   I think about others as I travel and move in a game.
4. When I Say Stop/Cuando Digo ¡Ya! (Song 29)

   I use words to set boundaries and respect myself and others.

Caring

1. Sleeping Hands/Los Pajaritos Duermen (Song 23)

   I convey my care as I pat the backs of my classmates.
2. Creeping Mouse (Song 9)

   I can carefully touch the hands of my friends.
3. Grandmother Spider (Song 19)

   I feel what it means to be unified with others and to know that we care about each other.
4. Peace is Me Being Me (Song 43)

   I dance with others and create motions that communicate our interconnection.
5. Linking Up! (Song 46)

   I feel my connection to others and I believe that I am important in this world.

Trustworthiness

1. How Can We Be Friends Again?/Amigos de Nuevo (Song 25)
   I think about what helps friends trust each other.

2. Heart to Heart/Corazón a Corazón (Song 27)
   I connect to my friends with my hands.

3. Carry the Candle (Song 44)
   I can be trusted to carry a lit candle carefully.

Fairness

1. We Won't Leave Anyone Out (Song 20)
   I include all classmates.

2. Sing About Us/Cantemos de Nosotros (Song 21)
   I affirm our differences.

3. Speak Up (Song 17)
   I intervene when someone is treated unfairly.

4. In the Very Middle (Song 16)
   I know what I have in common with all other people.

Citizenship

1. I Want To Know Your Name (Song 18)
   I celebrate citizens of my community.

2. Full Circle (Song 24)
   I feel connected to others like in a village.

3. Two Hands Hold The Earth (Song 41)
   I take responsibility for the earth.

4. This Little Light of Mine (Song 3)
   I share the light of my heart.

HOW SONGS CAN TEACH READING

Using Charts

Post the lyrics of a song on chart paper. Underline the key words you'd like students to learn. First, play the recording while following along with the words on the chart. Then, read out loud in unison with your students while pointing to each word. Pause before an underlined word and ask students to identify it.

Partner Practice

Students work with copies of the lyrics. *You have permission from ESR to copy lyrics from this book for your language arts program. Students work in pairs and practice reading words to each other. They support each other to learn words they find difficult. Once both are successful, partners raise their hands to show they can both read the song.

Song Lyric Notebooks

Use bilingual songs with students to help them learn to read in both Spanish and English*.

1. Each time they present a song, they provide each student with their own copy of the lyrics. These are placed in individual notebooks.

2. Students sing or recite each song for the teacher to illustrate their facility.

3. Groups of four conference with their notebooks and choose whether they will read a song in Spanish or in English.

By the end of the year, their students can read forty to sixty songs.

*   *From Carlos Villegas, Simon Alvarez, and Tomas Butchart of Albuquerque, New Mexico.*

Reading Song Boards*

Provide incomplete lyrics and ask students to fill in the missing words using cards. Teachers can create song boards providing the partial lyrics of a song and leave spaces for key words. Two sets of cards can be developed—one with pictures of the missing words and the other with the key words themselves. The children then place the correct cards in the spaces.

Song Boards are described in the extension for:

> Good Morning to the Sky/Buenos Dias al Cielo (Song 2)

Other songs which easily lend themselves to Song Boards are:

> Step by Step/Paso a Paso (Song 13)
> Full Circle (Song 24)
> Build A Boat (Song 35)

You can create boards for any song that you select.

*   *This idea derives from the work of Spencer Kagan on cooperative learning. He teaches methods of using heterogeneous groups to study a song board and work together to lay out the cards in the appropriate spaces. For more information, contact Kagan Cooperative Learning, 1-800-933-2667.*

Cooperative Songwriting

Select a song with a clear pattern that provides an effective foundation for new words contributed by students. Examples:

> I Want to Know Your Name (Song 18)
>
> Sing About Us/Cantemos de Nosotros (Song 21)
>
> How Can We Be Friends Again/Amigos de Nuevo (Song 25)
>
> My Roots Go Down (Song 33)

Create worksheets that provide the song pattern. Provide one sheet for each small group of two or three students. Once the pattern is clear, ask children to work together to create new words and write them in the blank spaces. Provide guidance to help them break down the assignment step by step. Help them offer ideas and also listen to what each other say, working interdependently with all members participating. This method is described in depth in Sarah Pirtle's book, *Songwriting Together*, available from the Discovery Center.

Class Books

Encourage children to extend the meaning of a song through drawing and writing. Ask them to create drawings related to a song. For example, after listening to "En la Feria/At the Fair" (Song 14) which focuses upon instruments heard at a town fair, students select an instrument to draw. After playing the "Creeping Mouse Game" (Song 9), they draw the images from the story.

Next, help children add words to describe their drawings, and then group their work to create a class book. These songs lend themselves to this process:

> The Colors of Earth (Song 1)
>
> Good Morning to the Sky/Buenos Días al Cielo (Song 2)
>
> Creeping Mouse (Song 9)
>
> Across the Wide Ocean/A Través del Inmenso Mar (Song 10)
>
> Pajarito/Little Bird (Song 12)
>
> En la Feria/At the Fair (Song 14)
>
> My Roots Go Down (Song 33)

Gather as a class to read the book together and enjoy each contribution.

HOW SONGS DEVELOP THE SOCIAL HEALTH OF A CLASS

- Song that help children move comfortably in their own personal bubble of space:
    - My Space/Mi Espacio (Song 6)
    - My Roots Go Down (Song 33)
    - Step by Step/Paso a Paso (Song 13)
    - Shake, Shake, Freeze (Song 36)
    - Cloud Hands (Song 38)
    - Sitting in the Soup (Song 7)
    - Grandmother Spider (Song 19)

- Songs that help children have the self-awareness to initiate movements that they themselves enjoy:
    - Across the Wide Ocean (Song 10)
    - My Roots Go Down (Song 33)
    - My Space/Mi Espacio (Song 6)
    - Cloud Hands (Song 38)

- Songs that help children feel physically connected and anchored to the earth:
    - Two Hands Hold the Earth (Song 41)
    - My Roots Go Down (Song 33)
    - My Space/Mi Espacio (Song 6)

- Songs that help children use gentle touch to connect with other children:
    - Creeping Mouse (Song 9)
    - Sleeping Birds/Los Pajaritos Duermen (Song 23)
    - Let's Get Together (Song 40)
    - Pajarito / Little Bird (Song 12)
    - We Won't Leave Anyone Out (Song 20)

- Songs that help children provide words that describe their feelings, their playtime activities, and important events in their lives:
    - Come Join in the Circle (Song 4)
    - Our Own Song (Song 8)
    - Jump, Jump, Jump (Song 7)
    - Sing About Us (Song 21)

- Songs that help children respond to the movements and words of others:
    - Cloud Hands (Song 38)
    - Heart to Heart / Corazón a Corazón (Song 27)
    - Come Join in the Circle (Song 4)
    - In the Very Middle (Song 16)
    - ¡Dilo!/ Talk to Me (Song 31)

- Songs that help children mirror and lead movements with a partner:
    - Across the Wide Ocean (Song 10)
    - Cloud Hands (Song 38)

- Songs that help children move respectfully in a shared group space:
    Shake, Shake, Freeze (Song 36)
    Sitting in the Soup (Song 7)
    Jump, Jump, Jump (Song 7)
    Peace is Me Being Me (Song 43)
    Under the Bridge (Song 39)
    My Roots Go Down (Song 33)
    Step by Step/Paso a Paso (Song 13)

- Songs that help children collaborate with others to make a shape together:
    Build A Boat (Song 35)
    Let's Get Together (Song 40)
    Under the Bridge (Song 39)

- Songs that help children collaborate with others to create a story dance:
    Across the Wide Ocean (Song 10)
    El Caracol / The Snail's Dance (Song 32)
    Canción de La Nube / Song of the Cloud (Song 22)
    Peace is Me Being Me (Song 43)
    My Roots Go Down (Song 33)
    Night Critters Game (Song 34)
    Build A Boat (Song 35)

TEACHER TRAINING FOR LINKING UP

Here are ten ways you can get ready to teach this material.

1. Examine the group agreements you use with your class or create new group agreements. Think about ways the children can be involved in the process.

   a. Think about the space you use for Circle Time, the provisions you make for doing large active movement, and any group customs you want to establish.

2. Try Lesson Plans with Song Sequences

   a. As adults, try some of the Song Sequences in the book.

   b. Select one of the Song Sequences for the children with whom you work. Modify it to fit their needs. Try it and take notes on how it went. Use this evaluation time not to criticize yourself but to reflect on what you learned about the children and to record what occurred.

3. Study Methods of Interaction

   a. Choose anecdotes from the book and read them out loud or dramatize as role plays. Discuss the method of interaction that is illustrated. Discuss any ways in which you might have handled the situation differently than the anecdote portrays. Define the goal of the teacher.

   b. Select one of the methods of interaction described in the book. Think of a situation from your own work with children— but don't pick the hardest one. Meet with another teacher and discuss how to apply this method of interaction to your situations.

   c. In your own words describe what "information + affirmation" means to you.

4. Use the following questions to journal, discuss with a partner, and/or discuss as a group

   a. What is your personal history with the expressive arts?

   b. What touchstone can you use to remember your ability to "hold" the group of children you work with? What are the underlying messages you want to say when you are "holding" children?

   c. Who is a compassionate person you know that can be your role model as you give guidance to children?

   d. What messages did you receive about differences as you were growing up?

   e. How were conflicts handled in your family?

5. Focus on Unity and Diversity

   a. How have you seen misinformation, bias or pre-prejudice come up during your work with children pertaining to:
      - family differences,
      - gender,
      - physical differences,
      - ability differences,
      - racial and ethnic identity,

Note: *ESR offers comprehensive training to help you implement this curriculum. For more information, see "Professional Development for Linking Up!" or call ESR at 1-800-370-2515.*

- economic differences,
- religious differences.

   b. Pick one of the situations you have identified and brainstorm what kinds of discussions, interactions, songs, and other activities would help supply information + affirmation.

   c. Discuss ways you can help children understand and experience their underlying unity. Choose one to try.

   d. Discuss ways you can help children talk about, recognize, respect, and value their great diversity. Choose one to try.

6. Focus on Conflict Resolution

   a. Study the two tools in the beginning of chapter five.

   b. Examine the conflict resolution lesson plans and Song Sequences of conflict resolution songs. Choose plans to try together. Experience how they work and modify them for your own class.

7. Focus on Teaching Goals

Select an element from Five Key Elements in Teaching Social Skills and focus on developing it in your teaching. First read over the examples and discuss the meaning of each element. Next, choose one element and think of a concrete goal for yourself related to that element Discuss it with a partner. After you try the goal, meet back with your partner to discuss how it went.

8. Study the Social Health of Your Group

Instead of thinking about the qualities or problems of individuals, generalize to the classroom community as a whole. To build toward social health, evaluate first what your group is doing well. Then focus not on what isn't working but rather on what potential can be developed. Look for the skills that individuals and groups are ready to develop next.

9. Develop a New Lesson Plan (Song Sequence)

Construct a song sequence of 3, 4 or 5 songs.

Picture each stage of the lesson you have designed.

Visualize the room of children and what they will be doing. See each activity in its most successful form. As you study the plan in your imagination, learn any changes you need to make or any instructions you will need to give to help with transitions.

10. Prepare Three Songs

Pick three things you want a song to do for your group from the various skills listed above or found throughout the book. Memorize three songs (from here or another collection of songs), one from each of the three categories you've selected.

Examples:

Reinforce personal space.	My Space / Mi Espacio
Provide stop and go practice.	Shake, Shake, Freeze
Provide a joyful cooperation game.	Let's Get Together
Give opportunity for creative movement.	Across the Wide Ocean /A Través del Inmenso Mar

Professional Development for Linking Up!

Educators for Social Responsibility offers comprehensive training for early childhood educators. In the Peaceable Early Childhood Classroom training, preschool through grade 3 teachers develop a framework for understanding how violence affects young children, practice conflict resolution skills, and explore a range of teaching strategies for promoting pro-social values in early childhood settings. Our workshops focus on developing a classroom community that infuses age-appropriate cooperation, caring communication, appreciation of diversity, expression of feelings, and conflict resolution into daily classroom practice.

Some of the topics addressed in ESR's early childhood workshops include:

- how violence in society, both in real life and in the media, is affecting children, families, and schools;
- ways to help children appreciate a wide range of differences;
- ways to help children work through experiences, ideas, and feelings about violence;
- strategies for infusing violence prevention and conflict resolution into daily classroom life, as well as developing an action plan for implementation in your own setting;
- the developmental, political, and cultural issues surrounding the violence in children's lives;
- practical activities and ideas such as using dialogue, graphs, puppetry, games, play, class charts, and curriculum webs to create a Peaceable Classroom;
- how to design developmentally appropriate activities for your classroom;
- how to develop an action plan for implementing conflict resolution in your own setting.

A team of professionals with a wide range of early childhood experience, including author Sarah Pirtle, are available for introductory and advanced training for developing a Peaceable Early Childhood Classroom.

For more information call ESR at
1-800-370-2515

ABOUT THE AUTHOR

Sarah Pirtle provides social skills training for children and teachers across the country through school residencies, staff development workshops, conferences, and concerts. She received four national awards for her children's recordings produced by A Gentle Wind: "Magical Earth," "The Wind is Telling Secrets," and "Two Hands Hold the Earth," including the Parents' Choice Award, the Oppenheim Gold Seal Award and the American Library Association Notable Award.

Her young adult novel, *An Outbreak of Peace*, (New Society Publishers, 1987) received the Olive Branch Award for the outstanding book on world peace. She is also the author of *Discovery Time for Cooperation and Conflict Resolution: Grades K–6* (Children's Creative Response to Conflict, Nyack, NY 1998). She teaches music in the Creative Arts in Learning Program at Lesley College and has taught graduate education courses on conflict resolution skills for the University of Vermont and the University of Syracuse. She was one of the main founders of the Children's Music Network.

To contact Sarah: The Discovery Center for the Expressive Arts
                              63 Main Street, Shelburne Falls, MA 01370
                              (413)625-2355

Send for a catalog about Sarah's three other recordings or to find out more about the programs she provides.

ABOUT THE CHILDREN'S MUSIC NETWORK

Classroom teachers, music teachers, songwriters, parents, performers, radio hosts, and children themselves link up with each other through this national organization. The network is founded on the belief that children's music is an important force for building community and for teaching cooperative values. Through local, regional, and national gatherings and through the journal *Pass it On!* which was launched by Sarah, people learn about new songs and teaching methods and meet inspiring people of all ages.

To contact the Children's Music Network: P.O. Box 1341
                                                           Evanston, IL 60204-1341
                                                           (847)733-8003

ABOUT ESR

Educators for Social Responsibility seeks to make social responsibility an integral part of education in our nation's schools. We create and disseminate new ways of teaching and learning that help young people participate in shaping a better world.

Our programs and products present divergent viewpoints, stimulate critical thinking about controversial issues, teach creative and productive ways of dealing with differences, promote cooperative problem solving, and foster informed decision making. We help young people develop a personal commitment to the well-being of other people and the planet, and encourage participation in the democratic process.

For more information about our products and training programs call 1-800-370-2515 or write to ESR, 23 Garden St., Cambridge MA 02138.

OTHER EARLY CHILDHOOD RESOURCES FROM ESR

Early Childhood Adventures in Peacemaking
William J. Kreidler with Nan Doty, Claudia Logan, Laura Parker Roerden, Cheryl Raner, and Carol Wintle

Early Childhood Adventures in Peacemaking is a unique activity guide designed to help early childhood educators help young children learn effective, nonviolent ways to resolve conflict. The guide addresses vital issues such as cooperation, the expression of feelings, anger management, and communication through hundreds of developmentally appropriate activities.

The guide assists providers in:
- developing approaches for resolving conflict in your program;
- implementing direct instruction in key conflict resolution concepts;
- developing children's skills through games, music, art, drama, storytelling, and other activities.

In addition to hundreds of activities, the guide contains an extensive discussion of ways to develop a "Peaceable Program," including strategies for building community, ways to listen to children and observe behavior, how to plan for anti-bias work, and opportunities for involving parents/guardians in your program.

A section on bullying and name-calling helps providers effectively address these issues. Scripts help providers use Peace Puppets to address conflicts among children. Discussion pictures provide another way to spark discussions about conflict in your program.

A provider kit will soon be available containing many items to use in conjunction with the activity guide, as well as numerous children's books, cassettes, and more.

Preschool–Grade 3 ESR 1997, 372 pages AIPECH
$22.00 Nonmembers $19.80 Members
Provider kit available soon. Call for more information.

Teaching Young Children in Violent Times: Building a Peaceable Classroom
Diane E. Levin, Ph. D.

Teaching Young Children in Violent Times helps preschool through grade 3 teachers create a classroom where children learn peaceful alternatives to the violent behaviors modeled for them in society.

Part I of this essential guide explores the developmental roots of young children's thinking and behaviors on issues ranging from conflict to prejudice to violence and provides a cultural context for the violence in children's lives. Highly-effective dialogs between young children and teachers are offered with a framework for teachers to extend children's thinking in developmentally appropriate ways.

Part II includes practical guidelines and activities for creating a Peaceable Classroom.

Learn how to use puppetry, games, play, class charts, curriculum webs, and graphs to help young children resolve their conflicts peacefully and respect one another's differences. This highly-acclaimed book is a must for early childhood educators, parents, and policy makers.

Preschool-Grade 3 193 pages, ESR 1994 TEACHV

$21.95 Nonmembers $19.76 Members

Elementary Perspectives: Teaching Concepts of Peace and Conflict
William J. Kreidler

This outstanding curriculum offers more than 80 activities that help teachers and students define peace, explore justice, and learn the value of conflict and its resolution.

Students read, write, draw, role-play, sing, and discuss their way through a process that helps them acquire the concrete cooperative and conflict resolution skills needed to become caring and socially responsible citizens.

Grades K-6 269 pages, ESR 1990 EPERS1

$30.00 Nonmembers $27.00 Members

School-age Adventures in Peacemaking: A Conflict Resolution and Violence Prevention Curriculum
William J. Kreidler and Lisa Furlong with Libby Cowles and IlaSahai Prouty
How do you create a program that fosters mutual respect and the creative resolution of conflict? *Adventures in Peacemaking* includes hundreds of activities, ideas and tips for creating a Peaceable Program—designed to meet the unique needs of afterschool programs, camps, and recreation centers.

Adventures in Peacemaking blends ESR's innovative conflict resolution curricula with Project Adventure's activity-based programming. The complete program includes an activity guide, kit of manipulatives, lending library, and training.

The **activity guide** can be used alone, or along with the kit of manipulatives. The guide includes hundreds of hands-on, engaging activities that teach basic conflict resolution skills through drama, cooperative challenges, cooking, and art.

The **provider kit** includes a broad range of manipulatives to use in conjunction with the activity guide. Hard-to-find items such as foam "lily pads," spot markers, buddy ropes, Feelings Cards, and much more are at your fingertips. Rather than wasting valuable program time looking for materials, you can bring *Adventures in Peacemaking* "out of the bag" and directly into your children's hands. Two versions of the kit are offered: a full kit and a mini-kit. The full kit includes key materials needed for the activities and optionally also includes three, six-week "clubs" (thematic, sequenced activities). The mini-kit contains the most-difficult-to-find and most-often-used items.

The **lending library** includes valuable resources such as specially selected books, games, videos, and cassettes for helping families create "Peaceable Homes."

Activity Guide Grades K-6, 330 pages ESR 1996, ADVENP

$22.00 Nonmembers, $19.80 Members
Full kit of manipulatives without clubs

ADVKI2
$1,050.00 Nonmembers $945.00 Members
Full kit of manipulatives with clubs

ADVKIT
$1,200.00 Nonmembers $1,080.00 Members
Mini-kit of manipulatives

ADVMIN
$300.00 Nonmembers, $270.00 Members
Parent Lending Library

ADVLIB
$660.00 Nonmembers, $594.00 Members

Creative Conflict Resolution: More Than 200 Activities for Keeping Peace in the Classroom, K-6
William J. Kreidler

Creative Conflict Resolution is a definitive manual that provides elementary school teachers with thoughtful, effective ideas for responding to everyday classroom conflicts. Teachers learn to turn conflict into productive opportunity, helping students to deal nonviolently and constructively with anger, fear, aggression, and prejudice.

Creative Conflict Resolution offers over 200 classroom-tested activities and games and over 20 different techniques with examples. This book is widely used and highly recommended.

Grades K-6 216 pages Scott, Foresman and Company 1984 CREATI
$13.00 Nonmembers $11.70 Members

Roots and Wings: Affirming Culture in Early Childhood Programs
Stacy York

Help young children soar beyond prejudice and discrimination—give them *Roots and Wings*. This highly recommended resource for early childhood educators includes over 60 activities to support young children wtih an awareness of their cultural roots and the skills to respect differences. Learn how to respond to children's questions about race, culture, and discriminatory behaviors, and take advantage of teachable moments. Ideas are included for integrating cultural awareness and prejudice reduction into all aspects of your program.

Preschool-Grade 3 205 pages, Redleaf Press 1991
ROOTSA
$24.95 Nonmembers $22.46 Members

ORDER FORM

Call, mail, or fax your order
Tel. (800) 370-2515
Fax (617) 864-5164

esr

EDUCATORS
for
SOCIAL
RESPONSIBILITY

23 Garden Street
Cambridge, MA 02138
(617) 492-1764

Bill to: _____

Address _____

City, State, Zip _____

Phone _____

☛ Use street address for UPS delivery. Please allow two to four weeks for delivery. Rush service available, please call for details.

Ship to: _____

Street Address _____

City, State, Zip _____

Phone _____

❏ Enclosed is my check or money order in U.S. funds

❏ Enclosed is a purchase order

❏ Charge my order to ❏ MasterCard ❏ Visa

Card # _____ Exp. _____

Signature _____

Phone _____

Qty.	Code	Description	Unit Price	Total Price

Remember to add 10% for shipping and handling ($3.50 minimum) for U.S. orders.

LU

Subtotal	
S&H ($10%, $3.50 min)	
Total	